Contents

You will sit <u>two exam papers</u> at the end of your AQA GCSE Computer Science course.
<u>Paper 1</u> will cover the content in <u>sections 1-5</u> and <u>Paper 2</u> will cover the content in <u>sections 4-7</u>.

Published by CGP

Editors: Liam Dyer, Sammy El-Bahrawy, Michael Weynberg.

Contributors: Colin Harber-Stuart, Shaun Whorton.

With thanks to Shaun Harrogate for the proofreading.

With thanks to Jan Greenway for the copyright research.

Android is a trademark of Google Inc.

Photo on p.82 iStock Editorial / Getty Images Plus / valio84sl

ISBN: 978 1 78908 271 5

Printed by Elanders Ltd, Newcastle upon Tyne.
Clipart from Corel®

GCSE AQA

Computer Science

No doubt ab   AQA's Grade 9-1 GCSE Computer Science exams are
seriously   ack. But this CGP book is the perfect user guide…

It's f   led notes, clear diagrams and useful examples,
not to m   ty of exam-style questions to test your performance.

There's also a f   ractice papers, with answers and a complete mark scheme,
so there'   mpatibility errors when you finally face the real thing.

How to access your free Online Edition

This book includes a free Online Edition to read on your PC, Mac or tablet.
You'll just need to go to **cgpbooks.co.uk/extras** and enter this code:

4241 4325 5665 4629

By the way, this code only works for one person. If somebody else has used
this book before you, they might have already claimed the Online Edition.

Complete
Revision & Practice

<u>Everything</u> you need to pass the exams!

Contents

Computational Thinking

Welcome to the world of Computer Science — first things first is to get you thinking like a computer scientist. <u>Computational thinking</u> is all about the steps you take to find the best solution to a complex problem.

Three Key Techniques for Computational Thinking

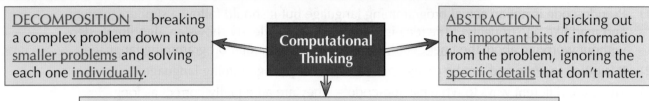

DECOMPOSITION — breaking a complex problem down into <u>smaller problems</u> and solving each one <u>individually</u>.

Computational Thinking

ABSTRACTION — picking out the <u>important bits</u> of information from the problem, ignoring the <u>specific details</u> that don't matter.

ALGORITHMIC THINKING — a <u>logical way</u> of getting from the <u>problem</u> to the <u>solution</u>. If the <u>steps</u> you take to solve a problem follow an <u>algorithm</u> then they can be reused and adapted to solve <u>similar problems</u> in the future.

These techniques are all used in Real-Life...

Computational thinking is something you'll do <u>all the time</u> without even noticing.

For example, when deciding which film to watch at the cinema with your family:

Decomposition	Abstraction	
Things to look at	Details to ignore	Details to focus on
What type of films are on?	Plot details, actors and director.	Film genre and age rating.
What times are the films on?	Days other than the date you're going.	Start and end times on the date you're going.
What are the reviews like?	In depth analysis of the characters and plot.	Ratings

<u>Algorithmic thinking</u> may involve coming up with some logical steps to reach a decision. E.g. listing all of the films that are showing, then deleting all the age restricted films and ones with poor ratings. Getting each family member to vote for their favourite, then picking the film with the most votes.

If the family went to see a film the following week they could use the <u>same processes</u> of decomposition, abstraction and algorithmic thinking, but they would have to <u>do the research</u> and <u>make the decisions</u> again.

... and the Same Skills can be used in Computer Science

Computer scientists rely on decomposition, abstraction and algorithmic thinking to help them turn a complex problem into <u>small problems</u> that a computer can help them to solve.

See p.7-8 for more on sorting algorithms.

Imagine the task is to sort a list of product names into alphabetical order:
- One part of the <u>decomposition</u> might decide what <u>alphabetical order</u> means — letters are straightforward but what if some entries in the list contain numbers and punctuation?
- Another part of the <u>decomposition</u> might look at <u>comparing the entries</u> — this could be decomposed further into how you could compare two entries, three entries, etc.
- <u>Abstraction</u> will help the programmer focus on the important bits — it doesn't matter what the entries are and what they mean. The important information is the <u>order of the characters</u> in each entry.
- <u>Algorithmic thinking</u> will put the tasks into a step by step process. For example, you might compare the first two entries and order them, then compare the third entry to each of the first two and put it in the correct place, then compare the fourth entry to each of the first three, etc.

Break your big problems down into small manageable tasks...

Think about a recent decision you've made, or a problem you've solved. How did you decompose the problem? What information did you ignore/focus on? How did you reach the final solution?

Writing Algorithms — Pseudo-code

Algorithms are just sets of <u>instructions</u> for solving a problem. In real-life they can take the forms of recipes, assembly instructions, directions, etc. but in computer science they are often written in pseudo-code.

Algorithms can be written using **Pseudo-code**

1) Pseudo-code is not an actual programming language but it should follow a <u>similar structure</u> and <u>read like one</u> (roughly). The idea is that pseudo-code clearly shows an algorithm's steps without worrying about the <u>finer details</u> (syntax) of any particular programming language.

2) It is <u>quick to write</u> and can be <u>easily converted</u> into any programming language.

3) There are different ways to write pseudo-code — they are all <u>equally correct</u> as long as the person reading the code can <u>follow it</u> and <u>understand</u> what you mean.

 EXAMPLE: **Write an algorithm using pseudo-code to calculate the salary of a worker after a 10% pay increase.**

A <u>simple solution</u> to the problem would be:

```
Take worker's current salary
Multiply the salary by 1.1
Display the answer
```

This solution is perfectly adequate as the problem has been <u>split down</u> into steps and it is <u>obvious</u> to the reader what to do at <u>each stage</u>.

A more <u>useful solution</u> is shown here:

```
salary ← USERINPUT
newsalary ← salary * 1.1
OUTPUT newsalary
```

This solution is better as the <u>words</u> and <u>structure</u> resemble a real <u>programming language</u>. It can be more <u>easily adapted</u> into real code.

Make sure your pseudo-code isn't **Too Vague**

Even though pseudo-code isn't a formal <u>programming language</u> you still need to make sure it's <u>readable</u>, <u>easy to interpret</u> and not too <u>vague</u>.

EXAMPLE: **When registering on a website, a user's password should be more than 6 characters long and it must be different from their username. Write an algorithm to check if the password is valid. If it's invalid it should say why.**

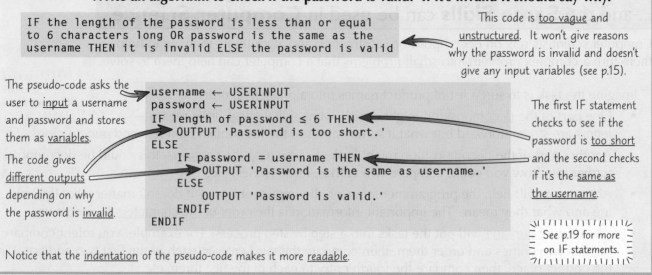

```
IF the length of the password is less than or equal
to 6 characters long OR password is the same as the
username THEN it is invalid ELSE the password is valid
```

This code is <u>too vague</u> and <u>unstructured</u>. It won't give reasons why the password is invalid and doesn't give any input variables (see p.15).

The pseudo-code asks the user to <u>input</u> a username and password and stores them as <u>variables</u>.

The code gives <u>different outputs</u> depending on why the password is <u>invalid</u>.

```
username ← USERINPUT
password ← USERINPUT
IF length of password ≤ 6 THEN
    OUTPUT 'Password is too short.'
ELSE
    IF password = username THEN
        OUTPUT 'Password is the same as username.'
    ELSE
        OUTPUT 'Password is valid.'
    ENDIF
ENDIF
```

The first IF statement checks to see if the password is <u>too short</u> and the second checks if it's the <u>same as the username</u>.

See p.19 for more on IF statements.

Notice that the <u>indentation</u> of the pseudo-code makes it more <u>readable</u>.

EXAM TIP

Pseudo-code isn't always everything it appears to be...

If you have to write an algorithm in your exam, pseudo-code is a great way to give your answer. You don't have to worry about the fiddly bits of syntax from a specific programming language.

Writing Algorithms — Flowcharts

Algorithms can also be shown using a flowchart, and just like for pseudo-code, there are different ways to write the same algorithm. You do get to draw some different shapes though, so things are looking up.

Flowcharts use **Different Boxes** for different **Commands**

Start / Stop — The beginning and the end of the algorithm are put in boxes with rounded corners.

Inputs/Outputs — Anything that's put into or taken out of the algorithm goes in a parallelogram box.

Processes — General instructions, processes and calculations go in rectangular boxes.

Decision — Decisions, often a 'yes' or 'no' question, are put in diamond boxes.

Subroutine — Subroutines are references to other flowcharts (see p.31-32).

Arrows connect boxes and show the direction you should follow. Some boxes might have multiple arrows coming in or going out of them.

Algorithms can be written as **Flowcharts**

Flowcharts can show sequences, selections, iterations or a combination of them.

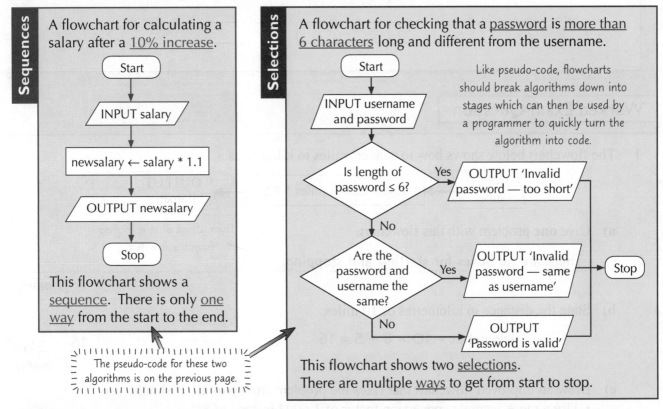

Sequences

A flowchart for calculating a salary after a 10% increase.

Start → INPUT salary → newsalary ← salary * 1.1 → OUTPUT newsalary → Stop

This flowchart shows a sequence. There is only one way from the start to the end.

The pseudo-code for these two algorithms is on the previous page.

Selections

A flowchart for checking that a password is more than 6 characters long and different from the username.

Like pseudo-code, flowcharts should break algorithms down into stages which can then be used by a programmer to quickly turn the algorithm into code.

Start → INPUT username and password → Is length of password ≤ 6? — Yes → OUTPUT 'Invalid password — too short' → Stop

No → Are the password and username the same? — Yes → OUTPUT 'Invalid password — same as username' → Stop

No → OUTPUT 'Password is valid'

This flowchart shows two selections. There are multiple ways to get from start to stop.

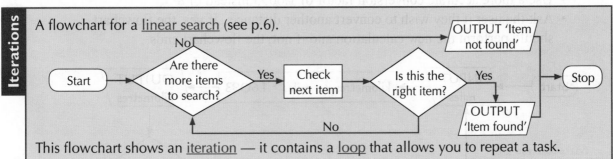

Iterations

A flowchart for a linear search (see p.6).

Start → Are there more items to search? — No → OUTPUT 'Item not found' → Stop

Yes → Check next item → Is this the right item? — Yes → OUTPUT 'Item found' → Stop

No → (loop back to Are there more items to search?)

This flowchart shows an iteration — it contains a loop that allows you to repeat a task.

EXAM TIP

Flowcharts should show the general flow of the algorithm...

You don't need to pack flowcharts with all the details. If you get a flowchart question in your exam, make sure you use the correct boxes and that all paths in your chart lead to the end.

Warm-Up and Worked Exam Questions

Now it's time to practise your computational thinking, pseudo-code and flowchart skills.
Work through these warm-up questions then have a go at the exam questions.

Warm-Up Questions

1) Give the names of the three key techniques used for computational thinking.

2) What is meant by an 'algorithm'?

3) Which of these statements are true?

> A: Pseudo-code is a formal programming language.
>
> B: There are lots of different ways to write pseudo-code.
>
> C: The more vague that pseudo-code is the better.
>
> D: Indentation helps to make pseudo-code easier to follow.

4) Draw lines matching the commands below to the correct flowchart symbol.

Start   Output   Decision   Subroutine   Process

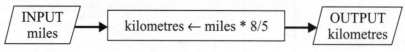

Worked Exam Question

1   The flowchart below shows how to convert miles to kilometres.

INPUT miles → kilometres ← miles * 8/5 → OUTPUT kilometres

a) Give **one** problem with this flowchart.

Think about what is missing from the flowchart.

There are no boxes for starting and stopping.

[1 mark]

b) State the distance in kilometres of 10 miles.

kilometres = 10 × 8 ÷ 5 = 16

................16........ km
[1 mark]

c) Draw an improved flowchart that fixes the problem from part a). It should also:
   • Use a more accurate conversion factor of 1.6093 instead of 8/5.
   • Ask the user if they wish to convert another distance. If yes, the flowchart
     should perform the new calculation and if not, the flowchart ends.

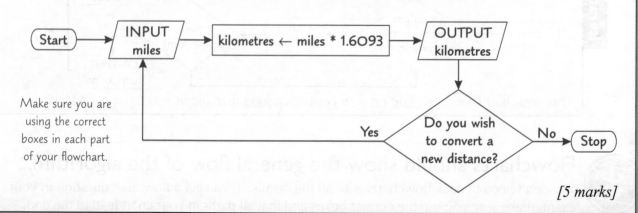

Make sure you are using the correct boxes in each part of your flowchart.

[5 marks]

Exam Questions

2 Bernard has written the algorithm on the right using pseudo-code.

```
OUTPUT 'Enter the height.'
height ← USERINPUT
OUTPUT 'Enter the width.'
width ← USERINPUT
area ← height * width
OUTPUT area
```

a) Describe what Bernard's algorithm does.

Go through the pseudo-code line by line and describe what each bit does.

....

....

....

[3 marks]

b) What would the output of the algorithm be if the inputs were 5 and 10? Shade **one** oval only.

A 2 ⬭   **B** 5 ⬭   **C** 15 ⬭   **D** 50 ⬭

[1 mark]

3 A file uploading service won't allow two files with the same file name to be uploaded.
If a file name already exists, it will ask the user to change the file name.

a) Describe with examples how abstraction can help decide how to compare the files.

....

....

....

[3 marks]

b) Describe with examples how decomposition could be used to help program this task.

....

....

....

[3 marks]

4 A robot moves on the 4 × 4 square grid shown below.
A subroutine, SqMove, is part of a flowchart that tells the robot how to move.

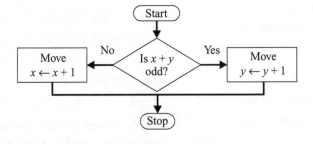

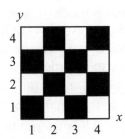

Draw a flowchart to show how the robot moves. The flowchart should:
- Ask the user to enter which square the robot starts on.
- Run the subroutine SqMove on a loop.
- Stop when the robot reaches the top or the right of the grid.

This is when x is 4 or y is 4.

[6 marks]

6

Search Algorithms

Computers need to follow search algorithms to find items in a list — the ones you'll need to know about are binary search and linear search. Now, if only someone could make a search algorithm to find my keys.

A **Binary Search** looks for items in an **Ordered List**

BINARY SEARCH ALGORITHM

1) Find the <u>middle item</u> in the ordered list. ◄━━━ To find the <u>middle item</u> in a list of n items do $(n + 1) \div 2$ and round up if necessary.

2) If this is the item you're looking for, then <u>stop</u> the search — you've found it.

3) If not, <u>compare</u> the item you're <u>looking for</u> to the <u>middle item</u>. If it comes <u>before</u> the middle item, get rid of the <u>second half</u> of the list. If it comes <u>after</u> the middle item, get rid of the <u>first half</u> of the list.

4) You'll be left with a list that is <u>half the size</u> of the original list. Repeat steps 1) – 3) on this <u>smaller list</u> to get an even smaller one. Keep going until you find the item you're looking for.

EXAMPLE: **Use the binary search algorithm to find the number 99 in the following list.**

| 7 | 21 | 52 | 59 | 68 | 92 | 94 | 99 | 133 |

There are 9 items in the list so the middle item is the $(9 + 1) \div 2$ = 5th item.
The 5th item is 68 and 68 < <u>99</u> so get rid of the first half of the list to leave:

| 92 | 94 | 99 | 133 |

There are 4 items left so the middle item is the $(4 + 1) \div 2$ = 2.5 = 3rd item.
The 3rd item is 99. You've found the item you're looking for so the search is complete.

A **Linear Search** can be used on an **Unordered List**

A linear search checks <u>each item</u> of the list in turn to see if it's the correct one.
It stops when it either <u>finds the item</u> it's looking for, or has <u>checked every item</u>.

LINEAR SEARCH ALGORITHM

1) Look at the <u>first item</u> in the unordered list.

2) If this is the item you're looking for, then <u>stop</u> the search — you've found it.

3) If not, then look at the <u>next item</u> in the list.

4) Repeat steps 2) – 3) until you find the item that you're looking for or you've checked <u>every item</u>.

EXAMPLE:

Use a linear search to find the number 99 from the list above.

Check the first item: 7 ≠ 99
Look at the next item: 21 ≠ 99
Look at the next item: 52 ≠ 99
Look at the next item: 59 ≠ 99
Look at the next item: 68 ≠ 99
Look at the next item: 92 ≠ 99
Look at the next item: 94 ≠ 99
Look at the next item: 99 = 99

You've found the item you're looking for so the search is complete.

1) A linear search is much <u>simpler</u> than a binary search but not as <u>efficient</u> (see p.41). The biggest advantage of a linear search is that it can be used on <u>any type</u> of list, it doesn't have to be ordered.

2) For <u>small ordered lists</u> the difference in efficiency doesn't really matter so the run time of both algorithms will be <u>similar</u>.

3) For <u>large ordered lists</u> the run time of binary search will generally be <u>much quicker</u> than linear search.

EXAM TIP

Write out every step of a search algorithm, don't skip ahead...

The binary and linear search algorithms might seem like a faff for you to follow when you can just look at a list and pick out the item you want. Sadly computers are more systematic and they need to follow every step of an algorithm — in your exam you'll need to show every step too.

Sorting Algorithms

I'm sure you all know how to sort things into numerical or alphabetical order but try telling a computer that. You'll need to be able to follow and carry out the two sorting algorithms on the next two pages.

A **Bubble Sort** compares **Pairs** of items

The bubble sort algorithm is used to sort an unordered list of items.
The algorithm is very simple to follow but can often take a while to actually sort a list.

BUBBLE SORT ALGORITHM

1) Look at the first two items in the list.
2) If they're in the right order, you don't have to do anything. If they're in the wrong order, swap them.
3) Move on to the next pair of items (the 2nd and 3rd entries) and repeat step 2).
4) Repeat step 3) until you get to the end of the list — this is called one pass. The last item will now be in the correct place, so don't include it in the next pass.
5) Repeat steps 1) – 4) until there are no swaps in a pass.

Each pass will have one less comparison than the one before it.

EXAMPLE:  **Use the bubble sort algorithm to write these numbers in ascending order.**

| 66 | 21 | 38 | 15 | 89 | 49 |

First pass:

66 21 38 15 89 49	Compare 66 and 21 — swap them.
21 66 38 15 89 49	Compare 66 and 38 — swap them.
21 38 66 15 89 49	Compare 66 and 15 — swap them.
21 38 15 66 89 49	Compare 66 and 89 — no swap.
21 38 15 66 89 49	Compare 89 and 49 — swap them.
21 38 15 66 49 89	End of first pass.

After the 2nd pass the order of the numbers will be: 21 15 38 49 66 89

After the 3rd pass the order of the numbers will be: 15 21 38 49 66 89

There are no swaps in the 4th pass so the list has been sorted: 15 21 38 49 66 89

The bubble sort is considered to be one of the simplest sorting algorithms as it only ever focuses on two items rather than the whole list of items.

Pros
- It's a simple algorithm that can be easily implemented on a computer.
- It's an efficient way to check if a list is already in order. For a list of n items you only have to do one pass of $n - 1$ comparisons to check if the list is ordered or not.
- Doesn't use very much memory as all the sorting is done using the original list.

Cons
- It's an inefficient way to sort a list — for a list of n items, the worst case scenario would involve you doing $\frac{n(n-1)}{2}$ comparisons.
- Due to being inefficient, the bubble sort algorithm is pretty slow for very large lists of items.

In the bubble sort, items bubble up to the end of the list...

A common mistake is to forget the final pass because you realise that the list is already in order — remember that you should always show a pass when nothing changes to complete the algorithm.

Sorting Algorithms

The other sorting algorithm you'll need to learn is the merge sort — it splits a list apart and then magically merges it back together in the correct order. I really hope you're ready to see something special.

A **Merge Sort Splits** the list apart then **Merges** it back together

The merge sort algorithm is an example of a <u>divide-and-conquer</u> algorithm and takes advantage of two facts:

- Small lists are <u>easier to sort</u> than large lists.
- It's easier to merge <u>two ordered lists</u> than two unordered lists.

> **MERGE SORT ALGORITHM**
>
> 1) <u>Split</u> the list in <u>half</u> (the smaller lists are called <u>sub-lists</u>)
>   — the second sub-list should start at the <u>middle item</u> (see p.6).
> 2) Keep repeating step 1) on each sub-list until <u>all the lists</u> only contain <u>one item</u>.
> 3) <u>Merge pairs</u> of sub-lists so that each sub-list has twice as many items.
>   Each time you merge sub-lists, <u>sort the items</u> into the right order.
> 4) Repeat step 3) until you've merged <u>all the sub-lists</u> together.

EXAMPLE: **Use the merge sort algorithm to write these letters in alphabetical order.**

1) <u>Split</u> the original list of 8 items into <u>two lists</u>, the second list should start at the (8 + 1) ÷ 2 = 4.5 = <u>5th item</u>.

2) Carry on <u>splitting</u> the sub-lists until each list only has <u>one item</u> in it.

3) <u>Merge</u> and <u>order</u> sub-lists back together. E.g.

> Compare F and A — <u>move A</u> to the new list.
> Compare F and L — <u>move F</u> to the new list.
> Compare P and L — <u>move L</u> to the new list.
> P is the <u>last item</u> in the new list.

Note that merging is always performed on <u>two ordered lists</u> and is <u>very simple</u> to do.

4) Keep <u>merging</u> sub-lists until you only have <u>one list</u>.

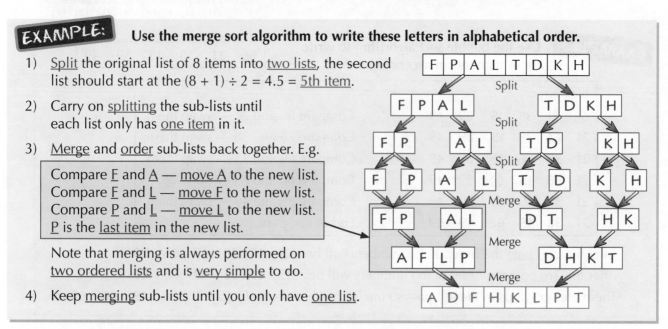

You'll often be unable to <u>split</u> or <u>merge</u> lists <u>evenly</u>. For example, sometimes you'll have to merge a list containing <u>two items</u> with a list containing <u>one item</u> to make a list of <u>three items</u>.

Pros	Cons
• In general, it's much <u>more efficient</u> and <u>quicker</u> than the bubble sort algorithm (p.7) for <u>large lists</u>, and has a <u>similar running time</u> for <u>short lists</u>.	• Even if the list is <u>already sorted</u>, it still goes through the <u>whole splitting</u> and <u>merging</u> process, so a bubble sort may be <u>quicker</u> in some cases.
• It has a very <u>consistent running time</u> regardless of how ordered the items in the original list are.	• It uses <u>more memory</u> than the bubble sort because it has to create <u>additional lists</u>.

Due to its efficiency, the merge sort algorithm (or variations of it) are used in many programming languages such as Java™, Python and Perl as the primary sorting algorithm.

 EXAM TIP

To do the merge sort, split things down before sorting them...

When doing a merge sort it's important that you show the splitting process <u>and</u> the merging process — if you only show the merging process then you've only shown half the algorithm.

Warm-Up and Worked Exam Questions

There are lots of searching and sorting algorithms for you to learn, so here are some questions to test your knowledge. Start off with the warm-up questions then have a go at the exam questions.

Warm-Up Questions

1) Here is a list of the ages of Maya's sons and daughters:

| 3 | 6 | 8 | 11 | 13 | 15 | 18 |

   a) Use a binary search to find "8" in the list.
   b) Use a linear search to find "11" in the list.

2) Describe how a bubble sort works.

3) Here are the names of the four pupils at a chess club: | Chris | Beth | Dalia | Ahmed |

   a) Show the steps of a bubble sort to put the names in ascending alphabetical order.
   b) Show the steps of a merge sort to put the names in descending alphabetical order.

4) Which sorting algorithm is best to use on a large list of items, bubble sort or merge sort?

Worked Exam Questions

1 Nicola has a list of numbers: 2, 3, 7, 5, 13, 11.

   a) She says, "I can't use a binary search to find 13." Why is this the case?

   A binary search only works on ordered data.

   [1 mark]

   b) Show the steps of a linear search to find 13 in the list above.

   Check the first item: 2 ≠ 13.
   Check the second item: 3 ≠ 13
   Check the third item: 7 ≠ 13
   Check the fourth item: 5 ≠ 13.
   Check the fifth item: 13 = 13.   Stop searching as item has been found.

   The linear search is straightforward but make sure you show every single step of the algorithm to get full marks.

   [2 marks]

2 A musician is sorting his CD collection by year released, from oldest to newest. A sample of the sorted list is shown below.

| 1989 | 1990 | 1992 | 1998 | 2000 |

   a) Show all comparisons of a bubble sort algorithm to show that the list above is already in order.

   Compare 1989 and 1990 and don't swap.
   Compare 1990 and 1992 and don't swap.
   Compare 1992 and 1998 and don't swap.
   Compare 1998 and 2000 and don't swap.

   Pass completed with no swaps so list is ordered

   [2 marks]

   b) By looking at the number of comparisons, explain why a bubble sort is useful for checking if a list is ordered.

   A bubble sort is efficient, as a list of n items only requires n − 1 comparisons.

   [2 marks]

Exam Questions

3 Sonia has a sorted list of ice cream flavours that she sells in her shop.

a) Show the stages of a binary search to find the word 'butterscotch' in the list below.

butterscotch	chocolate	mint	strawberry	vanilla

[4 marks]

b) Give **one** advantage of using a binary search over a linear search.

....

....

[1 mark]

c) Six more flavours are added to Sonia's list. The list is still in alphabetical order. Explain why it would only take two iterations of a binary search to find the ninth item in the list.

....

....

....

[3 marks]

4 Kim has a hand of playing cards, all of the same suit: 3, 7, 6, 2, 5.

a) Arrange the cards in order from highest to lowest using a merge sort.

[4 marks]

b) Which of these statements about the merge sort algorithm are true? Shade **two** ovals only.

A A merge sort is efficient for sorting lists with lots of items.   ◯

B A merge sort is always less efficient than a bubble sort.   ◯

C Merge sorts on two lists of the same length will have similar running times. ◯

D A merge sort is efficient for checking if a list is already in order.   ◯

[2 marks]

Revision Questions for Section One

Well that's <u>algorithms</u> all <u>done</u> and <u>dusted</u>. Or so you thought — just wait until you start <u>Section Two</u>.

- Try these questions and <u>tick off each one</u> when you <u>get it right</u>.
- When you've done <u>all the questions</u> for a topic and are <u>completely happy</u> with it, tick off the topic.

Computational Thinking (p.1) ☑

1) What is meant by: a) decomposition?   b) abstraction?

2) Why is using algorithmic thinking useful when solving a problem?

3) Outline the decomposition, abstraction and algorithmic processes for choosing a film at the cinema.

Pseudo-code and Flowcharts (p.2-3) ☑

4) What is pseudo-code? Give three features of well-written pseudo-code.

5) What are the benefits of writing algorithms in pseudo-code rather than a programming language?

6) Draw the five box types used on flowcharts and say what each one is used for.

7) What do sequences, selections and iterations look like on a flowchart?

8)* Draw a flowchart to check if a new username is valid. Usernames should be at least 5 characters long and unique. If it's invalid, the algorithm should give the reason why and get the user to enter another username.

Search Algorithms (p.6) ☑

9) What are the four steps of the binary search algorithm?

10) What are the four steps of a linear search algorithm?

11)* Here's a fascinating list of British towns and cities:

| Ashington | Brecon | Chester | Dagenham | Morpeth | Usk | Watford |

   a) Use a binary search to find "Morpeth" in the list above.
   b) Now do the same using a linear search.

12) What are the benefits and drawbacks of using a linear search over a binary search?

Sorting Algorithms (p.7-8) ☑

13) a) What are the five steps of the bubble sort algorithm?
    b)* Use the bubble sort algorithm to sort these fruit into alphabetical order:

| Orange | Banana | Apple | Peach | Grape | Lime |

14) What are the four steps of the merge sort algorithm?

15)* Here is a list of numbers:

| 8 | 7 | 5 | 1 | 3 | 6 | 4 | 2 |

   a) Use the merge sort algorithm to sort this list into ascending order.
   b) Use the bubble sort algorithm to sort this list into descending order.

16) Outline the strengths and weaknesses of the following sorting algorithms:
    a) bubble sort   b) merge sort

*Answers on p.139

Programming Basics — Data Types

Ah my favourite section of the book — it's time to get to grips with some programming...

Everything we cover in this section will work slightly differently in different programming languages, but the principles are the same and that's what you need to learn for the exam.

In this section, examples of code will be given in these boxes and will be written in pseudo-code (p.2).

The output of the code will be shown in this box.

Programming languages have **Five Main Data Types**

1) Programming languages store data as different types. You need to learn the ones in this table...

Data type	Pseudo-code	Characteristics	Examples
Integer	INT	Whole numbers only.	0, 6, 10293, –999
Real (or float)	REAL	Numbers that have a decimal part.	0.15, –5.87, 100.0
Boolean	BOOL	Can only take one of two values, usually TRUE or FALSE.	True/False, 1/0, yes/no
Character	CHAR	A single letter, number, symbol.	'A', 'k', '5', '–', '$'
String	STRING	Used to represent text, it is a collection of characters.	'FsTmQ2', '$money$'

2) Each data type is allocated a different amount of memory.

3) Using the correct data types makes code more memory efficient, robust (hard to break) and predictable.

Programming languages can be weakly typed or strongly typed.
- Weakly typed languages will try to convert data types to avoid errors, however this can lead to unpredictable results.
- Strongly typed languages won't try to convert data types and so will produce more errors but more predictable results.

Data type	Typical amount of memory taken up
Integer	2 bytes or 4 bytes.
Real	4 bytes or 8 bytes.
Boolean	1 bit is needed but 1 byte is usually used.
Character	1 byte
String	1 byte for every character in the string.

Using the **Correct Data Type** for different **Variables**

You should be able to choose the best data type to use in different situations.

 **EXAMPLE:** **Give the appropriate data type for each of the categories in this registration form.**

Initial of first name:	N
Surname:	Chapman
Age (in whole years):	27
Height (in metres):	1.64
Male or Female:	Female

Initial of first name should be stored as a character.

Surname should be stored as a string.

Age (in whole years) should be stored as an integer.

Height (in metres) should be stored as a real data type.

Male or Female could be stored as Boolean.

Using the wrong data type can lead to unexpected results...

Using the correct data types is a fundamental part of programming — sometimes a piece of data could take different data types and you'll have to decide which is best based on the context.

Programming Basics — Operators

Operators are special characters that perform certain functions. You'll already be used to using operators in maths, but it's important to know how they work in computer science too.

You can **Change** from one **Data Type** to another

1) Languages have functions (p.31) that let you manually convert between data types — this is known as casting. Different languages will do this in different ways but the principle is the same:

STRING_TO_INT('1') ◄—— Converts the string '1' to the integer 1.

STRING_TO_REAL('1.0') ◄—— Converts the string '1.0' to the real 1.0

INT_TO_STRING(1) ◄—— Converts the integer 1 to the string '1'.

REAL_TO_STRING(1.0) ◄—— Converts the real 1.0 to the string '1.0'

2) It's important to realise that the integer 1, the real 1.0 and the strings '1' and '1.0' are all different.

3) You can also find the ASCII code (see p.59) of characters and vice versa using these functions:

CHAR_TO_CODE('b') ◄—— Converts the character 'b' into its ASCII code 98.

CODE_TO_CHAR(98) ◄—— Converts the ASCII code 98 into its equivalent character 'b'.

The **Basic Arithmetic Operators** are straightforward

1) The arithmetic operators take two values and perform a maths function on them.

2) Addition, subtraction, multiplication and division operators do what you'd expect.

3) The DIV operator returns the whole number part of a division and the MOD operator gives the remainder.

Dividing integers might behave oddly in some programming languages, e.g. 5 / 2 may give the answer 2 instead of 2.5...

...using DIV and MOD can avoid these issues.

Function	Typical Operator	Example	Result
Addition	+	5 + 5	10
Subtraction	–	3 – 10	–7
Multiplication	*	4 * 8	32
Division	/	7.5 / 5	1.5
Integer division (quotient)	DIV	20 DIV 3	6
Remainder (modulus)	MOD or %	20 MOD 3	2

4) The first four operators in the table above work on integers and real data values (or combinations of the two). DIV and MOD are for integers only.

5) Computers follow the rule of BODMAS (Brackets, Other, Division, Multiplication, Addition & Subtraction) — so take care when using operators to make sure your code is actually doing what you want it to. E.g. 2 + 8 * 2 will give 18. To do the addition first, use brackets: (2 + 8) * 2 will give 20.

Arithmetic operators only work on integers and reals...

Get your head around these basic things now and you'll have a better chance of understanding the trickier stuff later on. The DIV and MOD operators might seem strange but they're really useful.

Programming Basics — Operators

Programming languages have other types of operator too —
this page covers the assignment operator and the comparison operators.

The Assignment Operator

The <u>assignment operator</u>, ← (or =), is used to <u>assign values</u> to <u>constants</u> or <u>variables</u> (see next page).

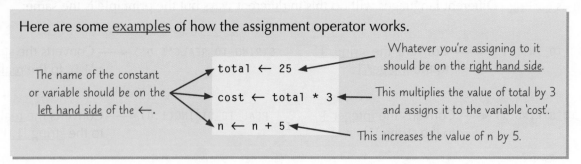

Here are some <u>examples</u> of how the assignment operator works.

The name of the constant or variable should be on the <u>left hand side</u> of the ←.

Whatever you're assigning to it should be on the <u>right hand side</u>.

```
total ← 25
cost ← total * 3
n ← n + 5
```

This multiplies the value of total by 3 and assigns it to the variable 'cost'.

This increases the value of n by 5.

The Comparison Operators

<u>Comparison operators</u> compare the expression on their <u>left hand side</u> to the expression on their <u>right hand side</u> and produce a <u>Boolean value</u> (either true or false).

Comparison operator	What it means	Evaluates to True	Evaluates to False
= (or ==)	Is equal to	5 = 5	5 = 8
≠ (or <> or !=)	Is not equal to	6 ≠ 7	6 ≠ 6
<	Is less than	4 < 10	3 < 2
>	Is greater than	15 > 9	10 > 12
≤ (or <=)	Is less than or equal to	7 ≤ 8	11 ≤ 10
≥ (or >=)	Is greater than or equal to	3 ≥ 3	9 ≥ 12

Don't get mixed up between = and ==...

1) Many programming languages use "=" for the assignment operator and "==" for the comparison operator. A <u>common mistake</u> is to get them the wrong way round — you'll know if you've used them <u>incorrectly</u> because your code won't do what you were expecting.

2) In this book we'll always use ← for assignment and = for "is equal to" so that it is clear when values are being assigned and when we are doing a comparison.

REVISION TASK

Comparison operators are used to compare two expressions...

Knowing what all the different operators are and what they do is essential to learning how to write simple programs. Close the book and see if you can write down all the arithmetic and comparison operators, explain what each operator does and give an example of it being used.

Constants and Variables

Now that you know about the different data types and operations it's time to look at constants and variables. As you can probably tell by the names, constants remain the same and variables can be changed.

Data Values can be **Constants** or **Variables**

1) Data values can be stored as constants or variables.

2) The name of the constant or variable is linked to a memory location that stores the data value. The size of the memory location depends on the data type (see p.12).

3) A constant is assigned a value at design time that can't be changed. If you attempt to change the value of a constant in a program then the interpreter or compiler (see p.42) will return an error.

4) Variables on the other hand can change value which makes them far more useful than constants.

5) In many programming languages, constants and variables need to be declared before you can use them. When writing pseudo-code they're often just declared when you want to assign a value to them. This can be done in different ways:

Here are two ways of declaring PRESSURE as a constant and assigning it the value of 30. Upper case letters are often used when naming constants.

Here are three ways of declaring temperature as a variable and assigning it the value of 20.5. The var keyword can be used to make it clear that it's a variable.

```
constant PRESSURE as INT ← 30
constant PRESSURE ← 30
```

The first example in each case specifies the data type as well.

```
var temperature as REAL ← 20.5
var temperature ← 20.5
temperature ← 20.5
```

To make code easier to follow, programmers usually give variables and constants descriptive names. They will also follow standard naming conventions when naming variables. For example, by capitalising the first letter of each word (apart from the first), like tempInOven or pressureInPot.

Identifying **Constants** and **Variables** in Programs

 **EXAMPLE:**

In a multi-event athletics competition, athletes get 5 points for winning an event and 2 points for coming second. Otherwise they get 0 points. This program calculates the total number of points that an athlete has.

```
firsts ← USERINPUT
seconds ← USERINPUT
OUTPUT (5 * firsts + 2 * seconds)
```

a) **Rewrite the program so that all the variables are declared with data types and initial values.**

The two variables are firsts and seconds. They should both be declared as integers as there are a whole number of events.

```
var firsts as INT ← 0
var seconds as INT ← 0
firsts ← USERINPUT
seconds ← USERINPUT
OUTPUT (5 * firsts + 2 * seconds)
```

The initial value of each variable is set to 0.

b) **Give two reasons for assigning the values 5 and 2 to constants.**
- They don't need to be changed during the running of the program.
- If the points awarded for each event was changed you'd only need to change the value given in the declaration of the constant.

This is an example of improving the maintainability (p.39) of the program.

A constant, a variable... and finally a constant. Time starts now...

You can't change the data type of a variable, only the value. But as you saw on p.13 you can use a casting function to return a different data type, which you can then assign to a new variable:

```
cost ← 50
stringCost ← INT_TO_STRING(cost)
```

This converts the integer 50 to the string '50' and stores it in stringCost.

Strings

Remember from page 12 that strings are a data type made up of characters — these characters are <u>alphanumeric</u> (letters, numbers, spaces, symbols, etc.). Now you'll see how you can manipulate them.

Strings are written inside **Quotation Marks**

In this book you'll see strings written inside <u>single quotation marks</u> ', but in some programming languages you might see <u>double quotation marks</u> being used ".

```
string1 ← 'Output me, I am a string.'
OUTPUT string1
```
```
Output me, I am a string.
```

Strings can be <u>joined together</u> to form new strings — this is called <u>concatenation</u>. It's often done using the <u>+ operator</u>.

```
string1 ← 'My favourite colour is'
string2 ← 'purple.'
newString ← string1 + ' ' + string2
OUTPUT newString
```
```
My favourite colour is purple.
```

The + operator joins the strings together.

A space character has been added between the two strings.

Programs let you **Manipulate Strings** in a variety of ways

1) Before getting started on string manipulation you should know that the <u>characters</u> in a string are usually numbered <u>starting at 0</u>.

```
0 1 2 3 4  5
S P Y I N G
```

2) Here are some common <u>string manipulation</u> functions that you'll need to learn for your exam.

Pseudo-code function	Operation	Example
LEN(string)	Returns the number of characters in the string.	LEN('Hello') returns 5
POSITION(string, character)	Returns the position of the first occurrence of a certain character in the given string.	POSITION('Hello', 'o') returns 4 POSITION('Hello', 'l') returns 2
SUBSTRING(x, y, string)	Extracts a substring from the original string starting at position x and finishing at position y.	SUBSTRING(0, 3, 'Hello') returns 'Hell'

EXAMPLE: **An electricity company generates a customer's 7 character username from:**
- **the first 3 letters of their town.**
- **the customer's age when they sign up (2 digits).**
- **the last letter of the customer's surname.**

Write an algorithm to generate a username for any customer given that their data is stored under the variables town, age and surname.

Start by working out how to <u>extract</u> the information from <u>each variable</u>...

1) `SUBSTRING(0, 2, town)` ← This extracts the <u>first 3 characters</u> from the customer's town.

2) `INT_TO_STRING(age)` ← <u>Converts</u> the customer's age to a <u>string</u> (p.13).

3) `n ← LEN(surname)`
   `SUBSTRING(n-1, n-1, surname)` ← Finds the <u>length</u> of the <u>surname</u> so that it can take the <u>last character</u>. Remember, the last character is in the n–1th position.

... then combine the code into a <u>single algorithm</u> at the end.

```
n ← LEN(surname)
username ← SUBSTRING(0, 2, town) + INT_TO_STRING(age) + SUBSTRING(n-1, n-1, surname)
```

I hope you don't just think I'm stringing you along...

EXAM TIP It's important that you know the string manipulations on this page. Examiners might throw some different ones at you in the exam — luckily they'll also show you exactly how they work.

Warm-Up and Worked Exam Questions

That's the first part of programming done — have a go at these questions to see how much you've understood.

Warm-Up Questions

1) What is the most appropriate data type for each of these items?
   a) The nickname of your best friend.
   b) The number on a rolled dice.
   c) The exact length of a car in metres.
   d) The answer to a yes/no question.

2) Work out the results of the following arithmetic operations:
   a) `5 * 8`
   b) `10 MOD 3`
   c) `28 DIV 6`
   d) `3 + 2 * 8`

3) Will the following pieces of code return true or false?
   a) `6 ≤ 10`
   b) `5 = 5`
   c) `14 > 15`
   d) `12 < 8 + 5`

4) What's the difference between a variable and a constant?

5) Given that `fish ← 'lobster'`, state what would be returned from the following methods:
   a) `LEN(fish)`
   b) `SUBSTRING(0, 2, fish)`
   c) `POSITION(fish, 'e')`
   d) `SUBSTRING(2, 4, fish)`

Worked Exam Questions

1 The program below calculates the cost of a burger in pounds at a fast food restaurant.
A standard burger costs £6.50 with additional costs for toppings and eating in the restaurant.

```
constant STANDARD ← 6.5
OUTPUT 'How many toppings?'
tops ← USERINPUT
OUTPUT 'Are they eating in? (Y/N)'
eat_in ← USERINPUT
IF eat_in = 'Y' THEN
    OUTPUT (STANDARD + 0.5*tops + 1)
ELSE
    OUTPUT (STANDARD + 0.5*tops)
ENDIF
```

a) List **all** the variables in this program.

   tops and eat_in

   [2 marks]

b) How much extra does it cost to eat your burger inside the restaurant?

   £1

   [1 mark]

c) The restaurant manager says that 0.5 should have been declared as a constant.
Give **two** reasons for declaring this value as a constant.

   1 *It doesn't need to be changed as the program is running.*

   2 *Updating the value of a constant once will update it everywhere in the program.*

   You could also mention that giving the value a name,
   e.g. toppingsCost will make the code more meaningful.

   [2 marks]

2 A digital radio stores the current date as a string under the variable name `date`.
The radio is broken and is stuck on the date: 8 January 2016

State the output from each of the following pieces of code:

a) `LEN(date)`

   14

   [1 mark]

b) `SUBSTRING(0, 0, date) + SUBSTRING(10, 13, date)`

   '8' + '2016'

   They are strings so use string
   concatenations instead of adding them.

   82016

   [1 mark]

Exam Questions

3 Millie has written a program that contains lots of constants and variables.
Which of the following can be changed as a program is running? Shade **one** oval only.

    A The data type of a variable. ⬯   **C** The value of a variable. ⬯

    B The data type of a constant. ⬯   **D** The value of a constant. ⬯

[1 mark]

4 A pedestrian crossing uses a button to request the traffic to stop. State the data type
that you would use to record each of these variables and give a reason for your answer.

a) A variable to record whether the button has been pressed or not.

Data type ....

Reason ....

[2 marks]

b) A variable to record how many whole seconds it's been since the button was pressed.

Data type ....

Reason ....

[2 marks]

5 A juice company generates a product ID for each of its fruit juices. The product ID
is generated using string concatenation on the first three letters of the fruit and the
volume of fruit juice in ml. E.g. a 500 ml carton of apple juice would be app500.

a) Define what is meant by string concatenation.

....

[1 mark]

b) What would the product code be for a 2000 ml carton of orange juice?

....

[1 mark]

c) Complete the algorithm below so that line 05 reassigns the first three letters of the fruit
to the `fruit` variable and line 06 assigns the final product ID to the `prodID` variable.

```
01  OUTPUT 'Enter the name of the fruit.'
02  fruit ← USERINPUT
03  OUTPUT 'Enter the volume of the juice.'
04  volume ← USERINPUT

05  fruit ← ...............................................................................

06  prodID ← ..............................................................................
07  OUTPUT prodID
```

[2 marks]

Program Flow — Selection

The flow of a program is the order that the steps are carried out in. One way that you can control the program flow is by using <u>selection statements</u> — but first, here's how to get your programs to interact with the user.

Programs need to be able to **Interact** with a **User**

1) It's really handy for programs to be able to get information from and give information to the <u>user</u> — this is done through the <u>input</u> and <u>output</u> devices.

2) <u>Inputs</u> can be received from many devices, e.g. keyboard, mouse, webcam or microphone.

3) <u>Outputs</u> are typically displayed visually on the monitor or as sound from the speakers.

4) When writing pseudo-code we usually assume that <u>inputs</u> are from a <u>keyboard</u> and <u>outputs</u> will be <u>displayed</u> on a monitor (typically as <u>text</u>).

When you ask a user for an <u>input</u>, you should assign it to a <u>variable</u> with a <u>descriptive name</u>.

```
OUTPUT 'Enter your age'
userAge ← USERINPUT
OUTPUT userAge
```

<u>Outputs</u> can be used to <u>communicate</u> with the user and <u>prompt</u> them to <u>input</u> data.

<u>Outputs</u> will usually be <u>strings</u> — to output data stored in a variable just use the <u>variable name</u>.

IF statements usually have an **IF-THEN-ELSE** structure

1) <u>IF statements</u> allow you to check if a <u>condition</u> is true or false, and carry out different actions depending on the outcome. You can think about them as a <u>flowchart</u>.

2) Here is a program that can verify if the user knows a certain passcode before granting access.

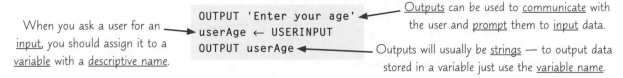

The first part of the <u>IF statement</u> is the condition that must be checked.

Indenting the actions for each condition makes the code more readable.

```
passcode ← USERINPUT
IF passcode = 'GO' THEN
        OUTPUT 'Unrestricted access.'
ELSE
        OUTPUT 'Access denied.'
ENDIF
```

The part after THEN tells the program what to do if the condition is true.

The part after ELSE tells the program what to do if the condition is false.

3) If there is <u>nothing</u> for the program to do when the <u>condition is false</u>, <u>leave out</u> the 'else' part.

Nested IF statements allow multiple outputs

1) More complex IF statements can be made by putting one IF statement <u>inside</u> another one — this type of selection statement is called a <u>nested IF statement</u>.

2) Nested IF statements allow you to <u>check more conditions</u> once you've established that the <u>previous condition</u> is <u>true</u> or <u>false</u>.

If the <u>first condition</u> is <u>true</u>, it will check the <u>second condition</u>.

If the <u>first condition</u> is <u>false</u>, it will run this <u>else statement</u> — all access is denied.

<u>Indentation</u> lets the reader see where each IF statement begins and ends.

```
userType ← USERINPUT
passcode ← USERINPUT
IF passcode = 'GO' THEN
    IF userType = 'Teacher' THEN
        OUTPUT 'Unrestricted access.'
    ELSE
        OUTPUT 'Restricted access.'
    ENDIF
ELSE
    OUTPUT 'Access denied.'
ENDIF
```

If the <u>second condition</u> is <u>true</u> then unrestricted access is allowed.

If the <u>second condition</u> is false then restricted access is allowed.

Program Flow — Selection

ELSE-IF statements check conditions until one is True

1) ELSE-IF statements are used to check multiple conditions and give different outputs depending on which condition is true.

2) They are different from nested IF statements as they only check more conditions if the previous condition is false — e.g. IF the first condition is true then they won't check the others.

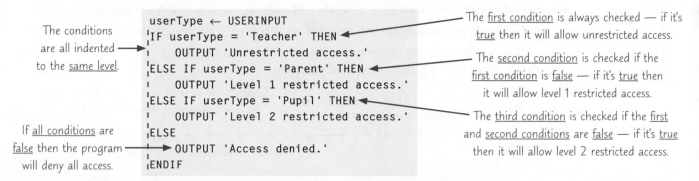

The conditions are all indented to the same level.

```
userType ← USERINPUT
IF userType = 'Teacher' THEN
    OUTPUT 'Unrestricted access.'
ELSE IF userType = 'Parent' THEN
    OUTPUT 'Level 1 restricted access.'
ELSE IF userType = 'Pupil' THEN
    OUTPUT 'Level 2 restricted access.'
ELSE
    OUTPUT 'Access denied.'
ENDIF
```

If all conditions are false then the program will deny all access.

The first condition is always checked — if it's true then it will allow unrestricted access.

The second condition is checked if the first condition is false — if it's true then it will allow level 1 restricted access.

The third condition is checked if the first and second conditions are false — if it's true then it will allow level 2 restricted access.

CASE Statements check the value of a Variable

1) Instead of checking to see if a condition is true or false, CASE statements (sometimes called SWITCH statements) can check if a variable has specific values.

2) They're used when you want a program to perform different actions for different values of the same variable.

3) Here is a program that can be used to count votes in an election.

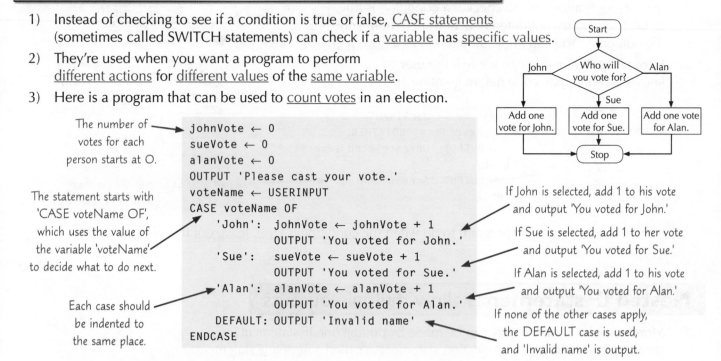

The number of votes for each person starts at 0.

```
johnVote ← 0
sueVote ← 0
alanVote ← 0
OUTPUT 'Please cast your vote.'
voteName ← USERINPUT
CASE voteName OF
    'John':  johnVote ← johnVote + 1
             OUTPUT 'You voted for John.'
    'Sue':   sueVote ← sueVote + 1
             OUTPUT 'You voted for Sue.'
    'Alan':  alanVote ← alanVote + 1
             OUTPUT 'You voted for Alan.'
    DEFAULT: OUTPUT 'Invalid name'
ENDCASE
```

The statement starts with 'CASE voteName OF', which uses the value of the variable 'voteName' to decide what to do next.

Each case should be indented to the same place.

If John is selected, add 1 to his vote and output 'You voted for John.'

If Sue is selected, add 1 to her vote and output 'You voted for Sue.'

If Alan is selected, add 1 to his vote and output 'You voted for Alan.'

If none of the other cases apply, the DEFAULT case is used, and 'Invalid name' is output.

4) CASE statements have a similar structure to ELSE-IF statements but they give a neater way to test different values of a variable — this makes them easier than ELSE-IF statements to maintain.

5) The drawback of CASE statements is that they can only check the value of one variable. ELSE-IF statements can check if multiple conditions are true.

> ELSE-IF and CASE statements can also be used to make more complex nested selection statements just like the nested IF statements on p.19.

Can't decide what to have for lunch? Use a selection statement...

CASE statements don't have to include a DEFAULT case, just like how IF statements don't need an ELSE. In some cases (like the example above) putting one in can help to make your program more robust.

Program Flow — Iteration

Here are some <u>indefinite</u> iteration statements — the number of times that they repeat depends on a <u>condition</u>.

All these **Loops** are controlled by **Conditions**

<u>REPEAT-UNTIL</u>, <u>WHILE</u> and <u>DO-WHILE</u> loops are easy to get mixed up — they're very similar but with subtle differences that you need to know:

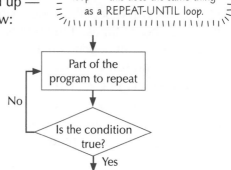

You might also see a DO-UNTIL loop — this does the same thing as a REPEAT-UNTIL loop.

REPEAT-UNTIL LOOPS
- Controlled by a condition at the <u>end of the loop</u>.
- Keep going <u>until</u> the condition is <u>true</u> (i.e. while it is false).
- <u>Always run</u> the code inside them <u>at least once</u>.
- You get an <u>infinite loop</u> if the condition is <u>never true</u>.

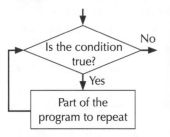

WHILE LOOPS
- Controlled by a condition at the <u>start of the loop</u>.
- Keep going <u>while</u> the condition is <u>true</u> (i.e. until it is false).
- <u>Never run</u> the code inside them if the condition is initially <u>false</u>.
- You get an <u>infinite loop</u> if the condition is <u>always true</u>.

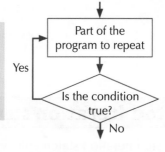

DO-WHILE LOOPS
- Controlled by a condition at the <u>end of the loop</u>.
- Keep going <u>while</u> the condition is <u>true</u> (i.e. until it is false).
- <u>Always run</u> the code inside them <u>at least once</u>.
- You get an <u>infinite loop</u> if the condition is <u>always true</u>.

EXAMPLE: Write an algorithm that a supermarket self-scan machine could use to check if enough money has been fed into it and output the right amount of change.

REPEAT-UNTIL Loop:

```
total ← 0
cost ← total cost in pence
REPEAT
  coinValue ← USERINPUT
  total ← total + coinValue
UNTIL total ≥ cost
change ← total - cost
OUTPUT change
```

The loop starts at <u>REPEAT</u> and ends when the <u>UNTIL</u> condition is <u>true</u> — when the total is greater than or equal to the cost.

WHILE Loop:

```
total ← 0
cost ← total cost in pence
WHILE total < cost
  coinValue ← USERINPUT
  total ← total + coinValue
ENDWHILE
change ← total - cost
OUTPUT change
```

The loop starts by checking the <u>WHILE</u> condition is <u>true</u> and keeps repeating until it is <u>false</u> — when the total is greater than or equal to the cost.

DO-WHILE Loop:

```
total ← 0
cost ← total cost in pence
DO
  coinValue ← USERINPUT
  total ← total + coinValue
WHILE total < cost
change ← total - cost
OUTPUT change
```

The loop starts at <u>DO</u> and repeats until the <u>WHILE</u> condition is <u>false</u> — when the total is greater than or equal to the cost.

All of these loops in the example above work exactly the same when cost > 0.
If the cost is 0, the <u>WHILE</u> loop won't expect an input, whereas the <u>REPEAT-UNTIL</u> and <u>DO-WHILE</u> loops will.

REVISION TIP

Keep looping through this page until it's stuck in your head...

As well as learning what each loop does, you should learn the difference between the different loops. The key thing is recognising exactly when the loop will start or stop.

Program Flow — Iteration

The final type of iteration statement you need to know about is the FOR loop — it's a type of <u>definite</u> iteration. A definite iteration statement will repeat for the exact number of times you tell it to.

FOR Loops are an example of a Count-Controlled Loop

1) <u>FOR loops</u> will repeat the code inside them a fixed number of times. The number of times that the code repeats will depend on an <u>initial value</u>, <u>end value</u> and sometimes a <u>step count</u>.

2) For example, FOR k ← 1 TO 10 STEP 3 will count up from 1 to 10 in steps of 3, so k ← 1, k ← 4, k ← 7 and k ← 10. If no step count is given the count will <u>increase by 1</u> each time.

3) The <u>number of times</u> the loop repeats can also be set as the <u>program runs</u> — e.g. FOR k ← 1 TO x, where x is a variable.

4) FOR loops can also use the count <u>within the loop</u> — in the example on the right, k is used to keep track of how many votes have been cast.

The FOR loop repeats the code between FOR and ENDFOR.

```
johnVote ← 0
sueVote ← 0
alanVote ← 0
FOR k ← 1 TO 100        Allows 100 votes to be cast.
  OUTPUT 'Please cast your vote.'
  voteName ← USERINPUT
  CASE voteName OF
    'John': johnVote ← johnVote + 1
            OUTPUT 'You voted for John.'
    'Sue': sueVote ← sueVote + 1
            OUTPUT 'You've voted for Sue.'
    'Alan': alanVote ← alanVote + 1
            OUTPUT 'You voted for Alan.'
  ENDCASE
  OUTPUT INT_TO_STRING(k) + ' total votes'
ENDFOR
```

Loops can contain other types of statement — the CASE statement used here is from p.20.

The value of k can be used anywhere within the loop.

Nested Iteration statements have Loops Within loops

1) Nested iteration statements will typically just have <u>one loop</u> inside <u>another loop</u> (an <u>outer</u> loop and an <u>inner</u> loop). But they can get quite complicated when you start <u>adding more loops</u> — you get loops within loops within loops... etc.

2) <u>Every time</u> the outer loop repeats, the inner loop completes a <u>full set</u> of iterations.

3) The example below shows a <u>FOR loop</u> inside a <u>REPEAT-UNTIL</u> loop. The algorithm is for a darts practice machine, where the player tries to get a score of <u>100 or more</u> in <u>3 darts</u>, and the machine counts <u>how many attempts</u> it takes them to do it.

Nested iteration is really useful when you're working with two-dimensional arrays — see p.28.

At the start of each iteration of the REPEAT loop, the number of attempts taken increases by 1 and the current total is reset to 0.

```
attempt ← 0
REPEAT
   attempt ← attempt + 1
   total ← 0
   FOR dart ← 1 TO 3
      OUTPUT 'Enter score for throw'
      score ← USERINPUT
      total ← total + score
   ENDFOR
UNTIL total ≥ 100
OUTPUT INT_TO_STRING(attempt) + ' attempts taken.'
```

Each time you go through the REPEAT loop, the FOR loop repeats 3 times.

The REPEAT loop ends when the player scores 100 points or more in one round.

On every iteration of the FOR loop, the player enters their score and it is added to their total for that attempt.

Use FOR loops when you know the number of repetitions...

When you're putting nested iteration statements into your own programs, you can use any combination of definite and indefinite loops. Just be careful that you don't get stuck looping around forever and ever.

Boolean Operators

Boolean operators work with Boolean values to produce a Boolean answer.

AND, OR and NOT are the only Boolean Operators you'll need

1) It doesn't make sense to use the arithmetic operators on things that are either true or false so instead you use the Boolean operators AND, OR and NOT.

Boolean operator	Examples that return true	Examples that return false
AND	3 < 5 AND 2 > 1	4 ≤ 5 AND 10 > 20
OR	1 > 8 OR 2 = 2	1 = 8 OR 2 < 2
NOT	NOT(5 > 8)	NOT(10 > 6)

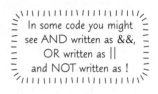
In some code you might see AND written as &&, OR written as || and NOT written as !

2) Just like with numerical operators, you can combine Boolean operators — it's important that you use brackets in long Boolean expressions to let the computer know which part to do first. Boolean operations are carried out in the following order: brackets, NOT, AND then OR.

Boolean Operators can be used in Conditions

Boolean operators can be used in selection and iteration statements (p.19-22) to check multiple conditions.

1. Karen and Stu are playing a 'best out of 10' game. The game should end when one of them wins 6 rounds or they both win 5 rounds. Write an algorithm to keep score in the game.

```
karenRounds ← 0
stuRounds ← 0
REPEAT
    OUTPUT 'Enter the name of the round winner'
    roundWinner ← USERINPUT
    CASE roundWinner OF
        'Karen': karenRounds ← karenRounds + 1
        'Stu':   stuRounds ← stuRounds + 1
    ENDCASE
UNTIL karenRounds = 6 OR stuRounds = 6 OR (karenRounds = 5 AND stuRounds = 5)
```

There's a CASE statement within the loop. This is where good indentation in your pseudo-code is key.

The REPEAT-UNTIL loop stops when one of these three conditions is met.

2. In a computer game a character's status depends on three variables: hunger, hydration and comfort. If any of the conditions on the right are met then the character dies, otherwise they are alive.
Write an algorithm to work out the status of the character.

- Any of the variables are equal to 0.
- Any two of the variables are less than 20.
- All three of the variables are less than 40.

```
IF hunger = 0 OR hydration = 0 OR comfort = 0 THEN
    alive ← false
ELSE IF (hunger < 20 AND hydration < 20) OR (hunger < 20 AND comfort < 20)
        OR (hydration < 20 AND comfort < 20) THEN
    alive ← false
ELSE IF hunger < 40 AND hydration < 40 AND comfort < 40 THEN
    alive ← false
ELSE
    alive ← true
ENDIF
```

The Boolean operators are AND, OR and NOT...

Using Boolean operators can save lots of work by letting you check many conditions at the same time.

Random Number Generation

Random numbers are really useful when you don't want your programs to do the same thing every time. They can be used to simulate random real-life events, e.g. rolling a dice, picking raffle tickets, etc.

Random Numbers are useful when making Games

1) Random numbers can be used in <u>simple games</u> when the programmer wants a number to be <u>unknown</u> — even the programmer themselves won't know what it's going to be.

2) Most programming languages have functions to <u>generate random numbers</u> — in pseudo-code, <u>random integers</u> can be generated using this function:

`RANDOM_INT(x, y)`

Generates a random integer between x and y (including x and y).

3) Here is an example of how random numbers can be used to simulate a roll of a <u>6-sided dice</u>.

Will randomly generate either 1, 2, 3, 4, 5 or 6 and assign it to the variable 'roll'.

```
roll ← RANDOM_INT(1, 6)
OUTPUT roll
```

Here, the number it has randomly generated is 2.

```
2
```

4) <u>FOR loops</u> can be used when you want to generate a <u>whole bunch</u> of random numbers.

This FOR loop will generate five random numbers from 1 to 10.

```
FOR i ← 1 TO 5
    roll ← RANDOM_INT(1, 10)
    OUTPUT roll
ENDFOR
```

The output will look something like...

```
4
9
4
2
10
```

Note that the same number can be randomly generated more than once.

You can use Random Numbers to make Random Selections

1) Instead of outputting the random number that you generated, you can use it to randomly generate <u>another event</u>.

2) Suppose you want to <u>simulate a coin toss</u> — there are two outcomes, <u>heads</u> or <u>tails</u> — we can simplify this in programming terms to 0 and 1 (where 0 = heads, 1 = tails).

```
number ← RANDOM_INT(0, 1)
IF number = 0 THEN
    OUTPUT 'Heads'
ELSE IF number = 1 THEN
    OUTPUT 'Tails'
ENDIF
```

Randomly generates either 0 or 1.

Technically, you could have an ELSE statement at the bottom without the condition, because there are only two possible outcomes.

3) Random numbers are really handy to use with <u>arrays</u> (see p.27-28). You can generate a <u>random number</u> then pick the element in that <u>position</u> of the array.

Uses the random number to select a piece of fruit from the array.

The random number generated was 3, so the fruit that was chosen was 'Peach' — as numbering in an array starts at 0.

```
fruits ← ['Mango', 'Banana', 'Pear', 'Peach']
number ← RANDOM_INT(0, 3)
chosenFruit ← fruits[number]
OUTPUT number
OUTPUT 'Today you should eat a ' + chosenFruit
```
```
3
Today you should eat a Peach
```

Randomly generates either 0, 1, 2 or 3.

Use random numbers to make your program more unpredictable...

The random numbers that are generated in a programming language are called pseudo-random numbers because they aren't completely random, they just look like they are. They are usually generated by following a complex algorithm which means that they will have a pattern — it's just very hard to see it.

Warm-Up and Worked Exam Questions

Time to see if all that information is sinking in. Have a go at these warm-up questions, then read through the worked exam questions before having a go at the questions on the next page yourself.

Warm-Up Questions

1) For each of the following, say if it is selection or iteration:
   a) REPEAT-UNTIL   b) IF-THEN-ELSE   c) CASE
   d) DO-WHILE   e) ELSE-IF   f) WHILE

2) Give one difference between a CASE statement and an ELSE-IF statement.

3) a) Name a type of a count-controlled loop and a type of condition-controlled loop.
   b) Explain the difference between the two loops given in part a).

4) Decide whether the following Boolean expressions are true or false:
   a) $12 > 4$ AND $8 = 5$ b) NOT$(11 = 3)$
   c) $12 \leq 4$ OR $10 \neq 5$ d) NOT$(9 > 4$ AND $5 < 2)$

5) List all the values that could be generated by RANDOM_INT(3, 8).

Worked Exam Questions

1 A garden centre has a climate monitoring system that gives warnings if the temperature and humidity aren't at suitable levels. The climate monitoring system contains this algorithm.

```
IF humidity = 50 AND (temperature > 16 AND temperature < 25) THEN
    OUTPUT 'Humidity and temperature at acceptable levels.'
ELSE IF temperature ≤ 16 OR temperature ≥ 25 THEN
    OUTPUT 'Warning — Please alter the temperature.'
ELSE
    OUTPUT 'Warning — Please alter the humidity.'
ENDIF
```

a) What will the output be if `humidity` is 30 and `temperature` is 16?

'Warning — Please alter the temperature.'

[1 mark]

b) What will the output be if `humidity` is 30 and `temperature` is 20?

'Warning — Please alter the humidity.'

[1 mark]

2 Salik needs a program that will ask users to create a password and then check if the password contains at least six characters. If it contains fewer than six characters the user must try again, otherwise the user is informed that their password is valid. Write an appropriate program for Salik.

```
REPEAT
        OUTPUT 'Please enter a password'
        password ← USERINPUT
UNTIL LEN(password) ≥ 6
OUTPUT 'Your password is valid'
```

Using a REPEAT-UNTIL loop will mean that the code in the loop always runs through at least once.

[4 marks]

Exam Questions

3 Jasminda has written the following program to convert minutes into hours and minutes.

```
OUTPUT 'Enter a number of minutes'
minutes ← USERINPUT
hours ← minutes DIV 60
mins ← minutes MOD 60
OUTPUT (INT_TO_STRING(hours) + ' hrs ' + INT_TO_STRING(mins) + ' mins')
```

   a) Which of these is the program an example of? Shade **one** oval only.

      A Validation ⬭   **C** Selection ⬭

      B Sequence ⬭   **D** Iteration ⬭

[1 mark]

   b) What would the program output if the input was 150?

....

[1 mark]

4 A developer has written the following code as part of a card game app. It is used to show 5 random playing cards from a standard deck (which is stored in an array called `deck`):

```
FOR x ← 1 TO 5
    randNum ← RANDOM_INT(0, LEN(deck)-1)
    drawnCard ← deck[randNum]
    OUTPUT drawnCard
ENDFOR
```

Explain **one** problem with the way this code uses random number generation to draw cards.

....

....

....

[2 marks]

5 A tumble dryer will only be allowed to start if all of the following conditions are met:
* the real variable `weight` is more than 1.5 and less than 15.0
* the boolean variable `doorClosed` is true.

Write an algorithm that checks these conditions before allowing the tumble dryer to start.

[3 marks]

6 Karl and John are playing snap. Write an algorithm that:
* Asks for the name of the winner of each game.
* After ten games, checks who has won more and displays the winner's name or tells them that it's a draw.

You'll need variables to keep track of the winner of each game and the number of games each player has won.

[6 marks]

Arrays

When you need to store data within a program you can do it using variables. But if you have lots of similar data to store, then using variables for each one is inefficient and that's where arrays come in.

Arrays are used to store multiple Data Values

1) An array is a <u>data structure</u> that can store a group of data values, of the <u>same type</u>, under <u>one name</u>.

2) Each piece of data in an array is called an <u>element</u> — each element can be <u>accessed</u> using its <u>position</u> (or <u>index</u>) in the array.

3) Arrays are <u>most helpful</u> when you have lots of <u>related data</u> that you want to store and it doesn't make sense to use <u>separate variables</u> — e.g. the names of pupils in a class, marks in a test, etc.

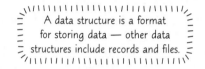
A data structure is a format for storing data — other data structures include records and files.

4) Just like variables, some languages require you to <u>declare arrays</u> before you use them.

One-Dimensional Arrays are like Lists

The easiest way to get your head around <u>one-dimensional arrays</u> is to picture them as <u>lists</u>.
Different languages have lots of fancy ways to <u>create</u> and <u>update arrays</u>.
Here are the ones you'll need to learn for your exam:

1) Creating arrays — just like variables, you start off with the <u>array name</u> and the <u>assignment operator</u>.
Then put your data values inside <u>square brackets</u> [ ] with <u>commas</u> separating each value.

```
rowers ← ['Mark', 'Adam', 'Shelly', 'Tobias']
```
Here the strings '<u>Mark</u>', '<u>Adam</u>', '<u>Shelly</u>' and '<u>Tobias</u>' are in positions <u>0</u>, <u>1</u>, <u>2</u> and <u>3</u> of the <u>rowers</u> array.

2) Retrieving elements from an array can be done by using the <u>name</u> of the array and the <u>element's position</u>. Remember that positions are numbered <u>starting at 0</u>.

```
OUTPUT rowers[0]
```
```
Mark
```

3) Changing elements is done by reassigning the array position to a different data value.

Replaces the rower in position 0 with 'Tamal'.

```
rowers[0] ← 'Tamal'
OUTPUT rowers
```
```
['Tamal', 'Adam', 'Shelly', 'Tobias']
```
Notice that 'Mark' has been completely removed from the array.

4) The <u>number of elements</u> in an array can be found using the LEN() function — just like for strings (see p.16).

```
LEN(rowers)
```
```
4
```

Combining these <u>array functions</u> with <u>FOR loops</u> (see p.22) will give you a <u>systematic way</u> of accessing and changing all of the <u>elements</u> in an array. Amongst other things, FOR loops can be used to <u>search</u> for specific elements, or make a similar change to <u>lots of elements</u>.

EXAMPLE: The numbers below are stored in an array called scores.
Write an algorithm that will add 3 to each element of the scores array.

| 4 | 12 | 32 | 18 | 21 | 11 | 9 | 14 | 24 |

FOR loop will run on each element of the array — i.e. from position 0 to position 8.

```
FOR k ← 0 TO LEN(scores)-1
    scores[k] ← scores[k] + 3
ENDFOR
```
Adds 3 to the element in position k of the array.

Think of one dimensional arrays as lists of similar objects...

In some languages (e.g. C, C++, Java™) you'll find that arrays can only store one data type and that you can't change their size once they've been declared. In others (e.g. PHP) arrays are much more flexible data structures — they can store different data types and their size can be altered.

Arrays

Now that you've covered one-dimensional arrays, the only way is up — that's right, two-dimensional arrays. Arrays can have even more dimensions, but luckily the examiners have decided that two is enough for now.

Two-Dimensional Arrays are like a List Of Lists

You can think of two-dimensional arrays as <u>one-dimensional arrays</u> where <u>each element</u> is also a <u>one-dimensional array</u>.

```
trees ← [['oak', 'ash'], ['beech', 'cedar'], ['pine', 'elm']]
```

You can visualise arrays as tables or grids.

	0	1
0	oak	ash
1	beech	cedar
2	pine	elm

The <u>position</u> of an element is usually written as [a][b] or [a, b], where <u>a</u> represents the position of the one-dimensional list that the element is in and <u>b</u> represents its position within that one-dimensional list.

```
OUTPUT 'My favourite tree is ' + trees[0][0]
OUTPUT 'My 2nd favourite tree is ' + trees[2][1]
```

```
My favourite tree is oak
My 2nd favourite tree is elm
```

You can <u>change elements</u> in exactly the same way as you saw for <u>one-dimensional arrays</u> (p.27).

You can also use the <u>LEN()</u> function on an <u>array</u> or on an <u>element</u> in the array.

```
LEN(trees)
```
```
3
```

```
LEN(trees[1])
```
```
2
```

 **EXAMPLE:** The 'scores' array has been used to store four test scores for five pupils, as shown. E.g. scores[2][0] will return the test 2 score for pupil 0, which is 5.

		Pupils				
		0	1	2	3	4
Tests	0	15	5	13	12	7
	1	2	14	11	14	9
	2	5	4	12	7	13
	3	6	8	18	19	15

a) **Evaluate scores[3][2] / scores[1][0].**

scores[3][2] = 18 and scores[1][0] = 2

So scores[3][2] / scores[1][0] = 18/2 = 9

b) **Write an algorithm to count the total score of any given pupil.**

As there aren't very many scores you could just add them together. E.g. for pupil 0 you could do scores[0][0] + scores[1][0] + scores[2][0] + scores[3][0]. But it's <u>better practice</u> to use a <u>loop</u> as it is easier to edit.

```
total ← 0
OUTPUT 'Enter the number of the pupil'
pupil ← USERINPUT
FOR i ← 0 TO 3
    total ← total + scores[i][pupil]
ENDFOR
OUTPUT total
```

c) **The pass mark on every test was 9 or above. Write an algorithm to count the number of passes in the original array.**

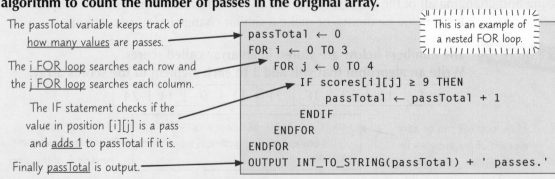

The passTotal variable keeps track of <u>how many values</u> are passes.

The <u>i FOR loop</u> searches each row and the <u>j FOR loop</u> searches each column.

The IF statement checks if the value in position [i][j] is a pass and <u>adds 1</u> to passTotal if it is.

Finally <u>passTotal</u> is output.

This is an example of a nested FOR loop.

```
passTotal ← 0
FOR i ← 0 TO 3
    FOR j ← 0 TO 4
        IF scores[i][j] ≥ 9 THEN
            passTotal ← passTotal + 1
        ENDIF
    ENDFOR
ENDFOR
OUTPUT INT_TO_STRING(passTotal) + ' passes.'
```

Two-dimensional arrays are really just an array of arrays...

Two-dimensional arrays can be used to store information about a digital image — each pixel's information can be stored as an element in the array. Programmers can then manipulate the image using array commands, e.g. changing the values of pixels, cutting rows and columns out of the image, etc.

Records

Records are another useful data structure — you need to know what they are and how to use them.

Records can contain Different Data Types

1) A record is a type of data structure (like an array — see p.27), which means that it is used to store a collection of data values.

In the context of a database table, a record is just a row of data.

2) One of the things that makes records so useful is that, unlike arrays, they can store values with different data types (see p.12), such as strings, integers and Booleans.

3) Each item in a record is called a field, and each field is given a data type and a field name when the record is created. The field name can help to describe the data stored in that field of the record.

Different programming languages have slight variations on record data structures. E.g. Python has dictionaries, and C has structures.

4) Records are fixed in length, which means that you can't add extra fields to them once they've been created.

Records can keep Related Information in one place

1) When you create a record structure, you can assign a data type and a name to each field:

Each field has its own data type.

```
RECORD recipes
    INT recipeNumber
    STRING recipeName
    BOOL tested
    INT score
ENDRECORD
```

The record is called 'recipes'.

'recipeNumber', 'recipeName', 'tested' and 'score' are the fields of the record.

2) Once you've created the structure of your record, you can assign it to variables:

'recipe1', 'recipe2' and 'recipe3' are all variables with the 'recipes' record structure.

```
recipe1 ← recipes(1, 'Chocolate Cake', True, 3)
recipe2 ← recipes(2, 'Lemon Slice', False, 0)
recipe3 ← recipes(3, 'Coconut Cookies', True, 8)
```

The data in each field needs to have the correct data type. E.g. the last one, 'score', should be an integer.

3) You can use the variable name to access a whole record. Or you can use the variable name with a field name to access a particular item of a record.

```
OUTPUT recipe1
OUTPUT recipe3.recipeName
```
```
(1, 'Chocolate Cake', True, 3)
Coconut Cookies
```

Individual items in a record can be accessed and changed.

```
recipe2.tested ← True
recipe2.score ← 6
OUTPUT recipe2.recipeName + ' scored '
        + INT_TO_STRING(recipe2.score)
```
```
Lemon Slice scored 6
```

Arrays are handy if you want to Group Records together

If you have multiple variables with the same record structure, you can collect them in an array.

```
recipeBook ← [recipe1, recipe2, recipe3]
FOR i ← 0 TO 2
    IF recipeBook[i].score ≥ 7 THEN
        OUTPUT recipeBook[i].recipeName
    ENDIF
ENDFOR
```
```
Coconut Cookies
```

This will output the names of all recipes with a score ≥ 7.

You can visualise the recipeBook array as a table:

	recipeNumber	recipeName	tested	score
0	1	Chocolate Cake	True	3
1	2	Lemon Slice	True	6
2	3	Coconut Cookies	True	8

Well, we got through all that in record time...

You might see records presented differently to this, but the key concepts will be the same. You'll still need to understand what records and fields are, and how they are used in programming.

File Handling

File handling is all about how a program can access data and change data stored in an external file.

Files allow Permanent Data Storage

1) Storing data in arrays (p.27-28) and records (p.29) is useful when the program is running, but all the data will be lost when the program is closed.

2) It's often useful for programs to store data permanently and then access it at a later date — this is done by writing data to an external file.

3) Programming languages typically have their own commands for handling files. Most languages will have commands to open files, close files, read text from a file and write text to a file.

Always start by Opening the External File

Some programming languages have separate open commands depending on whether you want to read from or write to the file.

1) Before you can do anything with a file you need to open it. This is done by using an OPEN() command and assigning it to a variable.

This will open the file so that you can read or write to it.

```
newFile ← OPEN('newFile.txt')
```

This is the name of the file you want to open. Sometimes you'll have to give the whole file path.

2) Once a file is opened the program will start reading or writing from the beginning. As you read from or write to the file, the program keeps its place in the file (think of it like a cursor).

3) When you're finished reading or writing to a file you should always close it using CLOSE(). If you forget to close it then the file can remain locked and prevent others from editing it.

Read or Write to a file after it is Opened

1) After you have opened a file you can read or write to it.

2) You can write text to a file using the WRITE() or WRITELINE() commands. If the file already contains some text then you'll need to be careful that you don't overwrite it.

The WRITE() and WRITELINE() commands take two parameters. The first is the variable storing the file and the second is the text you want to write.

```
winners ← OPEN('victory.txt')
names ← ['Jenny', 'Carlos', 'Matty', 'Anna']
FOR i ← 0 TO 3
    textToWrite ← INT_TO_STRING(i) + ' ' + names[i]
    WRITELINE(winners, textToWrite)
ENDFOR
CLOSE(winners)
```

The text file will look like this.

```
0 Jenny
1 Carlos
2 Matty
3 Anna
```

3) You can read text from a file using READ() or READLINE().

Reads the first line of the text file as programs always start reading from the start of the file. After this command is called, the 'cursor' will be at the beginning of the second line.

```
winners ← OPEN('victory.txt')
firstLine ← READLINE(winners)
secondLine ← READLINE(winners)
CLOSE(winners)
```

Reads the second line of the file as that's where the program is up to. After this command is called, the 'cursor' will be at the beginning of the third line.

4) ENDOFFILE() is another useful command. It returns 'true' if the 'cursor' is at the end of the file. It's really handy for using as the condition to tell a loop when to terminate.

```
winners ← OPEN('victory.txt')
REPEAT
    currentLine ← READLINE(winners)
    OUTPUT currentLine
UNTIL ENDOFFILE(winners)
CLOSE(winners)
```

Learning to read and write, it's like being back at primary school...

Data is stored externally so that it's not lost when the program is closed. E.g. a computer game will save your progress externally — if it was saved internally you'd lose your progress when the game was closed.

Subroutines

Subroutines (or sub programs) can be used to save time and to simplify code. By now you'll definitely have come across them even if you don't know what they are yet — all is explained on the next two pages.

Subroutines help to avoid Repeating Code

1) Subroutines are sets of instructions stored under one name — when you want your program to do the whole set of instructions you only need to call the name of the subroutine.

2) Subroutines can be either functions or procedures — the main difference is that functions always return a value and procedures do not.

3) Subroutines are very useful when you have sets of instructions that you need to repeat in different places within a program. They give your program more structure and readability whilst cutting down on the amount of code you actually need to write.

4) High-level programming languages (see p.42) have common subroutines built into them. If you want one that does something more specific you can create them yourself.

```
# The max() subroutine returns the highest value.
x ← max(12, 21, 8, 9, 19)
```

5) In most subroutines you'll encounter parameters.

> Parameters are special variables used to pass values into a subroutine.
> For each parameter you can specify a name, a data type and a default value.

The actual values that the parameters take when the subroutine is called are sometimes called arguments.

Subroutines can carry out a Set Of Instructions

1) Subroutines don't have to take parameters... ...but they sometimes will.   *'name' is a parameter.*

```
SUBROUTINE welcome()
   OUTPUT 'Hello and welcome.'
   OUTPUT 'This is a procedure.'
ENDSUBROUTINE
```

```
SUBROUTINE betterWelcome(name)
   OUTPUT 'Hello ' + name + ' and welcome.'
   OUTPUT 'This is a procedure.'
ENDSUBROUTINE
```

2) Subroutines are called by typing their name (and giving parameters if necessary).

```
welcome()
```
```
Hello and welcome.
This is a procedure.
```

```
betterWelcome('Pablo')
```
```
Hello Pablo and welcome.
This is a procedure.
```

The string 'Pablo' is passed into the betterWelcome subroutine.

3) Note that subroutines that don't return a value are called procedures.

Functions will always Return a Value

1) Subroutines that return a value are called functions.

2) When a function is called it should be assigned to a variable or used in a statement otherwise the value that it returns will not be stored anywhere and will be lost.

See p.16 for a reminder on string manipulation.

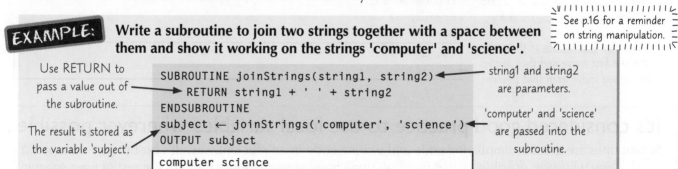

EXAMPLE: **Write a subroutine to join two strings together with a space between them and show it working on the strings 'computer' and 'science'.**

Use RETURN to pass a value out of the subroutine.

```
SUBROUTINE joinStrings(string1, string2)
   RETURN string1 + ' ' + string2
ENDSUBROUTINE
subject ← joinStrings('computer', 'science')
OUTPUT subject
```
```
computer science
```

string1 and string2 are parameters.

'computer' and 'science' are passed into the subroutine.

The result is stored as the variable 'subject'.

Subroutines

Subroutines can contain anything covered in this Section

 **EXAMPLE:** Orla has been given a maths problem to add together all of the numbers between two integers (including the integers themselves) and work out if the total is divisible by 7.
Write a subroutine that Orla could use to solve the maths problem for any pair of integers.

The variable 'total' is defined inside the subroutine so it's a local variable (see below).

The IF statement checks if the total is divisible by 7. Remember, MOD will give the remainder of a division (p.13).

x and y are the parameters of the subroutine.

The FOR loop is used to add up all the integers from x to y.

The subroutine is a function as it returns a value.

```
SUBROUTINE addIntegers(x, y)
    total ← 0
    FOR i ← x TO y
        total ← total + i
    ENDFOR
    IF total MOD 7 = 0 THEN
        RETURN true
    ELSE
        RETURN false
    ENDIF
ENDSUBROUTINE
```

Variables can be Local or Global

All parameters have local scope to the subroutine.

1) All variables have a <u>scope</u> (either local or global) — the scope of a variable tells you <u>which parts</u> of the program the variable can be used in.

> <u>Local variables</u> can only be used <u>within the structure</u> they're declared in — they have a <u>local scope</u>.
> <u>Global variables</u> can be used <u>any time</u> after their declaration — they have a <u>global scope</u>.

2) Variables declared inside a <u>subroutine</u> are <u>local variables</u>. They are <u>invisible</u> to the rest of the program — this means that they can't be used <u>outside</u> the subroutine.

3) The <u>advantage</u> of local variables is that their scope only extends to the subroutine they're declared in. They <u>can't affect</u> and are not affected by anything outside of the subroutine. It also doesn't matter if you use the <u>same variable name</u> as a local variable defined elsewhere in the program.

4) Variables in the <u>main body</u> of a program can be made into global variables using the 'GLOBAL' keyword — these variables can then be used anywhere in the program. It can be difficult to keep track of the <u>value</u> of global variables in <u>larger programs</u>.

5) The example below shows how <u>global variables</u> are used to store data outside of the subroutine.

x and y are defined <u>globally</u> — if they were declared inside the subroutine then they'd <u>reset to 0</u> each time the subroutine was called.

The subroutine is a <u>procedure</u> as it <u>doesn't</u> return a value.

The <u>parameters</u> a and b are added to the <u>global variables</u> x and y.

The program <u>keeps track</u> of the position after the first move and then applies the second move from that position.

```
# A subroutine to keep track of a character's x and y position.
GLOBAL x ← 0
GLOBAL y ← 0
SUBROUTINE move(a, b)
    x ← x + a
    y ← y + b
    OUTPUT '(' + INT_TO_STRING(x) + ', ' + INT_TO_STRING(y) + ')'
ENDSUBROUTINE
move(3, 5)
move(4, 7)
```

<u>a</u> and <u>b</u> are parameters so they have <u>local scope</u> to this procedure — they're <u>invisible</u> elsewhere in the program.

```
(3, 5)
(7, 12)
```

It's considered good practice to use local variables wherever possible...

Subroutines are great at simplifying code and writing code in an efficient way. It's best to give variables a local scope wherever possible — that way you don't have to worry about them in the rest of your program.

Warm-Up and Worked Exam Questions

That's all the learning done for the programming section — perfect time for some practice. Here are some warm-up questions to get you started, followed by a whole bunch of exam questions on the next two pages.

Warm-Up Questions

1) The top 5 high scores in an arcade game are stored in the highscores array shown below:

	0	1	2	3	4
Score	510 000	453 000	442 000	440 500	429 000

Give the output for the following:
   a) OUTPUT highscores[3]   b) OUTPUT highscores[0] - highscores[4]

2) Explain what the following commands will do with the array footballers.
   a) player ← footballers[3]   b) footballers[5] ← 'Pele'

3) Write the pseudo-code command that will:
   a) Open a file.   b) Write text in a file.
   c) Close a file.   d) Read text from a file.

4) Give two reasons why a programmer may choose to use a record to store data.

5) Give three benefits of using subroutines when you are writing code.

Worked Exam Question

1 Frances uses a program to create a list of jobs she has to do and store it in the ToDoList.txt file, shown on the right.

> 1. Clean my room.
> 2. Computer Science homework.
> 3. Organise my stamp collection.

   a) Give **two** reasons why a programmer might choose to store data in an external file.

   1 Data would not be lost when the program is closed.

   2 Multiple programs can access the data.

   They could also store the data in a file to send to someone else, or to create a backup.   *[2 marks]*

Frances wants to add more features to this program. She writes the following code:

```
01  myList ← OPEN('ToDoList.txt')
02  OUTPUT READLINE(myList)
03  CLOSE(myList)
```

   b) Describe what each line of the above code does.

   Line 01 Opens the file and assigns it to the variable myList.

   Line 02 Outputs the first line of the file (1. Clean my room.)

   Line 03 Closes the file.

   [3 marks]

   c) Explain why it is good practice to use CLOSE() when working with external files.

   Leaving files open may prevent other users or other programs from accessing them.

   [1 mark]

Exam Questions

2 Write a subroutine that takes an integer as a parameter and returns
the difference between the integer's cube and its square.

[3 marks]

3 A 2D array is used to store the names of the top 3 pupils in each event of a sports day.

a) What data type should each element of the array be assigned?

....
[1 mark]

b) Give **three** reasons for using a 2D array to store this data.

1 ....

2 ....

3 ....
[3 marks]

4 A comic book shop stores information about each of its comics in records.
The table below shows two records stored in the `comics` table.

ID Number	Title	Publication date	Length	Genre	Rating
0001	Hike of hope	04-05-2015	82	Adventure	5
0002	Voyage of Destiny	05-09-2015	65	Science Fiction	4

a) What data type should be used for the "Genre" field?

....
[1 mark]

b) Explain why they have chosen to store this information in records rather than an array.

....

....
[2 marks]

5 Omar has written an adventure story in the file adventure.txt.

Write an algorithm that allows a user to output Omar's adventure story one line at a time.
- Each time the user presses the 'y' key, the next line of the story should be outputted.
- The algorithm should end and close the file when it outputs the string 'THE END'.

[5 marks]

Exam Questions

6 John and three of his friends are training to run a marathon.
John records how many miles he and three friends ran each day last week.
John stores the data in a 2D array called distanceRun.

			Days of the week				
		0	**1**	**2**	**3**	**4**	**5**	**6**
Runner	**0**	9	10	8	12	0	6	9
	1	10	12	15	15	0	0	10
	2	15	14	13	16	0	8	9
	3	6	8	9	10	12	12	0

The distance run on day 0 by runner 2 is given by distanceRun[0][2].

a) Write the code to display the distance run on day 4 by runner 3.

....

....
[1 mark]

b) Write an algorithm that takes a runner number as an input and
outputs the total number of miles that they ran over the week.
[4 marks]

c) John has written the function milesConvert() which takes a distance in miles
and returns the equivalent distance in km. E.g. milesConvert(5) would return 8.
Write an algorithm to convert all distances in the array to km.
[3 marks]

7 Noel has written the subroutine rollTwo(n), which simulates the outcome of two random rolls
of an n-sided dice, returning the results as an array. E.g. rollTwo(6) might return [5, 3].

a) Noel has declared a local variable inside the subroutine.
Explain **two** reasons why it is good practice to use local variables.

1 ....

....

2 ....

....
[4 marks]

b) Noel wants to use his function in a dice game where two identical dice are rolled together.
- The player can choose the number of sides that the dice have.
- The player's score is the number of rolls it takes until both dice land on the same number.

Write a subroutine that takes the number of sides of the dice as a parameter,
uses the rollTwo subroutine to simulate a game, and returns a player's score.

[5 marks]

Revision Questions for Section Two

Well, that just about wraps up the programming section — perfect time to try some revision questions I think.

- Try these questions and <u>tick off each one</u> when you <u>get it right</u>.
- When you've done <u>all the questions</u> for a topic and are <u>completely happy</u> with it, tick off the topic.

Data Types, Operators, Constants, Variables and Strings (p.12-16) ☑

1) Define the following data types: integer, real, boolean, character and string. ☑

2)* Write a piece of pseudo-code that converts:
   a) the string '1234' into an integer.   b) the real 0.578 into a string.
   c) the integer 8 into a string.   d) the string '0.75' into a real. ☑

3) In pseudo-code, what do each of these operators do?
   a) =   b) MOD   c) *   d) ←   e) DIV ☑

4) What is meant by: a) a constant?   b) a variable? ☑

5) a) Define string concatenation and give an example of it being used.
   b)* What will each of the following pieces of pseudo-code return if colour ← 'magenta'?
       (i) LEN(colour)   (ii) POSITION(colour, 'g')   (iii) SUBSTRING(0, 3, colour) ☑

Program Flow, Boolean Operators and Random Numbers (p.19-24) ☑

6) In 20 words or less, outline what each of these statements does:
   a) IF statement   b) CASE statement. ☑

7) What is the main difference between ELSE-IF statements and nested IF statements? ☑

8) Compare the features of the three condition-controlled loops, REPEAT-UNTIL, WHILE and DO-WHILE. ☑

9)* Write an algorithm that outputs the number of Mondays in a 30-day month
    when the user inputs the day of the week that the month started on. ☑

10)* Write an algorithm to simulate 100 rolls of an 8-sided dice and output the result of each roll. ☑

Arrays, Records and File Handling (p.27-30) ☑

11) Why are arrays useful? ☑

12)* Write commands to perform the following operations on this array. The name of the array is 'chars'.
    ['3', 'T', 'P', '2', 'M', 'e', '4', 'q', 's', '3'].
    a) Output the character 'M'.
    b) Replace the 'P' in the chars array with a 'D'.
    c) Replace every element in the chars array with an 'N'. ☑

13)* Write an algorithm to create a two-dimensional array with 10 rows and 10 columns where each
    element is an integer and its value is given by the row number multiplied by the column number.
    (Hint: Remember that rows and columns are numbered starting at 0.) ☑

14) In programming, data can be stored in records:
    a) What is a record?   b) Give two differences between a record and a field. ☑

15) Give one benefit of storing data in an external file. ☑

16) Briefly describe what each of the following functions do:
    a) OPEN()   b) CLOSE()   c) WRITELINE()   d) READLINE() ☑

Subroutines (p.31-32) ☑

17) What is a subroutine? ☑

18) What is the difference between a function and a procedure? ☑

19) Define these terms: a) parameter   b) local variable   c) global variable ☑

*Answers on p.141

Structured Programming

On p.31-32 you saw how subroutines could be used to store a whole set of instructions under one name. Well, a single program will typically use lots of subroutines that each perform specific and simple tasks.

Structured Programming makes Coding much Easier

1) Structured (or modular) programming involves decomposing (see p.1) the program that you want to write into manageable modules. Each of those modules is then decomposed even further into smaller modules and eventually into modules that perform individual tasks.

2) Simple subroutines can be written to carry out each individual task. Then the bigger modules and main program can be written using these subroutines.

3) It's important to clearly document the interface of each module. This means listing the module's name, any inputs (i.e. parameters), processes (what the module does) and the output/return value (if any).

4) For example, to design a program simulating a game of noughts and crosses you might have:

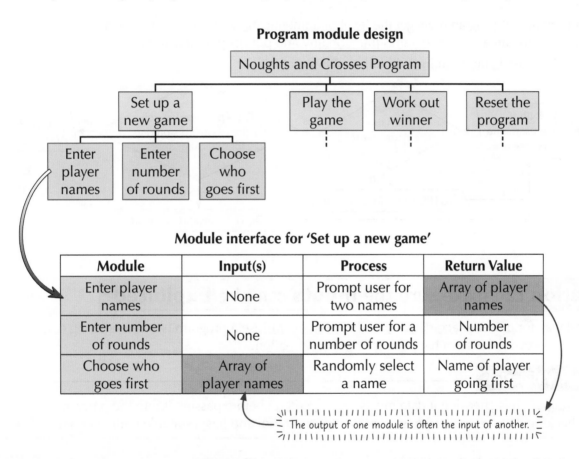

Program module design

Module interface for 'Set up a new game'

Module	Input(s)	Process	Return Value
Enter player names	None	Prompt user for two names	Array of player names
Enter number of rounds	None	Prompt user for a number of rounds	Number of rounds
Choose who goes first	Array of player names	Randomly select a name	Name of player going first

The output of one module is often the input of another.

Advantages of Structured Programming

- Coding is easier because you're only writing subroutines that carry out very simple tasks.
- Lots of programmers can work on one program as each module can be written independently.
- It's easier to test structured programs as each module can be tested individually (see p.40).
- Individual subroutines and modules can be fixed and updated without affecting the rest of the program.
- You will be able to reuse the subroutines and modules in programs you write in the future.

Planning your programming can make it more manageable...

The key to a well-structured program is planning — decomposing the program into modules is always an important step. Try finishing off the design for the noughts and crosses program above.

Robust Programming

Authentication and validation are used to improve the security and robustness of your programs.

Authentication can help Protect your programs

1) Authentication can confirm the identity of a user before they're allowed to access certain pieces of data or features of the program. A common way that programs do this is using passwords.

2) Passwords are usually associated with a username. When someone tries to access a protected part of the program, it should ask them for their password to check that they are who they claim to be.

3) Here are some common ways to increase the security of a password-based authentication system:

    • Force users to use strong passwords (p.100) and get them to change their passwords regularly.
    • Limit the number of failed authentication attempts before access to an account is lost.
    • Ask for a random selection of characters from the password on each authentication.

4) It's important that programmers get the level of authentication correct — too much authentication can affect a program's functionality and put people off using it.

5) A typical authentication routine will follow this structure:

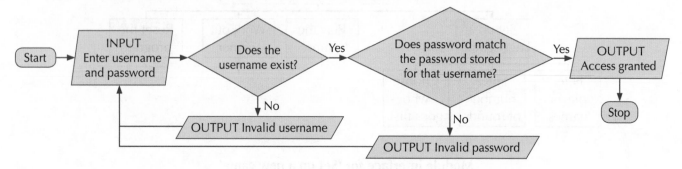

Validation can make sure the Inputs can't be Exploited

The easiest way for a user to accidentally or intentionally misuse a program is when entering data. You can try to prevent this from happening by using validation.

Input Validation

Input validation is checking if data meets certain criteria before passing it into the program.
E.g. checking that an email address contains an @ symbol and has a suitable ending (.com, .co.uk, etc).

Here are a few common types of input validation check you can use:

Range check	Checks the data is within a specified range.
Presence check	Checks the data has actually been entered.
Format check	Checks the data has the correct format (e.g. a date).
Look-up table	Checks the data against a table of acceptable values.
Length check	Checks the data is the correct length.

These are important ways of keeping programs secure...

You should be able to write subroutines to do simple authentication and validation checks (see next page). Think about who you want to access your programs and what data you want them to be able to enter.

Robust Programming

Example of Input Validation

You can use the things you saw in <u>Section Two</u> to write an <u>authentication</u> or <u>validation algorithm</u>.

 **EXAMPLE:**
Karen wants to validate usernames for an online forum.
She wants each username to be longer than 5 characters,
shorter than 12 characters and start with an uppercase letter.

a) **Give two validation checks Karen would need to use.**

- Length check to make sure the username is not longer or shorter than the lengths allowed.
- Format check to make sure the username starts with an uppercase letter.

b) **Write a subroutine that will check if a username is a valid length.**

```
SUBROUTINE validateUsername(username)
    usernameLength ← LEN(username)
    IF usernameLength > 5 AND usernameLength < 12 THEN
        RETURN true
    ELSE
        RETURN false
    ENDIF
ENDSUBROUTINE
```

Use the LEN() function (see p.16) to find the length of the username.

Use comparison operators (see p.14) to see if the length is valid.

Use a selection statement (see p.19-20) and return true or false depending on whether or not the length is valid.

Your program should be Easy To Maintain

1) When using structured programming, it's important that your code is <u>well-maintained</u>.

2) A well-maintained program makes it <u>easy</u> for other programmers to understand what the code does. They should also be able to <u>change</u> parts of the source code without the risk of causing problems elsewhere in the code (e.g. knock on effects).

3) The following features can <u>improve</u> the maintainability of source code:

Too many comments can leave your programs looking cluttered and unreadable.

- <u>Comments</u> (usually written after # or //) are useful for <u>explaining</u> what the <u>key features</u> of a program do — <u>well written</u> and <u>clear</u> comments are fundamental for helping other programmers <u>understand your programs</u>.

- <u>Indentation</u> can be used to separate <u>different statements</u> in a program. This allows other programmers to see the flow of the program more <u>clearly</u> and pick out the <u>different features</u>.

- <u>Variables</u>, <u>subroutines</u> and <u>parameters</u> should be named so that they refer to what they actually are. This helps programmers to understand what they do, and makes it easier to <u>keep track</u> of them.

- Only use <u>global variables</u> (see p.32) when <u>necessary</u> as they could affect the rest of your code. Variables with a <u>local scope</u> will only affect the subroutines that they are <u>declared in</u> — other programmers will know that <u>changing these variables</u> won't affect <u>other parts</u> of the program.

 REVISION TASK

Keep your revision notes well-maintained, too...

Keeping code well-maintained isn't rocket science, but sometimes programmers can get lazy and their code ends up in a bit of a mess. Have a look back at some code you've written. Write down some ways that you could have improved the maintainability of your code.

Testing

When you're writing programs, remember that the testing is just as important as the programming itself. Have a look at this page to test your knowledge of testing — it will prepare you for being tested in the tests.

Programming Errors can be **Syntax Errors** and **Logic Errors**

1) It's quite typical for a program to contain <u>errors</u> during its development — these errors need to be <u>found</u> and <u>corrected</u> as soon as possible.

2) The first task is to figure out what <u>type of error</u> has occurred:

> SYNTAX ERRORS — when the compiler or interpreter <u>doesn't understand</u> something you've typed because it doesn't follow the <u>rules</u> or <u>grammar</u> of the programming language.
>
> LOGIC ERRORS — when the compiler or interpreter is able to <u>run the program</u>, but the program does something <u>unexpected</u>.

3) <u>Syntax errors</u> can be <u>diagnosed</u> by compilers and interpreters (see p.42) — they'll be unable to turn the <u>source code</u> into <u>machine code</u> and a syntax error (with its location) will be returned.

4) <u>Logic errors</u> are more <u>difficult to diagnose</u> and <u>track down</u> — compilers and interpreters <u>won't</u> pick them up. Logic errors are found through general use of the program and by systematically <u>testing</u> it using a <u>test plan</u> (see below).

A **Test Plan** should be made **Before Implementation**

1) A <u>test plan</u> will outline exactly what you're going to test and how you're going to test it. It should cover all the <u>possible paths</u> through a program.

2) A <u>good test plan</u> will anticipate potential issues with the program and select appropriate <u>test data</u> to test for these issues.

Possible paths are all the branches of the flowchart (p.3) for your program.

3) The <u>test data</u> that you use in your test plan should fall into one of three categories:

- <u>Normal (typical) data</u> — things that a user is <u>likely</u> to input into the program.
- <u>Boundary (extreme) data</u> — values at the <u>limit</u> of what the program should be able to handle.
- <u>Erroneous data</u> — inputs that the program <u>should not accept</u>.

4) The table below shows an example of a test plan for setting an alarm system. Users should be able to set their own 3-5 digit alarm code.

Type of data	Test data	Reason for testing	Expected outcome
Normal	2476	To see how the alarm copes with normal usage.	Code accepted.
Normal	No input	To see if the alarm prompts an input.	Prompt to enter a code.
Boundary	000	To see if the smallest code is accepted.	Code accepted.
Boundary	99999	To see if the largest code is accepted.	Code accepted.
Erroneous	23aY	To see if the system accepts non-digits.	Error: The code contains non-numeric data.
Erroneous	12	To see if the alarm accepts fewer than 3-digit inputs.	Error: The code is too short.
Erroneous	632191	To see if the alarm accepts more than 5-digit inputs.	Error: The code is too long.

5) During testing, the tester can add "<u>actual outcome</u>" and "<u>pass or fail</u>" columns to the table.

6) <u>Trace tables</u> (see p.41) can be used when you've <u>identified</u> that there is a logic error. They will help you <u>trace the values</u> that the variables take as you go through the program so you can <u>pin-point exactly</u> where something has <u>gone wrong</u>.

EXAM TIP

Luckily for you, this page flew through its testing stage...

In the exam, you might have to design suitable testing procedures for a given scenario. This could include coming up with your own test plan and test data.

Trace Tables and Time Efficiency

Trace tables are really useful when you're learning the fundamentals of programming.
They help you to follow a piece of code in a systematic way to see if it's doing what you expect.

Trace Tables help you to find Logic Errors

1) <u>Trace tables</u> give a simple way of testing that a piece of code is <u>working correctly</u>.
   They <u>keep track</u> of the <u>values</u> that <u>certain variables</u> take as you go through the code.

2) Their main use is to '<u>dry run</u>' a subroutine or algorithm to make sure there are <u>no logic errors</u>
   — they can also be used to help you figure out what a piece of code is actually doing.

3) The <u>columns</u> of a trace table usually represent <u>variables</u>. Each <u>row</u> of a trace table
   represents the <u>values</u> that the variables take at a <u>particular point</u> in the algorithm.

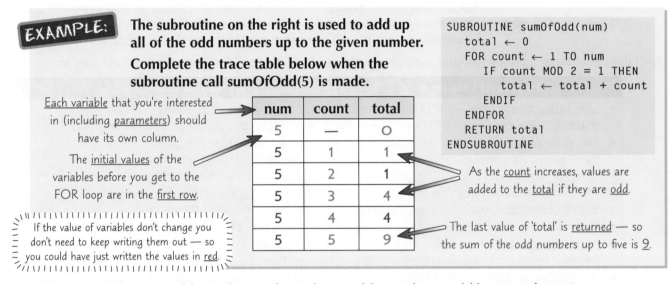

EXAMPLE: The subroutine on the right is used to add up all of the odd numbers up to the given number.
Complete the trace table below when the subroutine call sumOfOdd(5) is made.

<u>Each variable</u> that you're interested in (including <u>parameters</u>) should have its own column.

The <u>initial values</u> of the variables before you get to the FOR loop are in the <u>first row</u>.

num	count	total
5	—	0
5	1	1
5	2	1
5	3	4
5	4	4
5	5	9

```
SUBROUTINE sumOfOdd(num)
   total ← 0
   FOR count ← 1 TO num
      IF count MOD 2 = 1 THEN
         total ← total + count
      ENDIF
   ENDFOR
   RETURN total
ENDSUBROUTINE
```

As the <u>count</u> increases, values are added to the <u>total</u> if they are <u>odd</u>.

The last value of 'total' is <u>returned</u> — so the sum of the odd numbers up to five is <u>9</u>.

If the value of variables don't change you don't need to keep writing them out — so you could have just written the values in <u>red</u>.

4) The <u>columns</u> of a trace table might not always be variables — they could be any information
   that the programmer is <u>interested in</u>. For example, they might have a column for the length
   of an array or for the output of the algorithm.

5) When testing a <u>larger program</u>, the tester will often use <u>debugging tools</u> — for example, breakpoints
   are used to stop the program at certain places so that you can look at the values of variables.

Algorithms are also tested for Time Efficiency

1) Many <u>different algorithms</u> can be constructed to perform the
   <u>same task</u> (e.g. the searching and sorting algorithms on p.6-8).

2) Each algorithm will take a certain amount of '<u>time</u>' to complete
   the task. Algorithms that take <u>less 'time'</u> to complete a task
   are said to have a <u>better time efficiency</u>.

3) When programmers talk about the amount of 'time' an algorithm takes,
   they usually don't measure the <u>real-life time</u>. They measure things like
   the number of times <u>memory was accessed</u>, the number of <u>CPU cycles</u>
   taken to <u>execute commands</u> or the number of times a <u>loop was executed</u>.

```
SUBROUTINE sumOfOdd(num)
   n ← (num + 1) DIV 2
   total ← n * n
   RETURN total
ENDSUBROUTINE
```

This subroutine does exactly the same as the one above but it doesn't have a loop. For large values of the parameter this algorithm would have a much better time efficiency.

Programmers are often interested in the <u>space efficiency</u> of an algorithm too — this is the amount of space in memory that an algorithm uses.

EXAM TIP

Trace tables can help you understand a program or algorithm...

If trace tables crop up in your exam, you might not be told the purpose of the algorithm
you're tracing — don't worry, just work your way through the algorithm step-by-step.

Translators

For computers to process any computer language it needs to be <u>translated</u> into <u>machine code</u>.

Computer Languages can be **High-Level** or **Low-Level**

1) Most of the programming languages that you'll be familiar with (e.g. Python, C++) are <u>high-level languages</u>. The source code is <u>easy</u> for humans to write, but computers need to <u>translate it</u> into <u>machine code</u> before they can read and run it.

2) On the other hand, <u>low-level languages</u> are <u>tricky</u> for humans to read and write but are <u>easier</u> for a computer to run. They consist of <u>machine code</u> and <u>assembly languages</u>:

    000000 00010 00011 00100 00000 100000 ⟵ <u>Machine code</u> is very tricky for humans to understand. Each <u>processor</u> (or family of processors) will have its own <u>specific</u> machine code.

    ADD r4, r2, r3 ⟵ <u>Assembly code</u> is more <u>readable</u> for humans and easier to <u>remember</u>, so programmers are <u>less likely</u> to make mistakes writing assembly code than machine code. It's often used when <u>developing software</u> for <u>embedded systems</u> (see p.70) and when programmers need <u>more control</u> over specific hardware.

3) High-level languages are popular with programmers, but low-level languages have their uses too:

High-Level Languages	Low-Level Languages
• <u>One instruction</u> of high-level code represents <u>many instructions</u> of machine code.	• <u>One instruction</u> of assembly code usually only represents <u>one instruction</u> of machine code.
• The same code will work for <u>many different</u> machines and processors.	• Usually written for <u>one type of machine</u> or <u>processor</u> and won't work on any others.
• The programmer can easily <u>store data</u> in lots of different structures (e.g. lists and arrays) <u>without knowing</u> about the <u>memory structure</u>.	• The programmer needs to know about the <u>internal structure</u> of the CPU (see p.71-72) and how it manages the memory.
• Code is easy to <u>read</u>, <u>understand</u> and <u>modify</u>.	• Code is very difficult to <u>read</u>, <u>understand</u> and <u>modify</u>.
• <u>Must be translated</u> into machine code before a computer is able to understand it.	• Commands in <u>machine code</u> can be executed <u>directly</u> without the need for a translator.
• You <u>don't have much control</u> over what the CPU actually does so programs will be <u>less memory efficient</u> and <u>slower</u>.	• You <u>control</u> exactly what the CPU does and how it uses memory so programs will be <u>more memory efficient</u> and <u>faster</u>.

Translators convert programming languages into **Machine Code**

1) Computers only understand instructions given to them as <u>machine code</u>, so high level languages and assembly languages need to be <u>translated</u> before a computer is able to <u>execute</u> the instructions.

2) There are <u>three types of translator</u> that you need to know about: <u>assemblers</u>, <u>compilers</u> and <u>interpreters</u>.

3) Assemblers are used to turn <u>assembly language</u> into <u>machine code</u>. There are many different assembly languages (to support different CPU types) and each one needs its own <u>unique assembler</u>.

4) Compilers and interpreters are both used to turn <u>high-level code</u> into <u>machine code</u>.

Compiler	Interpreter
Translates <u>all</u> of the source code at the <u>same time</u> and creates <u>one executable file</u>.	<u>Translates</u> and <u>runs</u> the source code <u>one instruction at a time</u>, but doesn't create an executable file.
Only needed <u>once</u> to create the executable file.	Needed <u>every time</u> you want to run the program.
Returns a <u>list of errors</u> for the entire program once compiling is <u>complete</u>.	The interpreter will return the <u>first error</u> it finds and then <u>stop</u> — this is useful for <u>debugging</u>.
Once compiled the program <u>runs quickly</u>, but compiling can take a <u>long time</u>.	Programs will <u>run more slowly</u> because the code is being translated as the program is running.

5) The <u>type of translator</u> used will often be influenced by the <u>programming language</u> you're using.

6) However, sometimes programmers want to use a <u>specific type</u> of translator — <u>interpreters</u> are often used when you're <u>developing software</u> and <u>compilers</u> when you want to <u>distribute software</u>.

"Cette page est incroyable!" — call in the translators...

You should know the key features of low- and high-level languages, assemblers, compilers and interpreters.

Warm-Up and Worked Exam Questions

A whole section in one go — that's no mean feat. Make sure all of it has sunk in by having a go at these warm-up questions. Then, once you're happy, try the exam questions for some serious practice.

Warm-Up Questions

1) Suggest why a programmer may decompose a program into modules.

2) Name the type of input check that:
   a) checks that data has been entered.   b) checks data against a table of possible values.

3) Give three features that will improve the maintainability of code.

4) Are the following statements true or false?
   a) Syntax errors are harder to find than logic errors.
   b) Using the wrong Boolean operator is a logic error.
   c) Syntax errors will prevent code from running.
   d) Logic errors will prevent code from running.

5) What is meant by a high-level language?

6) Explain the purpose of a compiler.

Worked Exam Question

1   A retailer keeps a database of its loyalty card holders. The retailer stores the following data for each loyalty card holder: name, age, postcode and customer number.

First Name	Surname	Age	Postcode	Customer No.
Carol	Foreman	20	NE85 3TW	100278
Peter	Taylor	55	HA55 8PZ	223327

a) Describe **two** suitable input validation checks for an entry in the postcode field.

   1   Length check to make sure the input has a valid number of characters.

   2   Format check to make sure the input contains only letters and numbers.

   A format check could also do things like check that the postcode ends with a number and two letters.   *[2 marks]*

b) The retailer wants to use validation to check that each name is correctly capitalised. Write a subroutine that accepts a string as a parameter and returns true if it starts with a capital letter, or false if it doesn't. You should use the fact that the ASCII code for 'A' is 65 and 'Z' is 90.

Remember, you can use the command CHAR_TO_CODE() to find out a character's ASCII code.

```
SUBROUTINE initialCap(name)
       initial ← SUBSTRING(O, O, name)
       code ← CHAR_TO_CODE(initial)
       IF code ≥ 65 AND code ≤ 90 THEN
              RETURN true
       ELSE
              RETURN false
       ENDIF
ENDSUBROUTINE
```

[5 marks]

Exam Questions

2 Gordon wants to write a time-efficient subroutine to take two positive integer inputs and work out the difference between them. He writes two different subroutines, called `diffNums` and `numDiff`, shown on the right.

```
SUBROUTINE diffNums(a, b)
    WHILE a > 0 AND b > 0
        a ← a - 1
        b ← b - 1
    ENDWHILE
    RETURN a + b
ENDSUBROUTINE
```

a) Explain what is meant by the time efficiency of an algorithm.

....

....

....
[2 marks]

```
SUBROUTINE numDiff(a, b)
    IF a > b
        RETURN a - b
    ELSE
        RETURN b - a
    ENDIF
ENDSUBROUTINE
```

b) Complete the trace table to show the result of the subroutine call `diffNums(11, 4)`.

a	b

Check that your trace table has results you would expect.

[2 marks]

c) Gordon says, "Both subroutines contain the same number of lines of code, so they will have the same time efficiency." Do you agree with Gordon? Explain your answer.

....

....

....

....
[4 marks]

3 A company specialises in writing programs using low-level languages.

a) Give **two** reasons why some programmers still use low-level languages.

1 ....

2 ....
[2 marks]

b) Explain why programmers might prefer to use an assembly language over machine code.

....

....
[2 marks]

c) Which type of translator is used to translate assembly languages into machine code?
Shade **one** oval only.

A Interpreter ◯   **C** Assembler ◯

B Executor ◯   **D** Compiler ◯

[1 mark]

Exam Questions

4 A holiday company has written a simple program to calculate the price of its group holiday packages. The program asks the user to input the group size — if the group size is smaller than two or greater than 10 the program displays an error message. If not, the price (in £s) is calculated by multiplying the group size by 50 and then adding 10.

a) Describe how the company can use a test plan to check for logic errors in the program.

....

....

....

[3 marks]

b) Complete the test plan below by filling in the missing spaces.

Test Data	Expected Outcome	Reasons for test
Group_Size = 4		
	510	
Group_Size = 12		Check what happens if input too large.

[5 marks]

5 Pat is creating a program to manage user accounts on a company's network. He is using structured programming to help him develop his program.

a) Give **two** advantages of using structured programming when developing a program.

1 ....

2 ....

[2 marks]

b) One of the modules in Pat's program creates a new user account.

i) Suggest **two** other modules that Pat could include in his program.

....

[2 marks]

ii) Pat has designed a subroutine to get the user's details. He wants to design another that uses the user's details to create an email address. Complete the table to suggest suitable inputs, processes and return values for this subroutine.

Name	Inputs	Processes	Return Values
Enter user details	None	Prompt user to enter details	Array of user details
Generate email address			

[3 marks]

46

Revision Questions for Section Three

And just like that it's the end of <u>section three</u> — but before you move on, you've got one more task.

- Try these questions and <u>tick off each one</u> when you <u>get it right</u>.
- When you've done <u>all the questions</u> for a topic and are <u>completely happy</u> with it, tick off the topic.

Structured Programming (p.37) ☑

1) What is structured programming?
2) Give five advantages of using structured programming.

Robust Programming (p.38-39) ☑

3) What is authentication and why is it used?
4) Give three things that can be done to make a password-based authentication system more secure.
5) Draw a flowchart to show a standard username and password authentication routine.
6) Define the term input validation.
7) Give five types of input validation check and explain what each check does.
8)* The program below checks which year the user was born in.
What type of input validation check does it use? Explain your answer.

```
REPEAT
    OUTPUT 'Enter the year you were born'
    year ← USERINPUT
UNTIL year > 1900 AND year ≤ 2019
```

9) a) Give four features of maintainable source code.
    b) Explain how each feature can help other programmers to maintain your code.

Testing, Trace Tables and Time Efficiency (p.40-41) ☑

10) Define the following terms: a) Syntax Error   b) Logic Error
11) Explain why logic errors are more difficult to diagnose than syntax errors.
12) What are the three different types of test data?
13)* A software company is designing an anagram application. It will take a string
of letters and return all of the words that can be spelt using all of the letters exactly once.
Come up with five pieces of test data that the company could use to test their program.
14) What are trace tables used for?
15)* Complete the trace table for
the algorithm given on the right.
You may need to add more rows.

```
arr ← [2, 5, 1, 2, 3]
total ← 1
FOR x ← 0 TO LEN(arr)-1
    total ← total * arr[x]
ENDFOR
OUTPUT total
```

x	arr[x]	total

16) Describe what is meant by 'time efficiency'.

Translators (p.42) ☑

17) Define and give an example of the following: a) Machine code   b) Assembly Language
18) Give six differences between high-level languages and low-level languages.
19) What are the three types of translator?
20) Compare the functionality and uses of a compiler and an interpreter.

*Answers on p.142

Logic

Logic gates are pretty clever stuff. They take binary information and give an output based on the Boolean operations (p.23). Each Boolean operator (NOT, AND and OR) has its own logic gate.

Logic Gates apply Boolean Operations to Inputs

1) Logic gates are special circuits built into computer chips.
   They receive binary data, apply a Boolean operation, then output a binary result.

2) Logic diagrams are often drawn to show logic gates and circuits.
   Each type of logic gate is shown by a different symbol.

3) Each type of logic gate also has a corresponding truth table.
   Truth tables show all possible input combinations of 1s and 0s, and the corresponding outputs.

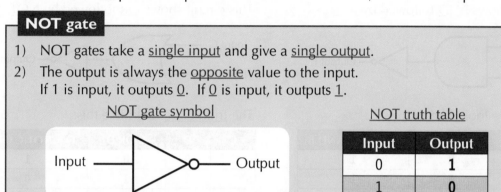

NOT gate

1) NOT gates take a single input and give a single output.
2) The output is always the opposite value to the input.
   If 1 is input, it outputs 0. If 0 is input, it outputs 1.

It can help to think of 1s as TRUE and 0s as FALSE.

NOT gate symbol

Input ———▷o——— Output

NOT truth table

Input	Output
0	1
1	0

AND gate

1) AND gates take two inputs and give one output.
2) If both inputs are 1, the output is 1, otherwise the output is 0.

AND gate symbol

Input A ———
Input B ——— } — Output

AND truth table

Input A	Input B	Output
0	0	0
0	1	0
1	0	0
1	1	1

OR gate

1) OR gates take two inputs and give one output.
2) If one or more inputs are 1, then the output is 1, otherwise the output is 0.

OR gate symbol

Input A ———
Input B ——— } — Output

OR truth table

Input A	Input B	Output
0	0	0
0	1	1
1	0	1
1	1	1

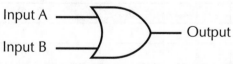

Logic isn't as scary as it looks...

REVISION TIP

These basic logic gates are the building blocks for bigger logic circuits. You should be able to draw each logic gate and the corresponding truth table — you might also see the symbols shown in this table as equivalent notation:

Gate	Expression	Notation
NOT	NOT A	¬A
AND	A AND B	A ∧ B
OR	A OR B	A ∨ B

Logic

You can make more interesting logic diagrams by combining logic gates. If you know the truth tables from the previous page you'll be able to create truth tables for much more complicated logic diagrams.

Logic Gates are Combined for More Complex Operations

1) Multiple logic gates can be added to the same logic circuit to carry out different operations.

2) You can work out the truth tables by working through each gate in order.
   For every input combination, follow them through each gate step-by-step, then write down the output.

3) By using brackets and the terms AND, OR and NOT, circuits can be written as logical statements, like NOT(A AND B) below. Operations in brackets should be completed first, just like in normal maths.

This circuit shows AND followed by NOT.

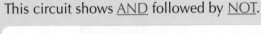

The truth table looks like this:

A	B	A AND B	P = NOT(A AND B)
0	0	0	1
0	1	0	1
1	0	0	1
1	1	1	0

This circuit shows OR followed by NOT.

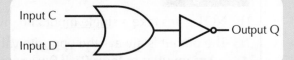

The truth table looks like this:

C	D	C OR D	Q = NOT(C OR D)
0	0	0	1
0	1	1	0
1	0	1	0
1	1	1	0

4) The two logic circuits shown above are examples of two-level logic circuits — they require the inputs to pass through a maximum of two logic gates to reach the output.

Logic Circuits can have More than Two Inputs

This is a two-level logic circuit with 3 inputs.

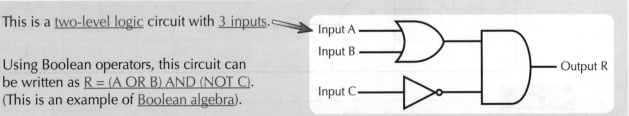

Using Boolean operators, this circuit can be written as R = (A OR B) AND (NOT C). (This is an example of Boolean algebra).

To cover every input combination, extra rows are needed in the truth table. There are 3 inputs and each can take one of 2 values, so $2 \times 2 \times 2 = 8$ rows are needed.

In general, the number of rows is 2^n, where n is the number of different inputs.

A	B	C	A OR B	NOT C	R = (A OR B) AND (NOT C)
0	0	0	0	1	0
0	0	1	0	0	0
0	1	0	1	1	1
0	1	1	1	0	0
1	0	0	1	1	1
1	0	1	1	0	0
1	1	0	1	1	1
1	1	1	1	0	0

To be OR NOT to be — literally covering all forms of being...

Once you've learned each gate's truth table, you can work out the truth tables of much more complicated circuits. If you take the inputs through each gate one step at a time you'll be fine — it's only logical...

Units

Just like you have units like centimetres, metres and kilometres for measuring distance, computers need units for measuring <u>digital information</u>. You'll need to learn all of the unit names on this page and their sizes.

Bits are the Smallest Measure of Data

1) Computers use 1s and 0s to represent the flow of electricity.
   <u>1</u> is used to show that electricity <u>is</u> flowing, and <u>0</u> shows that it is <u>not</u> flowing.

2) All the data we want a computer to process must be converted into <u>binary code</u> (1s and 0s).

3) Each 1 or 0 in a binary code is a <u>bit</u> (<u>b</u>inary dig<u>it</u>). For example, 1010 is 4 bits.

4) The table below shows <u>the size</u> of other units of data:

A <u>byte</u> is big enough to store one <u>character</u> (like x, e, M or £). See p.59 for more info.

Most <u>files</u> (like <u>songs</u>, <u>pictures</u> and <u>documents</u>) are measured in <u>kB</u> or <u>MB</u>.

High definition <u>videos</u> and complex <u>applications</u> are often measured in <u>gigabytes</u>.

<u>Secondary storage</u> capacity is measured in <u>gigabytes</u> or <u>terabytes</u>.

Name	Size
Bit (b)	A single binary digit (1 or 0)
Nibble	4 bits
Byte (B)	8 bits
Kilobyte (kB)	1000 bytes
Megabyte (MB)	1000 kilobytes
Gigabyte (GB)	1000 megabytes
Terabyte (TB)	1000 gigabytes

You might see each unit defined to be 1024 (not 1000) times bigger than the previous unit. The main reason is that 1024 is a power of 2 which is helpful when dealing with binary data.

5) Each <u>bit</u> can take one of <u>two different values</u> (either 1 or 0). This means that a <u>nibble</u> (4 bits) can take 2^4 = <u>16 different values</u>, and a <u>byte</u> (8 bits) can take 2^8 = <u>256 different values</u>.

You can Convert between Different Units

<u>Converting</u> between units of data is usually pretty straightforward — just watch out when you have to switch between <u>bits</u> and <u>bytes</u>.

EXAMPLE: **Ashley has downloaded some images to her computer. Each image is 300 kilobytes.**

a) How many bits are in each image?

1) First, convert to bytes by <u>multiplying by 1000</u>: 300 kB = 300 × 1000 = 300 000 Bytes

2) There are 8 bits in a byte, so <u>multiply by 8</u>: 300 000 Bytes = 300 000 × 8
   = 2 400 000 bits

b) She wants to copy 400 of these images onto her USB flash drive, which has 0.15 GB of free space left. Does she have enough space to store them all?

1) Work out the <u>total size</u> of all the images: 400 × 300 = 120 000 kB

2) Now convert this to GB — first, <u>divide by 1000</u> to get it in MB, then <u>again</u> to get it in GB: 120 000 kB = 120 000 ÷ 1000 = 120 MB
   120 MB = 120 ÷ 1000 = 0.12 GB
   So yes, she has enough space.

This page has me in bits...

Keep working your way through that unit table until the size order is clear in your head — it might just show up on your exam. A bit is smaller than a nibble, and a nibble is less than a full byte. I know, hilarious.

Warm-Up and Worked Exam Questions

Try these warm-up questions on logic and units — if there is anything you're unsure about, have a look back through the first part of this section before having a go at the exam questions on the next page.

Warm-Up Questions

1) Look at the three logic expressions in the box below:

> (NOT A) AND B   C OR (NOT D)   (E AND F) OR G

   a) Draw a logic circuit for each expression.
   b) Construct a truth table for each expression.

2) Which of these units is the largest? kB, TB, MB, GB

3) Convert these units:
   a) 10 kilobytes into bits.
   b) 3 terabytes into megabytes.

Worked Exam Questions

1   A logic gate can be written as P = A AND B.

   a) State the value of input B when input A is 1 and output P is 0.

   B = ...**0**......
   [1 mark]

   b) A NOT logic gate is placed after the AND logic gate to make the logic diagram below. State the input values when output P is 0.

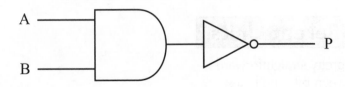

   For the NOT gate to output 0, the input of the NOT gate must be 1.

   A = ...**1**......   B = ...**1**......
   [1 mark]

2   Misha wants to save some music files onto a solid state drive (SSD).

   a) Which of these SSDs has the largest capacity? Shade **one** oval only.

   Convert all the values to the same unit and compare them.

A	250 gigabyte (GB)	⭘
B	200 000 megabyte (MB)	⭘ (200 000 MB = 200 GB)
C	0.3 terabyte (TB)	⬤ (0.3 TB = 300 GB)
D	40 000 000 kilobyte (kB)	⭘ (40 000 000 kB = 40 GB)

   [1 mark]

   b) Calculate how many 5 MB music files Misha could save onto a 250 GB SSD.

   1 GB = 1000 MB

   So 250 GB = 250 × 1000 = 250 000 MB

   250 000 ÷ 5 = 50 000 files

   ......**50 000**......
   [2 marks]

Exam Questions

3 Gigi is designing some images to be used in a video game. Each image file takes up 100 kB.

    a) Calculate how many bits there are in each image file.

.... bits

[2 marks]

    b) Gigi has made 5000 image files for the game. Calculate, in GB, the total size of these files.

.... GB

[2 marks]

    c) The images are stored on her computer using binary.
       Describe how binary is used to represent data in computers.

....

....

[2 marks]

4 A car uses a logic circuit to decide whether to start the engine or not.

    • The car has two buttons, labelled **S** (START) and **D** (DRIVE).
      If both buttons are on, the engine will start.
    • The engine also starts if the ignition switch **I** is turned on.

    a) Draw the logic circuit diagram for this system, with **Z** as an output.

[3 marks]

    b) Write a Boolean expression for this logic circuit.

....

[1 mark]

    c) State all possible values of the inputs and outputs if:
      i) Button D is on but the car doesn't start.

....

[1 mark]

      ii) Buttons I and S are both on.

....

....

[2 marks]

Binary Numbers

As computers only understand 1s and 0s, all data must be converted into binary to be processed.
Binary can be used to represent all numbers in our standard number system.

Counting in Binary is a bit like Counting in Decimal

1) In our standard number system we have ten different digits (0, 1, 2, 3, 4, 5, 6, 7, 8, 9).
   This is called <u>decimal</u>, <u>denary</u> or <u>base-10</u>.

2) <u>Binary</u> only uses <u>two</u> different digits (0 and 1) — we call this <u>base-2</u>.

3) Counting in binary is similar to counting in decimal, but the place values from <u>right</u> to <u>left</u>
   increase by <u>powers of 2</u> (e.g. 8, 4, 2, 1), instead of powers of 10 (e.g. 1000, 100, 10, 1).

4) The following table shows the <u>binary equivalents</u> of the <u>decimal numbers 0-15</u>:

0 = 0	4 = 100	8 = 1000	12 = 1100
1 = 1	5 = 101	9 = 1001	13 = 1101
2 = 10	6 = 110	10 = 1010	14 = 1110
3 = 11	7 = 111	11 = 1011	15 = 1111

Binary Numbers are easier to Convert using Tables

Drawing a table with binary <u>place values</u> in the first row makes binary to decimal conversion easier.

EXAMPLE: **Convert the 8-bit binary number 0011 0101 to a decimal number.**

1) Draw up a table with binary place values in the top row. Start with 1 at the right, then move left, <u>doubling</u> each time.

128	64	32	16	8	4	2	1
0	0	1	1	0	1	0	1

Each column is just a power of 2. i.e. 2^3, 2^2, 2^1, 2^0.

2) Write the binary number 0011 0101 into your table.

3) <u>Add up</u> all the numbers with a 1 in their column:

32 + 16 + 4 + 1 = 53. So 0011 0101 is 53 in decimal.

This works with all binary numbers — just draw as many columns as you need, doubling each time.

<u>8-bit</u> numbers can represent the decimal numbers 0 to 255. <u>16-bit</u> numbers can show the numbers 0 to 65 535, and <u>32-bit</u> can show the numbers 0 to 4 294 967 295.

Convert Decimal to Binary by Subtracting

When converting from <u>decimal</u> to <u>binary</u>, it's easier to draw a <u>table</u> of binary place values, then <u>subtract them</u> from <u>largest</u> to <u>smallest</u>. Have a look at this example:

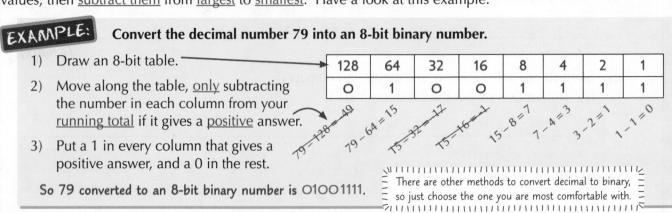

EXAMPLE: **Convert the decimal number 79 into an 8-bit binary number.**

1) Draw an 8-bit table.

128	64	32	16	8	4	2	1
0	1	0	0	1	1	1	1

2) Move along the table, <u>only</u> subtracting the number in each column from your <u>running total</u> if it gives a <u>positive</u> answer.

79 – 128 = -49   79 – 64 = 15   15 – 32 = -17   15 – 16 = -1   15 – 8 = 7   7 – 4 = 3   3 – 2 = 1   1 – 1 = 0

3) Put a 1 in every column that gives a positive answer, and a 0 in the rest.

So 79 converted to an 8-bit binary number is 0100 1111.

There are other methods to convert decimal to binary, so just choose the one you are most comfortable with.

Use powers of 2 to convert between binary and decimal...

There's an easy way to test yourself on this stuff. Write down a decimal number between 0 and 255 and convert it to binary. Then write down an 8-bit binary number and convert it to decimal.

Binary Numbers

More binary numbers coming right up, hope you're ready for another page full of 0s and 1s. Adding binary numbers is a lot like adding decimal numbers — have a look at this page of examples to see how it's done...

Add **Binary Numbers** using **Column Addition**

As binary only uses 1s and 0s we <u>can</u> comfortably do 0 + 0 = 0, 1 + 0 = 1 and 0 + 1 = 1.
Using binary we <u>can't</u> write 1 + 1 = 2. Instead, we have to write <u>1 + 1 = 10</u>.

EXAMPLES: **I.   Add the following 8-bit binary numbers together: 1000 1101 and 0100 1000**

1) First, put the binary numbers into <u>columns</u>.

2) Starting from the <u>right</u>, add the numbers in columns.

3) When doing <u>1 + 1 = 10</u>, carry the 1 into the next column.

So 1000 1101 + 0100 1000 = 1101 0101

```
  1 0 0 0 1 1 0 1
+ 0 1 0 0 1 0 0 0
  ───────────────
  1 1 0 1 0 1 0 1
              1
```

You can add <u>more binary numbers</u> together at the same time — just be careful when you get 1 + 1 + 1...

2.   Calculate the sum of the binary numbers 0100 1011, 1000 1001 and 0010 0101.

```
    0 1 0 0 1 0 1 1
    1 0 0 0 1 0 0 1
  + 0 0 1 0 0 1 0 1
    ───────────────
    1 1 1 1 1 0 0 1
        1 1 1 1
```

1) Put the numbers in <u>columns</u> and add from the <u>right</u> like before.

2) Sometimes you'll get something like 1 + 1 + 1 = 11, so you need to write 1, then carry 1 to the next column.

So 0100 1011 + 1000 1001 + 0010 0101 = 1111 1001

You can add binary numbers with <u>different numbers of bits</u> — just <u>add some 0s</u> to the <u>front</u> of the numbers with fewer bits.

3.   Calculate the sum of the binary numbers 11 0011, 110 1001 and 1 0110

1) <u>Add zeros</u> to the front of 11 0011 and 1 0110 so that all the numbers have <u>7-bits</u>.

2) Add up the numbers in the normal way.

3) The answer has <u>8-bits</u>.

So 11 0011 + 110 1001 + 1 0110 = 1011 0010

```
    0 1 1 0 0 1 1
    1 1 0 1 0 0 1
  + 0 0 1 0 1 1 0
    ───────────────
  1 0 1 1 0 0 1 0
    1 1 1 1 1 1 1
```

You can <u>check your answers</u> to binary addition by converting the numbers and answer to <u>decimal</u>, to make sure it still works. For example 3 above:

11 0011 = 51   110 1001 = 105
1 0110 = 22   1011 0010 = 178
51 + 105 + 22 = 178 so the answer is correct.

Adding binary numbers — as easy as 1, 10, 11...

The best way to learn how to add binary numbers is practice. It's a good idea to check your answer by converting all the binary numbers to decimal and adding them up.

Binary Numbers

Binary Shifts can be used to Multiply or Divide by 2

1) A binary shift (also known as a logical shift) moves every bit in a binary number left or right a certain number of places.

2) Gaps at the beginning or end of the number are filled in with 0s.

3) The direction of the binary shift indicates whether it multiplies or divides the binary number:

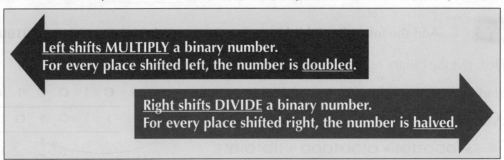

Left shifts MULTIPLY a binary number.
For every place shifted left, the number is doubled.

Right shifts DIVIDE a binary number.
For every place shifted right, the number is halved.

4) If a number is shifted 3 places right, it would be halved three times (i.e. divided by $2^3 = 8$).
If a number were shifted 4 places left, it would be doubled four times (i.e. multiplied by $2^4 = 16$).

5) If you're only working with 8-bit numbers, binary shifts can cause 1s to 'drop off' the end.
Losing 1s in a left shift will give a very different answer to the multiplication (see below).
Losing 1s in a right shift will give an inaccurate answer (rounded down to the nearest whole number).

Examples of Binary Shifts

EXAMPLE: Perform a 3 place left shift on the 8-bit binary number 00101001.
Explain the effect this will have on the number and problems that may occur.

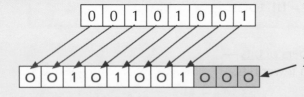

1) Write down the original binary number, then shift all digits 3 places to the left.

2) Fill in the gaps on the right with 0s.
The number has been doubled three times, so it has been multiplied by $2^3 = 8$.

If there are only 8 bits available to store the number, then a 1 will drop off the end — this will make the answer to the calculation wrong.

In decimal, this is 41 × 8 = 328, but the 8-bit answer is 72.

EXAMPLE: Perform a 2 place right shift on the binary number 00111100.
What effect will this have on the number?

1) Write down the original binary number, then shift all digits 2 places to the right.

2) Fill in the gaps on the left with 0s.

A 2 place right shift gives the binary number 00001111.
As this is a 2 place shift, the original number will have been halved twice (so divided by $2^2 = 4$).

Dividing using a right binary shift has the same effect as using the DIV operator (p.13) — your answer would not take into account any remainders.

Shift left to multiply and shift right to divide...

Binary shifts are really good for doing fast multiplication and division, but only by powers of 2.
If you're losing 1s on a right shift, your answer will be inaccurate (and on a left shift, it'll be way out).

Hexadecimal Numbers

Hexadecimal (hex) is another number system used regularly in programming.
Hex uses a combination of digits and letters in order to represent a number.

Hexadecimal numbers are Shorter than Binary

1) <u>Hexadecimal</u> (or <u>base-16</u>) uses sixteen different digits.

2) A single hex character can represent any decimal number from 0-15. To represent 0-15 in binary would require <u>4 bits</u> (a nibble), so each hex character equates to a <u>nibble</u> in binary.

3) The table shows the decimal and binary value of each hex character.

4) Programmers often <u>prefer</u> hex when coding, because:

- It's simpler to remember <u>large</u> numbers in hex — they're far shorter than binary numbers.
- Due to hex numbers being <u>shorter</u>, there's less chance of <u>input errors</u>.
- It's easier to convert between <u>binary</u> and <u>hex</u> than binary and decimal.

Computers themselves do not use hex — they still have to convert everything to binary to process it.

Decimal	Hex	Binary	Decimal	Hex	Binary
0	0	0000	8	8	1000
1	1	0001	9	9	1001
2	2	0010	10	A	1010
3	3	0011	11	B	1011
4	4	0100	12	C	1100
5	5	0101	13	D	1101
6	6	0110	14	E	1110
7	7	0111	15	F	1111

Convert Hex to Decimal by Multiplying each Character

In hex, moving right to left, place values increase in powers of 16.

4096	256	16	1

To convert from <u>hex to decimal</u>, draw up a table, fill in the boxes, then multiply — just like in this example:

EXAMPLES:

1. Convert the hexadecimal number 87 into decimal.

Luckily in the <u>exam</u> you'll only have to convert <u>two digit</u> <u>hex numbers</u> like in these examples.

1) First, <u>draw this table</u>, then write in your hex number.

16	1
8	7

2) <u>Multiply</u> the numbers in each column.

$8 \times 16 = 128$ $7 \times 1 = 7$

3) <u>Add up</u> the results: → $128 + 7 = 135$ So the hex number 87 is **135 in decimal.**

To convert from <u>decimal to hex</u>, draw the table but use division to fill it in.

2. Convert the decimal number 106 into hexadecimal.   *Remember, hex goes from 0-9, then A to F.*

1) Start at the <u>left</u>. <u>Divide</u> 106 by 16, then hold onto the <u>remainder</u>.

$106 \div 16 = 6 \text{ r } 10$

16	1
6	A

2) <u>Divide the remainder</u> from the last calculation by 1.

$10 \div 1 = 10 = A$

So the decimal number 106 is **6A in hexadecimal.**

Hex can be a blessing and a curse...

REVISION TASK

Hex and decimal can look fairly similar (as they both contain 0-9), so make sure you've got them the right way round when converting — 65 in hexadecimal is NOT the same as 65 in decimal. Memorise the hex table and its advantages, then cover it up and write everything you remember.

Hexadecimal Numbers

Convert **Binary** to **Hex** by splitting it into **Nibbles**

1) Each hex character is equal to a <u>nibble</u> in binary, so it is possible to convert from binary to hex by splitting the binary code into <u>4-bit chunks</u>.

2) Binary to hex conversions can be much <u>easier</u> than converting from binary to decimal, as you only have to deal with the nibbles <u>one at a time</u>.

EXAMPLE: **Convert the binary number 1011 1001 to hexadecimal.**

Remember, hex only uses letters for decimal values between 10-15.

1) Firstly, <u>split</u> the binary number into <u>nibbles</u>:   1011 1001

2) Draw a table with columns labelled 1, 2, 4, 8, then <u>repeat</u> the values for as many nibbles as you require.

3) Fill in the table with your binary number.

8	4	2	1	8	4	2	1
1	0	1	1	1	0	0	1

8 + 2 + 1 = 11   8 + 1 = 9
= B

4) For <u>each nibble</u>, add up the numbers with a 1 in the column, then convert this value to hex.

5) Finally put the hex values <u>together</u>.   The binary number 1011 1001 is B9 in hexadecimal.

If the binary number can't be split into nibbles, you'll have to stick some zeros on the front.

EXAMPLE: **Convert the binary number 11 1110 1000 to hexadecimal.**

1) Add <u>zeros</u> to the <u>front</u> of the binary number, so that you can split it into nibbles. 0011 1110 1000

2) Draw a repeating table of 1, 2, 4 and 8, as above.

3) Write your binary number in the table.

8	4	2	1	8	4	2	1	8	4	2	1
0	0	1	1	1	1	1	0	1	0	0	0

2 + 1 = 3   8 + 4 + 2 = 14   8 = 8
= E

4) Add up <u>each nibble</u> and <u>convert</u> each value to <u>hex</u>.

5) Put the hex values together.   The binary number 11 1110 1000 is 3E8 in hexadecimal.

For **Hex** to **Binary**, use each **Character's Decimal Value**

To convert the <u>opposite</u> way (from <u>hex</u> to <u>binary</u>) convert each hex character into binary, then just put the binary numbers together.

EXAMPLE: **Convert the hexadecimal number 8C to binary.**

1) First, find the <u>decimal value</u> of each character: 8 = 8 in decimal   C = 12 in decimal

2) Find the <u>binary value</u> of each decimal number:

8	4	2	1
1	0	0	0

8	4	2	1
1	1	0	0

8 = 1000 in binary   12 = 1100 in binary

3) Put the nibbles together to get the <u>equivalent binary number</u>.   The hexadecimal number 8C is 1000 1100 in binary.

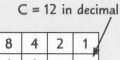

This page has so many nibbles it could spoil your lunch...

When converting binary to hex just remember to split the binary up into chunks of 4 bits, each with columns labelled 1, 2, 4 and 8. Then work out the individual hex values and put them together.

Warm-Up and Worked Exam Questions

Converting between binary, decimal and hexadecimal tests your maths skills just as much as your computing knowledge. Have a go at these warm-up questions before diving into the exam questions on the next page.

Warm-Up Questions

1) Convert:
   a) 01011001 from binary to decimal
   b) 69 from decimal to binary

2) Add the following 8-bit binary numbers together: 01101000 and 10001010

3) Perform a 3 place right shift on 10111000. Give your answer as an 8-bit number.

4) What is the effect of a 1 place left shift?

5) Convert:
   a) 48 from decimal to hex
   b) C6 from hex to decimal
   c) 10100010 from binary to hex
   d) 3D from hex to binary

Worked Exam Questions

1 Work out the following:

a) Convert the 8-bit binary number 10010011 into a decimal number.

128 + 16 + 2 + 1 = 147

.......147.......
[1 mark]

b) Convert the decimal number 252 into an 8-bit binary number.

Drawing an 8-bit table can help.

128	64	32	16	8	4	2	1
1	1	1	1	1	1	0	0

252 − 128 = 124
124 − 64 = 60
60 − 32 = 28
28 − 16 = 12
12 − 8 = 4
4 − 4 = 0

.......11111100.......
[1 mark]

2 Daniel is a programmer. He makes the following two claims about hex numbers.

Claim 1: "Hex is much easier to work with than binary."

Claim 2: "Converting from decimal to hex is easier than converting from binary to hex."

Would other programmers agree with Daniel's claims? Explain your answers.

Claim 1: _They're likely to agree with claim 1. Hex numbers are shorter so are easier to identify, remember, edit and share than binary codes._

Claim 2: _They're likely to disagree with claim 2. Converting binary to hex is easier as binary numbers can be split into nibbles to quickly read off the hex values._

[4 marks]

58

Exam Questions

3 Izzy is setting up a new user database for a business network.
Each user needs to be given a unique binary ID number.

    a) How many possible ID numbers are there, if each one is an 8-bit binary number?

....

[1 mark]

    b) Izzy finds out that the business only needs a maximum of 50 user accounts.
What is the minimum number of bits that Izzy could use for the ID numbers?

.... bits

[1 mark]

4 A security program encrypts passwords using a hexadecimal conversion.
The binary code of each letter for the password 'CAT' is shown below.

               01000011   01000001   01010100

    a) Convert each binary number above to a hexadecimal number to encrypt the password 'CAT'.

....

[3 marks]

    b) The password 'DOG' is encrypted as 44 4F 47.
       i) Convert the first encrypted letter to binary.

....

[1 mark]

       ii) What password would be encrypted as 43 4F 44 45?

Look back at previous
   question parts.

....

[2 marks]

5 The function `decimal()` converts one hexadecimal character to a decimal integer.
(e.g. `decimal(F)` = 15).

    a) Calculate the value of `decimal(A)` + `decimal(C)`.

....

[2 marks]

    b) Write an algorithm using `decimal()` to convert any 2-digit hexadecimal into decimal.
           Think about splitting the 2-digit hexadecimal into separate characters.

[4 marks]

Characters

Almost everything can be represented as binary code — words, images and sound can all be turned into bits and processed by a computer. Firstly let's look at words, which are made up of different characters.

Binary can be used to represent Characters

1) Alphanumeric characters are used to make words and strings (see p.16). They include uppercase and lowercase letters, the digits 0-9, and symbols like ? + and £.

2) Computers are unable to process these characters directly as they only process binary code. So they need a way of converting these characters to binary code and vice versa. They can do this using character sets.

> Character sets are collections of characters that a computer recognises from their binary representation.

Don't mistake a character set for a font. A character set is what determines the letter — the font you use just displays that letter in a certain way.

3) As well as the alphanumeric characters mentioned above, character sets also contain special characters which do certain commands (e.g. space, enter and delete).

4) So when you press a button on your keyboard it sends a binary signal to the computer telling it which key you pressed. The computer then uses the character set to translate the binary code into a particular character.

The number of Bits you'll need is based on the Character Set

Different character sets can have different amounts of characters. The number of characters in a character set determines how many bits you'll need. Here are some standard character sets you should know about:

ASCII

- ASCII is the most commonly-used character set in the English-speaking world. Each ASCII character is given a 7-bit binary code — this means it can represent a total of 128 different characters, including all the letters in the English alphabet, numbers, symbols and commands.

- An extra bit (0) is added to the start of the binary code for each ASCII character (see the table on the right). This means each ASCII character fits nicely into 1 byte.

- The codes for numbers, uppercase letters and lowercase letters are ordered (A comes before B comes before C...) with symbols and commands scattered around. E.g. From the table, the code for B is 66 in decimal. The code for E would be 3 after B, which is 66 + 3 = 69 in decimal or 01000101 in binary.

Character	Binary	Hex	Decimal
Backspace	0000 1000	8	8
0	0011 0000	30	48
1	0011 0001	31	49
=	0011 1101	3D	61
A	0100 0001	41	65
B	0100 0010	42	66
]	0101 1101	5D	93
a	0110 0001	61	97
b	0110 0010	62	98

Some examples of ASCII characters.

Extended ASCII uses 8-bit binary codes to represent 256 characters. The first 128 are the same as ASCII and the others are used for characters in other languages like French and German.

Unicode®

- Unicode® comes in several different forms and tries to cover every possible letter or symbol that might be written. Unlike ASCII, Unicode® uses multiple bytes for each character.

- The best thing about Unicode® is that it covers all major languages, even those that use a completely different alphabet like Greek, Russian and Chinese.

- The first 128 codes in Unicode® are the same as ASCII.

Character sets are used to turn binary data into characters...

You don't need to remember the ASCII codes for any specific characters, but if you're given the ASCII code of one character (e.g. T) you should be able to work out the ASCII code for another character (e.g. W).

Storing Images

Images and sounds are pieces of data stored on computers — so, naturally, they're made of bits (p.49).

Images are stored as a series of Pixels

1) The type of image you use most often is a <u>bitmap</u> —
they're mainly used for photos. Bitmap images are made up
of lots of tiny dots, called <u>pixels</u> (short for picture elements).

2) The <u>colour</u> of each pixel is represented by a <u>binary</u> code.
The number of colours available in an image is related to
the number of <u>bits</u> the code has.

3) <u>Black-and-white</u> images only use two colours, so they only
need <u>1-bit</u> to represent each pixel — <u>0 for white</u> and <u>1 for black</u>.

4) <u>2-bit images</u> can be made up of four colours. Each pixel
can be one of four binary values — <u>00</u>, <u>01</u>, <u>10</u> and <u>11</u>.

5) You can make a <u>greater range</u> of shades and colours
by <u>increasing the number of bits</u> for each pixel.

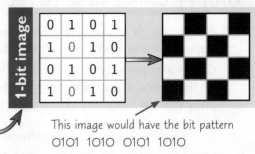

This image would have the bit pattern
0101 1010 0101 1010

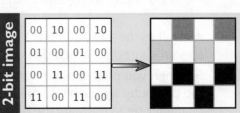

Computer screens are often divided into millions of pixels arranged in rows and columns.

Increasing Colour Depth and Resolution increases the File Size

1) The <u>colour depth</u> is the <u>number of bits</u> used for <u>each pixel</u>.

2) Given the colour depth you can work out <u>how many colours</u> can be made using this <u>formula</u>:

Total number of colours = 2^n (where n = number of bits per pixel, or bpp)

| 1-bit image: 2^1 = 2 colours | 4-bit image: 2^4 = 16 colours | 24-bit image: 2^{24} = 16 777 216 colours |

3) Most devices use a <u>24-bit colour depth</u>, with 8 bits used to indicate the levels of <u>red</u>, <u>green</u> and <u>blue</u>
needed for each pixel. It's estimated that the human eye can see around 10 million different colours,
so a 24-bit colour depth should cover every colour that you could possibly see.

4) The <u>image resolution</u> is the <u>number of pixels</u> in the image. It's sometimes given as <u>width × height</u>.
The <u>higher the resolution</u>, the more pixels the image is made of, so the <u>better the quality</u> of the image.
E.g. if an image has a resolution of 1200 × 800, it means that it is made up of 960 000 pixels.
If we decreased the resolution to 600 × 400, it would only have 240 000 pixels, so a lower quality.

5) To work out <u>how many bits</u> an image will take up, use the <u>formula</u>:

File size (in bits) = image resolution × colour depth = width × height × colour depth

6) Using a <u>greater</u> image resolution or colour depth means that there are <u>more bits</u> in the image.
This can give a <u>higher-quality image</u>, but also increases the <u>file size</u>.

EXAMPLE: **Calculate the file size, in MB, of an 8-bit image
that is 2000 pixels wide and 1000 pixels high.**

1) First, use the <u>formula</u> to find the <u>size in bits</u>:   2000 × 1000 × 8 = 16 000 000 bits

2) <u>Divide by 8</u> to convert to <u>bytes</u>:   16 000 000 ÷ 8 = 2 000 000 bytes

3) Finally, <u>divide by 1000 twice</u> to convert to <u>MB</u>:   2 000 000 ÷ 1000 ÷ 1000 = 2 MB

Images are stored as long strings of bits...

Remember that these types of images are called bitmaps — they're the ones made out of pixels. There
are also vector images — vectors are <u>not</u> made of pixels, and can be resized without loss of quality.

Storing Sound

Sound is made up of bits and stored in files on a computer. Or rather, digital sound is — the other type of sound, analogue, doesn't get on well with computers, so we've got to turn it into digital first.

Sound is Sampled and stored Digitally

1) Sound is recorded by a microphone as an analogue signal. Analogue signals are pieces of continually changing data.

2) Analogue signals need to be converted into digital data so that computers can read and store sound files. This is done by analogue to digital converters, which are found in most modern recording devices.

3) The process of converting analogue to digital is called sampling:

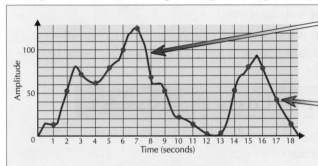

The blue line shows the analogue sound wave — it's one continuous piece of data which keeps changing.

To convert the analogue recording to digital data, we sample the amplitude of the wave at regular intervals (shown by dots on the graph). The amplitude can only take certain values depending on the sample resolution (see below).

Once the device has sampled the recording, it creates the curve digitally like this.

Each block of data matches where each sample was taken.

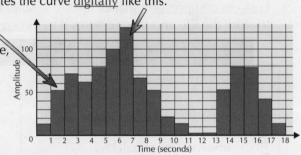

The digital data is about the same shape as the analogue wave, but it's not continuous. It's lost a lot of data — e.g. the last peak in the analogue wave is much flatter in the digital data.

The digital data can be improved by taking samples more regularly — most music isn't sampled every second but every couple of milliseconds.

Several factors affect the Size and Quality of Sound Files

1) Sample rate (or sampling frequency) is how many samples you take in a second — it's usually measured in hertz (Hz) or kilohertz (kHz). E.g. a common sample rate is 44 100 samples per second (44 100 Hz or 44.1 kHz).

2) Sample resolution is the number of bits available for each sample.

> Sample rate × sample resolution is often called the bit rate.

3) You can calculate the size of a sound file using this formula:

File size (in bits) = Sample rate (in Hz) × sample resolution × length (in seconds)

4) For example, if you were to sample 30 seconds of audio with a sample resolution of 8 bits and a sample rate of 500 Hz, your file would be 500 × 8 × 30 = 120 000 bits.

5) Increasing the sample rate means the analogue recording is sampled more often. The sampled sound will be better quality and will more closely match the original recording.

6) Increasing the sample resolution means the digital file picks up quieter sounds, even if they're happening at the same time as louder ones. This will also result in a sampled sound that is closer to the quality of the original recording.

7) However, increasing the sample rate or sample resolution will increase the file size.

You can change the size and quality of sound files...

Don't mix up sample resolution with image resolution from the previous page. Really, sample resolution is the sound equivalent of colour depth — it's the number of bits used for each piece of data.

Compression

How can we possibly store all of these images and sound files? Well, the answer is down to data compression.

Sometimes we need to **Compress** files

1) <u>Data compression</u> is when we make <u>file sizes smaller</u>, while trying to make the compressed file as <u>true to the original</u> as possible.

2) Compressing data files has many <u>uses</u>:

- Smaller files take up <u>less storage space</u> on a device.
- <u>Streaming</u> and <u>downloading</u> files from the Internet is quicker as they take up less <u>bandwidth</u>.
- It allows <u>web pages</u> to <u>load more quickly</u> in web browsers.
- <u>Email</u> services normally have restrictions on the size of the attachment you can send — compressing the file allows you to send the same content with a much smaller file size.

There are **Two Types** of compression — **Lossy** and **Lossless**

1) <u>Lossy compression</u> works by permanently <u>removing data</u> from the file — this limits the number of bits the file needs and so reduces its size.

2) <u>Lossless compression</u> makes the file smaller by <u>temporarily</u> removing data to store the file and then restores it to its <u>original state</u> when it's opened.

	Pros	Cons	E.g. of File Types
Lossy	• Greatly <u>reduced file size</u>, meaning more files can be stored. • Lossy files take up <u>less bandwidth</u> so can be downloaded and streamed more quickly. • <u>Commonly used</u> — lots of software can read lossy files.	• Lossy compression <u>loses</u> data — the file can't be turned back into the original. • Lossy compression <u>can't be used</u> on text or software files as these files need to retain all the information of the original. • Lossy files are <u>worse quality</u> than the original. But, this loss in quality is normally <u>unnoticeable</u>.	• MP3 (audio) • AAC (audio) • JPEG (image)
Lossless	• Data is only removed temporarily so there is <u>no reduction in quality</u> — the compressed file should look or sound like the original. • Lossless files can be <u>decompressed</u> — turned back into the original. • Lossless compression can be used on <u>text</u> and software <u>files</u>.	• Only a <u>slight reduction</u> in file size, so lossless files still take up quite a bit of space on your device. E.g. a lossless song may have a file size of around 30 MB, while the same song with lossy compression may be 5 MB.	• FLAC (audio) • TIFF (image) • PNG (image)

EXAMPLE: **Phil has just heard a new band on the radio. He wants to download fifty of their songs from the Internet and store them on his smartphone to take on holiday. State which type of compression would be most appropriate in this situation and explain why.**

<u>Lossy</u> compression would be the most appropriate. Lossy files are <u>smaller</u> so they would take up less bandwidth, meaning Phil could <u>download</u> the songs more quickly. Their smaller file size would also allow him to <u>store</u> them all on his smartphone without taking up too much storage space.

The best compression type? I'm afraid I'm at a loss...

Lossy files aren't as high quality as the originals, but the difference is normally unnoticeable to us unperceptive humans. This helps to explain why lossy file formats like JPEG (for photos) and MP3 (for music) are so popular — they save a lot of storage space and their inferior quality is hardly noticeable.

Encoding Data

So compression is important when storing and transmitting data — but the real question is, how do you do it? Run-Length Encoding (RLE) is one of the two compression techniques that you should know.

Run-Length Encoding looks for Repeating Data

1) Run-Length Encoding (or RLE for short) is a form of lossless compression (see previous page). This means that the process reduces a file's size without losing any data.

2) It looks for consecutive repeating data in a file — called a run. Instead of storing each piece of repeated data separately, it just stores the number of times it repeats, and one copy of the data.

- Take a look at the bitmap image below. It uses an 8-bit colour depth.

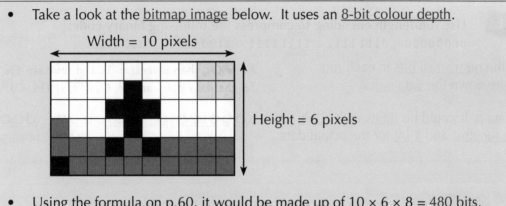

Width = 10 pixels

Height = 6 pixels

- Using the formula on p.60, it would be made up of 10 × 6 × 8 = 480 bits. This can be reduced by using RLE.

- First, count the number of times the same data is repeated in each run, and store this instead.

- So this image could be compressed to look like this: E.g. the top row has 8 white, then 2 yellow pixels.

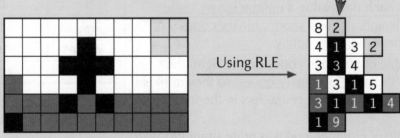

Using RLE →

- You can store this information as data pairs, which can be represented in the format (number of pixels, colour), e.g. (8, W) (2, Y) (4, W) (1, B) etc.

- In this example, we'd have 20 data pairs to store. Each data pair consists of a number, which could be stored as an 8-bit binary number (see p.52), and an 8-bit colour — so 16 bits total.

- The final compressed image would be 20 × 16 = 320 bits, rather than the 480 bits that we started with — that's a 33% decrease in file size.

3) Run-length encoding is pretty easy to understand, but it's not perfect. If the data doesn't have many runs of repeated data, then the file size will not be significantly decreased.

REVISION TIP

Learn how to use RLE — it will help you in the long run...

The size of each data pair will depend on what type of data you are trying to encode. E.g. if you are encoding a 24-bit image (see p.60), then each data pair might be 32 bits — 8 bits for the number of pixels in the run and 24 bits for the colour value of the pixel.

Encoding Data

First up, there's some more on RLE. Then it's on to another <u>lossless</u> compression technique — Huffman coding.

You can also use **RLE** to compress **Different Types** of **Data**

1) Run-length encoding can also be applied to <u>text</u>. For example, say we have the string 'wwwwwhtttt'. In <u>ASCII</u>, this would use <u>one byte</u> for each character, so <u>10 bytes</u> altogether.

2) Looking for runs, we can see that 'w' occurs 5 times, then 'h' once and then 't' four times. As <u>data pairs</u>, this would be: (5, w) (1, h) (4, t). So we can store this in <u>6 bytes</u> rather than 10.

3) You can also use RLE to encode <u>binary data</u>. But be warned — because 1s and 0s just take up <u>1 bit each</u>, you need <u>very long runs</u> of repeated data for it to actually <u>reduce</u> the size.

> **EXAMPLE:** **Use run-length encoding to compress the following binary code:**
>
> 0000 0000   0111 1111   1111 1111   1100 0000   0000 0000
>
> Count the <u>number of bits</u> in each <u>run</u> and write down the <u>data pairs</u>.
>
> Nine 0s, then seventeen 1s and fourteen 0s. So the data pairs are (9, 0) (17, 1) (14, 0).
>
> Each data pair could be <u>8 bits</u> with <u>7 bits</u> for the <u>run lengths</u>, and <u>1 bit</u> for the actual data:
>
> 0001001 0   0010001 1   0001110 0
> 9 written in binary 17 written in binary 14 written in binary

Huffman Coding uses the **Frequency** of each **Data Value**

1) Each <u>data value</u> in a <u>file</u> (e.g. a character in a text file) takes up the <u>same amount of space</u>. For example, text encoded in ASCII (see p.59) uses 1 byte per character, but this is often <u>inefficient</u>.

2) <u>Huffman coding</u> gives each data value a <u>unique binary code</u> but the codes <u>vary in length</u>. It gives <u>shorter binary codes</u> to data values that appear <u>more frequently</u>.

3) For example, in the <u>table</u> of Huffman codes on the right, the characters 'e', 'l' and 's' have <u>short binary codes</u>, so they're likely to appear <u>more frequently</u> than other characters in the file.

Character	Huffman code
e	00
l	01
s	11
space	100
a	1010
h	1011

<u>Decoding</u> data using a table of Huffman codes is quite straightforward:

> **EXAMPLE:** **Decode this binary string, using the Huffman code in the table above:**
>
> 1110110010011000101111001100101011101100010111
>
> 1) Starting on the left, find the <u>first code</u> — 1 isn't a code, but <u>11</u> is the code for '<u>s</u>'. <u>Draw a line</u> after 11, and write an '<u>s</u>'.
>
>
>
> 11|1011|00|100|1 1|00|01|01|11|100|1 1|00|101|0|11|1011|00|01|01|11
> s h e   s e l l s   s e a s h e l l s
>
> 2) Keep going until it's <u>completely decoded</u>.   **So the decoded string is she sells seashells.**

Huffman coding gives a unique binary code to each data value...

In the table of Huffman codes above, you'll also notice that each binary code doesn't start the same way as another code — and this is always true. E.g. 's' above has the code **11**, so no other character in the table can have a code starting **11**..., and 'h' has the code **1011**, so there won't be any other codes starting **1011**...

Encoding Data

Huffman trees can represent Huffman codes — they look daunting, but aren't so bad with a bit of practice.

Huffman Trees are made by ordering Frequencies

EXAMPLE: **Encode the string 'she sells seashells' using Huffman coding.**

1) Count the <u>number of times</u> each character occurs (its <u>frequency</u>).

Character	Frequency
s	6
h	2
e	4
space	2
l	4
a	1

2) Put the characters in an <u>ordered list</u>, starting with the character that appears <u>least frequently</u>. Each one is represented as a <u>node</u>.

1 (a)   2 (h)   2 (space)   4 (e)   4 (l)   6 (s)

3) Combine the <u>first two nodes</u> (the nodes with the lowest frequencies) to make a new node, <u>adding</u> the frequencies together, as shown.

4) Put the <u>combined node</u> back into the list, making sure it's <u>still in order</u>. Repeat this process until the main list contains only <u>one node</u>.

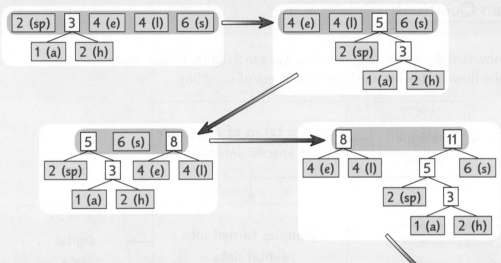

5) On the final <u>Huffman tree</u>, label each <u>left branch</u> with a <u>0</u>, and each <u>right branch</u> with a <u>1</u>. <u>Read off</u> the <u>Huffman codes</u> by following the path from the <u>final combined node</u> (19) to each character's node.

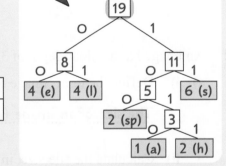

Character	's'	'h'	'e'	space	'l'	'a'
Huffman Code	11	1011	00	100	01	1010

6) Use the Huffman codes to <u>encode the string</u>.

So 'she sells seashells' would be encoded as 1110110010011000101111001100101011101100010111.

Encoding 'she sells seashells' in ASCII would need 19 x 8 = 152 bits. Or if you used another fixed-length encoding, you would need at least 3 bits per character (3 bits can encode up to 8 different characters), so the string would need 19 x 3 = 57 bits. However, Huffman coding gets it down to 46 bits, which is much better than either method.

Follow the nodes to read off the codes...

If you have to create a Huffman tree in the exam, make sure you work through the steps above carefully. If your table of frequencies is wrong, you could get a very different Huffman tree.

Warm-Up and Worked Exam Questions

That was a tricky bunch of pages to get your head around, so make sure it's all sunk in by trying these warm-up and exam questions. As always, make sure you look back over anything you're unsure about.

Warm-Up Questions

1) What is the difference between the character sets ASCII and Unicode®?
2) How many different colours are possible with a colour depth of 4?
3) What would be the effect on the file size of an image if:
   a) the colour depth was increased?　　　　b) the image resolution was decreased?
4) What would be the effect on the file size and quality of an audio sample if:
   a) sample rate was increased?　　　　b) the sample resolution was increased?
5) Name the two types of compression and give one reason why each one is useful.
6) Describe what is meant by 'run-length encoding'.
7) A text file is compressed using Huffman coding. The character 'e' has code 00, and the character 'z' has code 10100. What does tell you about the text file?

Worked Exam Questions

1 Sound is converted from an analogue sound wave to a digital format using sampling. Complete the flowchart below to show the process of sampling.

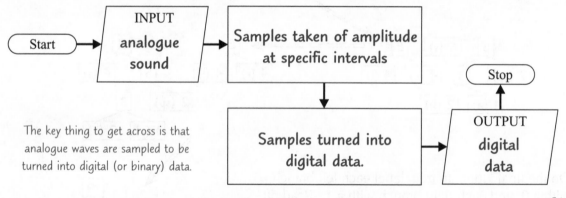

The key thing to get across is that analogue waves are sampled to be turned into digital (or binary) data.

[4 marks]

2 An image has a colour depth of 32 bits and an image resolution of 200 × 100.

a) i) Define the term 'image resolution'.

The size of an image (width × height) in pixels.

[1 mark]

ii) Calculate the file size, in bits, of this image.

200 × 100 × 32 = 640 000

640 000 bits

[2 marks]

b) Explain how decreasing the image resolution would affect the quality of the image.

A lower resolution would reduce the quality of the image because
it would have fewer pixels.

[2 marks]

Exam Questions

3   Helena is writing a news article using a word processor.

a)   Define the term 'character set'.

....

....
[1 mark]

b)   Complete the flowchart to explain how Helena's computer recognises characters she enters.

```
 ( Start )                                                        ( Stop )
    |                                                                ↑
    ↓                                                                |
+-----------+    +-----------------+    +-----------------+    +-----------+
|  INPUT    | →  |                 | →  |                 | →  | OUTPUT    |
| Key press |    |                 |    |                 |    | Display   |
+-----------+    +-----------------+    +-----------------+    | character |
                                                               +-----------+
```
[2 marks]

4   Jade has made two recordings of herself reading an extract from a novel to use in an audiobook.
The length, sampling rate and sample resolution of each recording are shown below.

	Length	Sampling Rate	Sample Resolution
Recording 1	102 seconds	20 000 Hz	4 bits
Recording 2	100 seconds	50 000 Hz	8 bits

a)   Explain which recording you would expect to have better sound quality.

....

....
[2 marks]

b)   Give **one** drawback of using recording 2 rather than recording 1 for the audiobook.

....
[1 mark]

5   Don has a file that contains the following binary data: 00000001 11111000 00000000

a)   Compress this data using run-length encoding.

....
[3 marks]

b)   In the compressed file, each data pair uses a total of 6 bits.
Calculate how many bits this compression will save.

.... bits
[2 marks]

Exam Questions

6 Three bitmap images are shown on the right.

Image A   Image B   Image C

1 bit is needed to represent either O (white) or 1 (black).

a) Explain which of the images would need the greatest number of bits to represent all of the pixels.

....

....

....

[4 marks]

b) Give the bit pattern for image A, using 0 to represent white and 1 to represent black.

....

[1 mark]

7 Mary has a string of text that only contains the letters L, A, M and B. The number of times each letter appears is shown in the table on the right. Mary uses Huffman coding to assign codes to each letter, such that the letter B has the Huffman code 100.

Letter	Frequency
L	6
A	5
M	2
B	1

a) Draw Mary's Huffman tree for this string.

Once you've constructed the tree, use the fact that B has the code 100 to decide where to put the 1s and Os.

[4 marks]

b) Complete the table to give Mary's Huffman code for each letter.

Letter	L	A	M	B
Huffman Code				100

[2 marks]

c) Use the same Huffman code to decode the following compressed section of the text:

001110111

....

[2 marks]

Revision Questions for Section Four

Section Four is done and dusted, so all you've got to do now is try these revision questions.

- Try these questions and <u>tick off each one</u> when you <u>get it right</u>.
- When you've done <u>all the questions</u> for a topic and are <u>completely happy</u> with it, tick off the topic.

Logic and Units (p.47-49) ☐

1) For each of the 3 main logic gates: a) Draw its symbol.
                                             b) State how many inputs and outputs it has.
                                             c) Draw its truth table.   Input A
                                    Input B   Output

2)* Draw the truth table for the logic diagram on the right.   Input C

3) Why is binary used by computers?

4) Put these units in order of size: Terabyte, Byte, Kilobyte, Gigabyte, Megabyte

5)* A hard drive has a storage capacity of 200 megabytes.
    a) How many gigabytes is this?   b) How many bits is this?

Binary and Hexadecimal (p.52-56) ☐

6)* Add the binary numbers 0101 1101 and 0011 0010.

7) What effect do left and right shifts have on binary numbers?

8)* Convert the following decimal numbers to: a) binary   b) hexadecimal
                                                      (i) 17   (ii) 148   (iii) 240

9)* Convert the following binary numbers to: a) decimal   b) hexadecimal
                                             (i) 0011 1000 (ii) 1001 1111 (iii) 10 1011

10)* Convert these hexadecimal numbers to: a) decimal   b) binary
                                          (i) 4A   (ii) 75   (iii) BD9

11) Give three reasons why programmers prefer hexadecimal over binary and decimal.

Characters, Images and Sound (p.59-61) ☐

12) What is the definition of a character set?

13) Give the four types of characters that are included in a character set.

14) What are the two main character sets? Give a feature of each.

15) Define the following terms: a) pixel   b) bitmap   c) colour depth   d) image resolution

16) Give two effects of choosing a greater image resolution or colour depth for an image.

17) In no more than four bullet points, explain how audio sampling works.

18) Give a definition for each of the following and explain what happens when you increase each of them:
    a) sample rate   b) sample resolution

Compression and Encoding Data (p.62-65) ☐

19) Give four reasons why you might want to compress data.

20) What is the difference between lossy compression and lossless compression?

21) Give three reasons why you might want to use: a) lossy compression   b) lossless compression

22)* The file letters.txt contains the string 'PPPPQQRRRSSSSSSPPPPPQQQ'.
    a) Encode this string using run-length encoding.
    b) Draw a Huffman tree for this string.
    c) Calculate the number of bits needed to store the string if it was encoded with:
        (i) ASCII   (ii) Huffman coding   (iii) Run-length encoding (if each data pair used 2 bytes).

*Answers on p.143

Computer Systems

Now it's time to take a step back and ask yourself the most important question — what even is a computer?

A **Computer** is a **Machine** that Processes **Data**

1) The purpose of a computer is to take <u>data</u>, <u>process</u> it, then <u>output</u> it.
   Computers were created to help process data and complete tasks <u>more efficiently</u> than humans.

2) A <u>computer system</u> consists of <u>hardware</u> and <u>software</u> that work together to process data / complete tasks.

   - Hardware is the <u>physical</u> stuff that makes up your computer   *External pieces of hardware like the keyboard,*
     system, like the CPU, motherboard, monitor and printer.   *mouse and printer are called <u>peripherals</u>.*
   - Software is the <u>programs</u> that a computer system runs. You can have <u>application software</u>
     (programs that help the user perform specific tasks, e.g. word processors, web browsers, email
     clients, games, etc.) and <u>system software</u> (operating systems, utilities, etc. — see p.81-84).

3) There are <u>many types</u> of computer system. These range from small devices like calculators and
   watches, up to large <u>supercomputers</u> used by banks or for scientific applications. Computers may
   be <u>general purpose</u> (designed to perform <u>many tasks</u>, e.g. PCs and tablets) or <u>dedicated systems</u>
   (designed for <u>one particular</u> function, e.g. controlling traffic lights or an aeroplane).

Embedded Systems are Computers inside a **Larger System**

1) <u>Embedded systems</u> are computers <u>built into other devices</u>, like dishwashers,
   microwaves and TVs. They are usually dedicated systems.

2) Embedded systems are often used as <u>control systems</u> — they <u>monitor</u> and <u>control</u> machinery
   in order to achieve a desired result. E.g. In a <u>dishwasher</u> the embedded system could
   control the water pumps and water release mechanisms, manage the various dishwasher
   cycles and control the thermostat to keep the water at an appropriate temperature.

3) As they're <u>dedicated</u> to a single task, embedded systems are usually easier to <u>design</u>,
   cheaper to <u>produce</u>, and more <u>efficient</u> at doing their task than a general purpose computer.

Computers contain **Components** which **Work Together**

This section is all about the main hardware components of a computer.
As a warm-up, let's take a look inside a <u>typical desktop PC</u>.

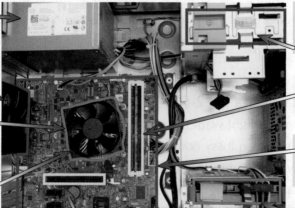

<u>Power supply</u> — supplies power
to motherboard, optical and
hard drives, and other hardware.

<u>Case cooling fan</u> — extracts
hot air from the computer case.

<u>CPU heat sink and cooling fan</u> —
keeps the CPU at a steady temperature
(CPUs generate a lot of heat).

<u>CPU</u> (hidden under the
heat sink) — the most
important component.
Does all the processing
(see p.71-72).

The <u>graphics card</u> slots in here (see p.76).

<u>Optical drive</u> —
for read/writing of
optical discs (see p.78).

<u>RAM sticks</u> (computer memory)
slot in here (see p.75-76).

<u>Motherboard</u> — the main circuit
board in the computer, where
the hardware is connected.

<u>Hard Disk Drive</u> — internal
secondary storage (see p.77).

If you know your computer, you need not fear defeat...

Familiarise yourself with these components as they'll crop up a lot throughout this section.

The CPU

The CPU is very important — it's the main component of a computer, so here are two whole pages about it.

The **CPU** is the **Central Processing Unit**

1) The CPU is the brain of the computer system.

2) It processes all of the data and instructions that make the system work.

3) The processing power of a CPU depends on different characteristics, like its clock speed, number of cores and cache size and type — see p.76.

4) The CPU architecture describes the main components of the CPU, how they interact with each other, and with other parts of the computer system. Von Neumann and Harvard are the two main types of architecture. You will need to know about Von Neumann — see next page.

CPUs contain 1000s of gold pins — some of these transmit data, others supply power to the CPU.

The CPU has **Five Main Parts**

The Control Unit (CU)

• The control unit is in overall control of the CPU. Its main job is to execute program instructions by following the fetch-decode-execute cycle (see next page).

• It controls the flow of data inside the CPU (to registers, ALU, cache — see below) and outside the CPU (to main memory and input/output devices).

The Arithmetic Logic Unit (ALU)

• The ALU basically does all the calculations.

• It completes simple addition and subtraction, compares the size of numbers and can do multiplications and divisions using repeated addition and subtraction.

• It performs logic operations such as AND, OR and NOT (p.47) and binary shifts (p.54) — remember, computers process binary data.

• Registers (see below) are used to store intermediate results of calculations.

The Cache

• The cache is very fast memory in the CPU. It's slower than the registers, but faster than RAM (p.75).

• It stores regularly used data so that the CPU can access it quickly the next time it's needed. When the CPU requests data, it checks the cache first to see if the data is there. If not, it will fetch it from RAM.

• Caches have a very low capacity and are expensive compared to RAM and secondary storage.

The Clock

• The clock sends out a signal that continually cycles between 1 and 0, usually at a constant rate.

• The signal is used to synchronise when instructions will be carried out (like a metronome).

• The number of clock cycles (or clock ticks) per second is called the clock speed (p.76).

Buses

• Buses are collections of wires that are used to transmit data between components of the CPU, and to other parts of the computer system.

• A processor may have separate buses for carrying data, instructions and memory addresses.

The CPU also contains various registers which temporarily hold tiny bits of data needed by the CPU. They are super-quick to read/write to, much quicker than any other form of memory.

REVISION TASK

That's a lot to remember, for something so small...

It's important that you know all about the different components of a CPU. Try learning everything you can about each one, then cover up the page and write down as many notes as you can.

The CPU

Now let's look at the Von Neumann architecture and what the CPU does in a bit more detail.
Von Neumann came up with his design in 1945 and it still describes how most computers work today.

Von Neumann's Design **Revolutionised** Computing

The Von Neumann architecture describes a system where the CPU runs <u>programs</u> stored in <u>memory</u>.
Programs consist of <u>instructions</u> and <u>data</u> which are stored in memory <u>addresses</u>.

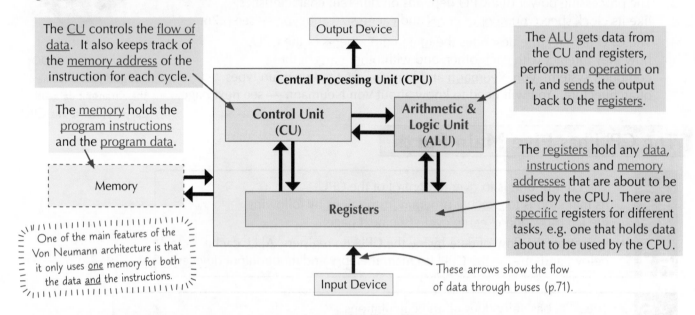

The <u>CU</u> controls the <u>flow of data</u>. It also keeps track of the <u>memory address</u> of the instruction for each cycle.

The <u>memory</u> holds the <u>program instructions</u> and the <u>program data</u>.

The <u>ALU</u> gets data from the CU and registers, performs an <u>operation</u> on it, and <u>sends</u> the output back to the <u>registers</u>.

The <u>registers</u> hold any <u>data</u>, <u>instructions</u> and <u>memory addresses</u> that are about to be used by the CPU. There are <u>specific</u> registers for different tasks, e.g. one that holds data about to be used by the CPU.

Output Device

Central Processing Unit (CPU)

Control Unit (CU)

Arithmetic & Logic Unit (ALU)

Registers

Memory

Input Device

One of the main features of the Von Neumann architecture is that it only uses <u>one</u> memory for both the data <u>and</u> the instructions.

These arrows show the flow of data through buses (p.71).

CPUs follow the **Fetch-Decode-Execute Cycle**

Essentially, <u>all a CPU does</u> is carry out instructions, one after another, billions of times a second. The <u>Fetch-Decode-Execute</u> cycle describes how it does it.

Each Fetch-Decode-Execute cycle will take multiple clock cycles (see previous page).

Fetch Instruction

1) The <u>control unit</u> reads the <u>memory address</u> of the next CPU instruction.
2) The <u>instruction</u> stored in that address is copied from <u>memory</u> to one of the <u>registers</u>.
3) The memory address in the <u>control unit</u> is <u>incremented</u> to point to the address of the <u>next</u> instruction, ready for the <u>next cycle</u>.

Execute Instruction

The instruction is <u>performed</u>. This could be: <u>load data</u> from memory, <u>write data</u> to memory, do a <u>calculation</u> or <u>logic</u> operation (using the ALU), change the address in the <u>CU</u>, or <u>halt</u> the program.

Decode Instruction

1) The instruction that was copied from memory is <u>decoded</u> by the control unit.
2) The control unit <u>prepares</u> for the next step, e.g. by loading other values into the registers.

REVISION TIP

Learn this with the Revise-Assess-Review cycle...

Keep going through the cycle until it sticks — the CPU uses the memory address to fetch the instruction, decodes it and gets everything ready for execution, and then it actually carries the instruction out. The parts of the CPU are important as well — the ALU does the calculations, the registers hold data and instructions waiting to be used, and the CU tells everything else what to do.

Warm-Up and Worked Exam Questions

There's a lot to learn on those pages — once you're happy with them, have a go at these questions.

Warm-Up Questions

1) Name five internal hardware components of a typical desktop computer.

2) Match the CPU component to the correct description of its function.

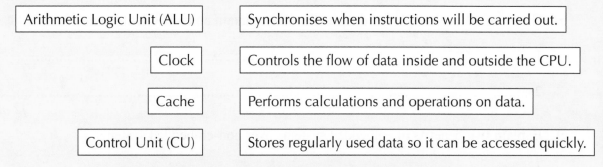

Arithmetic Logic Unit (ALU)	Synchronises when instructions will be carried out.
Clock	Controls the flow of data inside and outside the CPU.
Cache	Performs calculations and operations on data.
Control Unit (CU)	Stores regularly used data so it can be accessed quickly.

3) What should **A** and **B** be labelled as in the Von Neumann CPU architecture below?

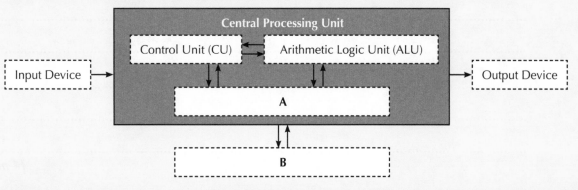

Worked Exam Question

1 Computer systems consist of hardware and software that work together.

   a) Define what is meant by hardware. Give **one** example.

   Definition .... The physical components that make up a computer system. ....

   Example .... A mouse ....

                                    There are loads of possible   *[2 marks]*
                                      examples for each of these
                                     — far too many to list.

   b) Define what is meant by software. Give **one** example.

   Definition .... The programs or applications that a computer can run. ....

   Example .... A word processor ....

                                             [2 marks]

   c) Explain the difference between system software and application software.

   .... Application software is run by the user to help perform particular tasks, ...

   .... while system software is run by the system to control or maintain the system. ....

                                             [2 marks]

Exam Questions

2 A microwave contains an embedded system which controls its cooking modes.

    a) What is an embedded system?

    ....

[1 mark]

    b) Give **two** other examples of devices that may contain an embedded system.

      1 ....

      2 ....

[2 marks]

    c) Explain **two** benefits of embedded systems over non-embedded systems.

      1 ....

      ....

      ....

      2 ....

      ....

      ....

[4 marks]

3 CPUs process data according to the fetch-decode-execute cycle.

    a) Describe what happens during each stage of the fetch-decode-execute cycle.

    ....

    ....

    ....

    ....

    ....

    ....

    ....

[6 marks]

The CPU contains wires that transmits data between components.

    b) What is the name given to these wires? Shade **one** oval only.

      A Cars   ⬭   **C** Trains   ⬭

      B Taxis   ⬭   **D** Buses   ⬭

[1 mark]

Memory

As you'll have gathered from earlier, memory is a pretty fundamental part of a computer. It contains all the instructions that the CPU follows. Without memory, a computer wouldn't know what to do with itself.

RAM is High Speed, Volatile memory

1) RAM (or Random Access Memory) is used as the main memory in a computer. It can be read and written to. RAM is volatile.

> - Volatile memory is temporary memory. It requires power to retain its data.
> - Non-volatile memory is permanent memory — it keeps its contents even when it has no power.

2) The main memory is where all data, files and programs are stored while they're being used.

3) When a computer boots up, the operating system is copied from secondary storage to RAM.

4) When software applications, documents and files are opened, they are copied from secondary storage to RAM. They stay in RAM until the files or applications are closed.

5) RAM is slower than the CPU cache, but much faster than secondary storage.

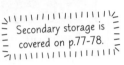

Secondary storage is covered on p.77-78.

ROM tells the CPU how to Boot Up

1) ROM ('Read Only Memory') is non-volatile memory. As it says on the tin, it can only be read, not written to.

2) ROM comes on a small, factory-made chip built into the motherboard.

3) It contains all the instructions a computer needs to properly boot up. These instructions are called the BIOS (Basic Input Output System).

The BIOS is a type of firmware — hardware-specific software built in to a device. Embedded systems (p.70) are controlled by firmware.

4) As soon as the computer is powered on, the CPU reads the instructions from ROM. This tells the CPU to perform self checks and set up the computer, e.g. test the memory is working OK, see what hardware is present and copy the operating system into RAM.

5) Although the CPU can only read ROM, it is possible to update ('flash') the BIOS on a ROM chip.

> ROM chips often use flash memory. This is a very common type of non-volatile memory that stores data in electrical circuits by trapping electrons. It's used in SD cards, USB sticks and solid state drives (SSDs). There's loads about flash devices on p.77.

Systems have Different RAM/ROM Requirements

The amount of RAM and ROM that a system needs depends on the purpose and type of the system.

Non-embedded systems

- Non-embedded systems usually have much more RAM than ROM because they often need to write data to main memory.
- ROM is typically only used for BIOS, which doesn't require much memory.
- ROM and RAM are usually stored on the motherboard, away from the CPU.

Embedded systems

- Embedded systems usually have more ROM than RAM because they don't write much (if any) data to memory.
- They don't tend to have secondary storage (p.77-78) so ROM is used to store all programs.
- ROM and RAM are often stored on the same chip as the CPU to reduce physical space needed and cost.

Get all this information stored on your brain's non-volatile memory...

RAM is where the computer puts everything it's working on. Don't confuse memory with secondary storage — if a computer has a 2 TB (see p.49) hard drive, that doesn't mean it has 2 TB of memory.

CPU and System Performance

All sorts of things affect the speed of a computer system, but the biggest factors are usually to do with the hardware. Choice of CPU, RAM and GPU (see below) can all have big effects on performance.

CPU Performance depends on Clock Speed, Cores and Cache

Clock speed

- For most desktop computers, clock speed (see p.71) is somewhere around 3.5 GHz (i.e. 3.5 billion clock cycles per second). This determines the number of instructions a single processor core can carry out per second — the higher the clock speed, the more instructions that can be carried out per second.
- Some CPUs can be overclocked to make them run at a higher clock speed than the factory-set rate. But it's risky if not done properly — it can make CPUs overheat, causing crashes or permanent damage to the system. High performance cooling systems (e.g. water cooling) are usually needed.

CPU Cores

- Each core in a CPU can process data independently of the rest.
- The more cores a CPU has, the more instructions it can carry out at once, so the faster it can process a batch of data.
- Most PCs and smartphones have 4 or more cores these days.

> It's not quite as simple as 'doubling the number of cores doubles performance'. Software needs to be designed to use multicore processing. And not all processing tasks can be split evenly between cores — some steps will depend on others, meaning one core may end up waiting for another core to catch up.

Cache Size

- The cache (p.71) is data storage inside the CPU that's much faster than RAM.
- A larger CPU cache gives the CPU faster access to more data it needs to process.

Cache Type

- There are different levels of cache memory — L1, L2 and L3. The higher the level, the more it can hold, but the slower it is.
- Cache speed is based on how far it is from the CPU. L1 is quick because it's on the CPU itself, while L3 is often on the motherboard so it's slower.

Generally, CPUs with higher clock speeds, more cores or larger caches of lower levels will have better performance, but will also be more expensive.

Overall Performance is affected by Other Components too

1) If a computer has too little RAM, it may not be able to keep all application data loaded at once, slowing the system down.
2) The more RAM, the more applications or more memory-intensive applications it can smoothly run, making it faster overall.
3) If the computer already has plenty of RAM to run everything the user wants, increasing RAM may make no difference to performance.

RAM comes on sticks which plug into slots on the motherboard.

- GPUs (graphics processing units) handle graphics and image processing. They relieve the processing load on the CPU, freeing it to do other things.
- Computers have basic GPUs integrated onto the motherboard or the CPU, but you can install a dedicated GPU (graphics card) to improve performance in graphics-intensive applications, e.g. PC gaming and design software.

Video Outputs — Cooling fan — PCI interface slots into motherboard.

High-end hardware tends to be very expensive...

There are other factors that affect CPU performance, but you don't need to worry about them at GCSE. Using SSDs rather than traditional hard drives is another way to speed up a computer — more info on p.77.

Secondary Storage

You might be thinking that we skipped primary storage — but we've already covered it, as you'll see...

There are **Two Main Tiers** of **Storage**

1) Primary storage refers to the memory areas that the CPU can access directly, like CPU registers, cache, ROM and RAM. Primary storage has the fastest read/write speeds and is mostly volatile (p.75).

2) Secondary storage is non-volatile storage that isn't directly accessible by the CPU. It's where all data (applications, user files and the OS) are stored when not in use. It includes magnetic hard disk drives, solid state drives, CDs and SD cards. Read/write speeds for secondary storage are much slower than primary storage.

There's also tertiary storage, which is used for long term data storage (mainly used for archives and backups of huge amounts of data).

Magnetic Hard Disks are **High-Capacity, Reliable Storage**

1) Hard disk drives (HDDs) are the traditional internal storage in PCs and laptops.

2) A hard disk drive is made up of a stack of magnetised metal disks spinning at a rate between 5400 and 15000 rpm (revolutions per minute).

3) Data is stored magnetically in small areas called sectors within circular tracks. Read/write heads on a moving arm are used to access sectors on the disks.

4) Portable HDDs are popular for backing up and transporting large amounts of data.

5) Despite their moving parts, HDDs are generally very long lasting and reliable, although they could be damaged by large impacts like being dropped.

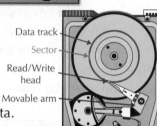

Data track
Sector
Read/Write head
Movable arm

Other types of magnetic storage

- Another type of magnetic storage is magnetic tape. It has a very high capacity and an extremely low cost per GB. It's often used by large organisations for backing up large amounts of data.
- Reels of tape are stored in plastic cassettes. Tapes are read/written sequentially by the tape drive i.e. from beginning to end. This means it can be slow when finding specific data stored on them, but once it's in the right place, reading/writing to the tape is very fast.

Solid State Drives are **Fast** and **Reliable Secondary Storage**

1) Solid State Drives (SSDs) are storage devices with no moving parts. Most of them use a type of flash memory (see p.75). SSDs are used for the same purpose as HDDs — for internal storage.

2) SSDs have significantly faster read/write times than HDDs. Using a SSD rather than traditional HDD can give much quicker times for booting up and opening programs and files.

3) Hybrid drives exist which use solid state storage for the OS and programs, and a hard disk for data.

4) Like HDDs, portable SSDs can be used to back up and transport data.

Other types of flash storage

- USB pen drives and memory cards (e.g. SD cards) are also flash-based, solid-state storage.
- They're much slower than SSDs and have a much shorter read/write life.
- They're used to expand the storage capacity of small devices like cameras, smartphones and tablets (which are too small for SSDs or HDDs). Their capacity is very high relative to their tiny size.

There are advantages to using HDDs and SSDs:

Advantages of HDDs	Advantages of SSDs
• HDDs are cheaper. • Both are high capacity, but HDDs are higher. • HDDs have a longer read/write life than SSDs — SSDs can only be written a certain number of times before they begin to deteriorate.	• SSDs are faster. • SSDs don't need defragmenting (see p.84). • SSDs are more shock-proof than HDDs. • HDDs make some noise, SSDs are silent.

Secondary Storage

Optical Discs are Cheap and Robust Secondary Storage

1) Optical discs are things like <u>CDs</u>, <u>DVDs</u> and <u>Blu-Ray</u>™ discs.

2) CDs can hold around 700 MB of data, DVDs can hold around 4.7 GB and Blu-Rays can hold around 25 GB.

3) Optical discs come in three forms:

> – <u>read-only</u> (e.g. CD-ROM / DVD-ROM / BD-ROM)
> – <u>write-once</u> (e.g. CD-R / DVD-R / BD-R)
> – <u>rewritable</u> (e.g. CD-RW / DVD-RW / BD-RW)

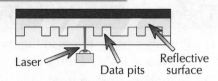
Laser   Data pits   Reflective surface

Data is stored as <u>microscopic indentations</u> on the shiny surface of the disc. Data is read by shining a laser beam on the surface and detecting changes in the position of the <u>reflected beam</u>.

4) Nowadays, their use is <u>declining</u>:
- <u>Streaming</u> and <u>download</u> services have reduced the need for optical discs.
- Modern devices like <u>phones</u> and <u>tablets</u> don't have optical drives.
- DVD-Rs and DVD-RWs used to be popular for backing up data, but they can't compete with flash storage devices due to their <u>low capacity</u> per disc, very <u>slow</u> read/write speeds and poor reliability of <u>RW</u> discs.

5) They do have some <u>advantages</u> — they're very cheap (per GB), portable, and won't be damaged by <u>water</u> or <u>shocks</u> (although they are easily <u>scratched</u>).

Cloud Storage uses the Internet to store files and applications

<u>Cloud storage</u> is a service where files can be <u>uploaded</u> via the <u>Internet</u> to a <u>remote server</u> (where it is usually stored on HDDs/SSDs). You normally pay a <u>subscription</u>, though some provide a <u>limited service</u> for <u>free</u> (p.107).

Pros of the cloud
- Users can access files from <u>any connected device</u>.
- Files can be <u>shared</u> with others or made <u>public</u>.
- Easy to <u>increase</u> how much <u>storage</u> is available.
- <u>No</u> need to buy <u>expensive hardware</u> to store data.
- <u>No</u> need to pay <u>IT staff</u> to manage the hardware.
- Cloud host provides <u>security</u> and <u>backups</u> for you.
- Can be <u>cheap/free</u> if <u>not much storage</u> is required.

Cons of the cloud
- Need <u>connection to the Internet</u> to access files.
- Upload/download speed depends on <u>bandwidth</u>.
- <u>Dependent on host</u> for security and backups.
- Stored data can be <u>vulnerable</u> to hackers (p.111).
- Unclear who has <u>ownership</u> over cloud data.
- Subscription fees for using cloud <u>storage</u> may be expensive in the <u>long term</u>.

A quick Summary...

Here's a summary of the relative <u>speeds</u>, <u>costs</u> and <u>capacities</u> of all these different types of storage.

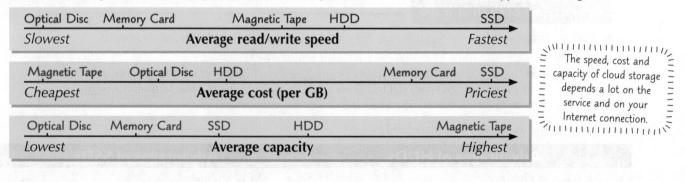

| Optical Disc | Memory Card | | Magnetic Tape | HDD | | SSD |
| Slowest | | | **Average read/write speed** | | | Fastest |

| Magnetic Tape | Optical Disc | HDD | | | Memory Card | SSD |
| Cheapest | | | **Average cost (per GB)** | | | Priciest |

| Optical Disc | Memory Card | SSD | | HDD | | Magnetic Tape |
| Lowest | | | **Average capacity** | | | Highest |

The speed, cost and capacity of cloud storage depends a lot on the service and on your Internet connection.

Be sure to learn the pros and cons of all these types of storage...
Be careful with your terminology. Storage <u>media</u> refers to the actual thing that holds the data, e.g. optical discs. Storage <u>devices</u> read/write data to media, e.g. HDDs or optical drive.

Warm-Up and Worked Exam Questions

Once you've got all the different memory and storage terms learnt, it's time to have a go at some questions. If you're confident with the warm-up questions, then test yourself against the exam questions.

Warm-Up Questions

1) What is the difference between RAM and ROM?
2) Explain what it means for a single-core processor to have "a clock speed of 3 GHz".
3) Name a type of secondary storage that:
   a) uses flash memory and has no moving parts   b) stores data as little pits on its surface
   c) stores data on a stack of magnetic disks
4) Give one advantage of storing data in cloud storage.

Worked Exam Questions

1   Tameeka runs a piece of software to analyse the performance of her computer.
    It recommends that she should install more RAM in her computer.

   a)   State the purpose of RAM in a computer system.

   RAM holds any data that is currently in use.

   [1 mark]

   b)   Give **two** reasons why Tameeka may need to install more RAM in her computer.

   1   Her computer may be running slowly.

   2   She may want to run more programs at once.

   [2 marks]

2   Shaun is on a skiing trip. Each night, he copies skiing videos to his laptop's secondary storage.

   a)   Give **three** characteristics to consider when choosing a suitable type
        of secondary storage for a computer system.

        You could also mention how quickly they transfer data, or how portable they are.

   1   Capacity

   2   Cost

   3   Durability   —   *Durability is how much physical damage it can take without breaking.*

   [3 marks]

   b)   Shaun uses a helmet-mounted action camera while skiing, which records onto a flash
        memory card. Give **two** reasons why this is a suitable storage type for an action camera.

   1   Flash storage is resistant to impacts, so is unlikely to be damaged

   when the action camera is in use.

   2   Flash storage can be very compact and lightweight.

   [2 marks]

Exam Questions

3 Diana has bought a new laptop. The laptop contains 3 GB RAM and 128 GB secondary storage.

a) Explain why secondary storage is needed in addition to RAM.

....

....

....

[3 marks]

Diana wants to back up the data on her laptop twice a week.

b) Give **two** advantages and **two** disadvantages of storing her backup data on optical discs.

Advantages 1 ....

2 ....

Disadvantages 1 ....

2 ....

[4 marks]

4 Jackson is considering upgrading his PC. Will offers to sell his old CPU to Jackson.
Will's CPU is the same type as Jackson's CPU but has a different specification.

Jackson's CPU	Will's CPU
8 cores	4 cores
6 MB cache	3 MB cache
1.6 GHz clock speed	2.8 GHz clock speed

a) Explain why using a CPU with a large cache capacity may increase CPU performance.

....

....

[2 marks]

b) Do you think Jackson should buy Will's CPU? Give reasons to justify your decision.

....

....

....

....

There's no wrong answer, as long as your answer is properly justified.   *[4 marks]*

c) Jackson increases the RAM in his PC from 4 GB to 8 GB, but is disappointed to find no
noticeable increase in his computer's performance. Explain why this may be the case.

....

....

[2 marks]

System Software — The OS

System software is software designed to run and maintain a computer system. By far the most important one is the operating system (OS). There's also utility software (p.84) but that's very much the runner up.

Operating Systems manage Hardware and run Software

An Operating System (OS) is a complex piece of software found on most computer systems.

Main Functions of an OS

- Communicate with input and output devices via device drivers (see below).
- Provide a platform for applications to run on, and a user interface (see p.82).
- Control memory management and allocation (see p.82).
- Organise the CPU and its processing tasks (see p.83).
- Deal with file management and disk management (see p.83).
- Manage system security and user accounts (see p.83).

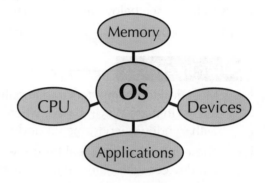

The OS Communicates with I/O Devices through Drivers

I/O (input/output) devices allow computers to take inputs (e.g. through a keyboard, microphone, webcam, etc.) and give outputs (e.g. through a monitor, speakers, printer, etc.). Operating systems use device drivers to communicate with I/O devices connected to the computer system:

- Every I/O device connected to the computer system requires a device driver. Drivers essentially act as a 'translator' for the signals between the OS and the device.

- When a computer is booted up, the OS will choose the correct device drivers for the device it detects. If new devices are connected to the computer, the system will install the new, matching driver.

- Device manufacturers may release updates to device drivers in order to fix bugs, add features or improve the performance of their device. Updates may be installed automatically by the OS or manually by the user.

Some OSs will automatically find and install the drivers when you plug in a new device.

A driver lets a computer speak to a mouse? If you say so...

Remember, the OS is the boss of the computer system. There's loads more to learn about the OS, so make sure you understand what device drivers do and how the OS manages them before moving on.

System Software — The OS

One of the most recognisable functions of an OS is its user interface. It's one of the first things you imagine when you think about a particular system. But there's much more to an operating system than how it looks...

The OS manages Applications

1) Operating systems provide a <u>platform</u> for applications to run on, and manage system resources to allow computers to run <u>multiple applications</u> at once — known as <u>multitasking</u>.

2) It also allows applications to <u>access hardware</u> and other peripheral devices as needed, including access to <u>RAM</u> (see below) and <u>secondary storage</u> (e.g. so files can be opened and saved).

3) The OS also provides a <u>user interface</u> that applications are accessed through:

User Interfaces

- Most desktop computers traditionally use <u>graphical interfaces</u> (GUIs) that are <u>WIMP</u>-based, where applications are displayed with <u>windows</u>, <u>icons</u>, <u>menus</u> and <u>pointers</u>.

- These interfaces are ideal for use with a <u>mouse and keyboard</u>, but devices with <u>different input</u> methods (e.g. smartphones with <u>touchscreens</u>) may have very different interfaces.

- Applications are usually <u>written</u> for a <u>particular</u> OS and will <u>take advantage</u> of its features. For example, using standard <u>windows</u> and <u>menus</u> in a WIMP interface, or allowing users to <u>tap, pinch and swipe</u> on a touchscreen device.

You can swipe between screens or tap an icon to open it on Android™.

The OS is in charge of Memory Management

1) When an application is <u>opened</u>, the OS copies the <u>necessary</u> parts of the application to <u>memory</u>, followed by <u>additional</u> parts when they are required.

2) The OS will decide if applications or features have been used recently — if <u>not</u>, they may be <u>removed</u> from memory.

3) The OS manages <u>how much</u> RAM a program has access to. This will depend on the program — for example, <u>image editing</u> software usually uses a lot of memory, while <u>text editors</u> need much less RAM. Certain things, like having <u>more documents</u> open, can make a program require <u>additional memory</u>.

4) When running <u>multiple</u> applications at once, the OS makes sure that they <u>don't overwrite</u> or <u>interfere</u> with each other by allocating certain applications certain memory addresses, keeping their processes in separate locations.

Make sure you understand how the OS manages memory...

Take a look at a few different types of OS (e.g. desktop computer, smartphone, game console). What differences can you see between the user interfaces? How have they been adapted to suit the device? How do applications take advantage of the features of the user interface?

System Software — The OS

The OS also interacts with the CPU — look back at p.71-72 if you want a reminder of what the CPU does.

The OS tells the CPU what to Process

1) When an application is launched, it creates one or more processes. Each process has instructions that it needs the CPU to execute. However, CPUs can only carry out instructions from one process at a time.

2) Operating systems deal with this by using scheduling to determine the most efficient order for the CPU to execute instructions.

3) Each process is allocated a 'priority' by the OS. The CPU carries out the instructions from the highest-priority processes first, and the other processes wait in a queue.

4) The OS may interrupt the current CPU process if a higher-priority process becomes available.

5) In order to allow multitasking, the CPU swaps between different processes very rapidly — remember, most CPUs can carry out billions of instructions in a second (p.76).

System software also creates processes, which run in the background.

The OS handles File and Disk Management

1) Computers store data as files. Images, music, videos and spreadsheets are all just collections of data. File extensions (for example .jpg, .mp3, .mpeg) tell the computer which software should be used to open the file.

2) The OS is responsible for file management — the organisation of data into a usable hierarchical structure. It also deals with the movement, editing and deletion of data.

3) The OS manages the hard disk. It splits the physical disk into storage sectors, decides which sectors to write data to, and keeps track of free space on the disk. Ideally, the data for a single file would be placed in adjacent sectors, but this isn't always possible (p.84).

4) The OS also organises and maintains the hard disk with utility software (see p.84) like defragmentation software.

Utilities like File Explorer allow users to navigate and edit the file structure or access their files.

Operating Systems manage System Security

Most popular OSs include ways of keeping data stored on a system secure.

1) One common way in which they do this is through user account control. User accounts allow different users to be granted or denied access to specific data or resources on a computer system.

2) On most desktop operating systems, each user has access to their own personal data and desktop, but cannot access other users' personal data, unless they are a system administrator.

3) Operating systems may have anti-theft measures to prevent other users from accessing locked devices or accounts to steal information. User accounts may be password, or pin protected. Some devices also require a user to draw a specific pattern on the screen, or have fingerprint or retina scanners.

That's all of the OS's main functions covered...

There's a lot to take in on those last few pages. Try going over the list on page 81 and explaining how the OS handles each one. Once you've learned them all, take a break — you've earned it.

System Software — Utilities

Operating systems are amazing things, but they'd be less amazing without the tools of their trade — utilities.

Utility Software helps to Maintain a computer

Utility system software refers to any software used to maintain or configure a computer. Many useful utilities are installed with the operating system, but you can install other ones to perform additional tasks.

Defragmentation

Files are stored on a hard disk in available spaces. Ideally, whole files would be stored together, but as files are moved and deleted, gaps appear on the disk. The OS has to split new files up to fill the gaps. This makes reading these files slower as the read/write head has to move back and forth across the disk. Defragmentation puts the files back into one block and collects the free space together:

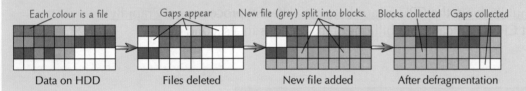

Each colour is a file   Gaps appear   New file (grey) split into blocks.   Blocks collected   Gaps collected

Data on HDD   Files deleted   New file added   After defragmentation

> As SSDs have no moving parts, fragmentation doesn't slow them down — in fact, defragmenting them can actually shorten their lifespan.

Disk Health

Over time, hard drives can start to deteriorate, causing corrupted data and slow read/write speeds. Disk health utilities scan the drive for problems and fix issues where possible.

System Cleanup

Programs like web browsers leave a lot of temporary files on your hard drive, which can end up taking up lots of space unnecessarily. System cleanup utilities go through and get rid of files like these.

Compression

Compression software reduces the size of files so they take up less disk space (see p.42). It's used loads on the Internet to make files quicker to download. Standard file formats include .zip and .rar. Compressed files need to be extracted before they can be used.

Backup

A backup is a copy of a computer system's files and settings stored externally that can be restored in the event of data loss. Data loss can happen for many reasons — fire, theft, flood, malware, hardware failure, or accidentally deleting files by mistake. A backup utility is software with facilities such as scheduling of regular backups, creating rescue disks, disk images, and options for how much data to backup.

Encryption

Encryption software (see p.64) scrambles (encrypts) data to stop third-parties from accessing it. Encrypted data can be decrypted using a special 'key'.

Virus Scanners

These inspect each file on your computer, looking for viruses. They usually have a list of known viruses to check for — they need to be updated regularly so they don't miss anything.

EXAM TIP

There are many more examples of utility software...

Remember, utility software helps maintain your system. There are plenty more you could mention in the exam, e.g. system restore, file managers, antispyware, firewalls, software auto-update, etc.

Warm-Up and Worked Exam Questions

Well, you've made it to the end of another section, which calls for a bit of a celebration. But not before having a go at these questions — better get them out of the way while it's all fresh in your mind...

Warm-Up Questions

1) Tick the correct box in each row of the table below.

	System Software	Not System Software
Operating System		
Word Processor		
Email Client		
Disk defragmenter		

2) Choose the utility software from the box that best matches each description below:

Compression	File manager	Backup	Virus scanner	Encryption	System cleanup

a) Removes unnecessary files from the hard drive.

b) Reduces the size of files and folders.

c) Searches the computer for malicious software.

d) Scrambles / encodes data so that only someone with a key can read it.

e) Creates copies of certain files and settings on your computer that can be restored.

Worked Exam Question

1 Selina has various I/O devices plugged into her computer, including a mouse, keyboard and a touchscreen monitor.

a) Which of the following statements are true? Shade **two** ovals only.

   A   The mouse and keyboard are both input devices. ⬤

   B   The mouse and keyboard are both output devices. ◯

   C   The touchscreen monitor is both an input and output device. ⬤

   D   The touchscreen monitor is only an output device. ◯

[2 marks]

b) Explain how the OS on Selina's computer manages the I/O devices.

The OS uses device drivers to translate signals between the computer software

and the I/O devices into a format that the other can understand.

[2 marks]

c) The OS on Selina's computer provides a graphical user interface (GUI). Give **two** features of a GUI that might allow users to interact with it using a mouse and keyboard.

1 Letting users drag windows around with the mouse.

2 Letting users use keyboard shortcuts to perform common tasks.

[2 marks]

Exam Questions

2   David has just installed a new operating system on his computer.

a)   State **three** functions of an operating system.

1 ....

2 ....

3 ....

[3 marks]

b)   Give **two** features the operating system may provide to help protect David's personal data.

1 ....

2 ....

[2 marks]

3   Annie has a three year old laptop. She is giving it a full service before selling it on.

a)   Annie runs some 'Disk Health' utility software to check for any problems with her HDD. Define what is meant by utility software.

....

....

[1 mark]

b)   The 'Disk Health' utility suggests that Annie should run a defragmentation utility on her laptop's HDD. Explain what defragmentation software is used for.

....

....

....

[3 marks]

4   Josephine opens up her email client and her web browser at the same time. The email client downloads her new emails while the web browser loads her home page.

Explain, with reference to memory and processor management, how the operating system on a computer manages applications and allows them to run at the same time.

....

....

....

....

....

....

[6 marks]

Revision Questions for Section Five

Well, that wraps up <u>Section Five</u>. You should be an expert on computer systems now, but we'd better check:

- Try these questions and <u>tick off each one</u> when you <u>get it right</u>.
- When you've done <u>all the questions</u> for a topic and are <u>completely happy</u> with it, tick off the topic.

Computer Systems and the CPU (p.70-72) ☑

1) What is a computer?
2) Define hardware and software.
3) Give one example of system software and one example of application software.
4) What is an embedded system?
5) What is a control system?
6) Explain the role of the control unit in the CPU.
7) What does ALU stand for and what does it do?
8) What is cache and what is it used for?
9) Describe the function of the clock.
10) What is a bus in a CPU?
11) Sketch a Von Neumann computer.
12) Describe what happens at each stage of the CPU fetch-decode-execute cycle.

Memory and Computer Performance (p.75-76) ☑

13) What is the difference between volatile and non-volatile memory?
14) What does RAM stand for? Describe how RAM is used in a computer system.
15) Could changing the amount of RAM affect the performance of the computer? Give reasons for your answer.
16) Explain why ROM is required by a computer system.
17) Which usually has more RAM: an embedded system or a non-embedded system?
18) Name three characteristics of a processor that may affect its performance.

Secondary Storage (p.77-78) ☑

19) Define primary and secondary storage and give an example of each.
20) List the advantages and disadvantages of HDDs and SSDs.
21) Why might someone choose magnetic tape as a form of storage?
22) List four uses of flash memory.
23) What are the pros and cons of:
    a) optical discs?   b) cloud storage?
24) Draw a diagram to summarise cost, speed and capacity for different types of secondary storage.

System Software (p.81-84) ☑

25) List six functions of an operating system.
26) Explain how device drivers are used in a computer system.
27) Describe how the OS manages:
    a) applications   b) memory   c) the CPU   d) files and disk space
28) Give three ways in which an OS might keep your files secure.
29) List seven types of utility software and explain what they do.

Networks

When you connect a device to another one, you're creating a network — networks allow devices to share information and resources. Here we'll look at the types of network you'll need to know for your exam.

A **LAN** is a **Local Area Network**

1) A LAN covers a <u>small geographical area</u> located on a <u>single site</u>.

2) All the hardware for a LAN is <u>owned</u> by the organisation that uses it.

3) LANs can be <u>wired</u> (e.g. with <u>Ethernet</u> cables — see next page) or <u>wireless</u> (see p.90).

4) You'll often find LANs in <u>businesses</u>, <u>schools</u> and <u>universities</u>.

5) Lots of homes have a LAN to connect various devices, such as <u>PCs</u>, <u>tablets</u>, <u>smart TVs</u> and <u>printers</u>.

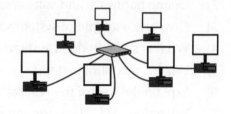

A **WAN** is a network that **Connects LANs**

1) WAN stands for <u>Wide Area Network</u>.

2) A WAN connects LANs that are in <u>different geographical locations</u>. For example, a business with offices in three different countries would need a WAN for all their devices to connect together.

3) Unlike a LAN, organisations <u>hire infrastructure</u> (e.g. communication lines) from telecommunications companies, who own and manage the WAN. This is because a WAN is much more <u>expensive</u> to set up than a LAN.

4) WANs may be connected using <u>telephone lines</u> (copper or fibre optic), <u>satellite links</u> or <u>radio links</u>.

5) The <u>Internet</u> is actually one big WAN.

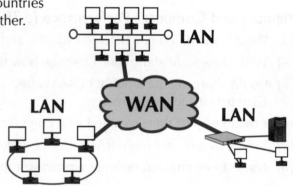

A **PAN** is a **Personal Network**

1) <u>Personal Area Networks</u> (PANs) connect devices over a <u>very short range</u>.

2) They're normally centred around a <u>single user</u>, and are often used to transmit between mobile/wearable devices (e.g. smartphones, smartwatches, headphones, etc.).

3) PANs often use common wireless technology (e.g. <u>Bluetooth</u>®) to connect devices. A Bluetooth® signal is <u>quite strong</u>, but has a very <u>short range</u> which makes it ideal for connecting devices in the <u>same room</u>.

4) PANs are handy as they usually <u>don't</u> require any <u>additional hardware</u>, just the devices themselves. This also means you can create a PAN <u>on the move</u>.

Don't LANguish at the bottom of the class — learn this page...

Make sure you're absolutely clear about the differences between the three types of network before moving on. Remember, companies use their own cables for LANs, but they almost always hire lines for WANs.

Networks

Connecting devices doesn't magically happen. To create a network, you need certain pieces of hardware...

Networks require lots of **Hardware**

1) A Network Interface Card (NIC) is a piece of hardware inside a device that allows it to connect to networks. NICs exist for both wired and wireless connections.

2) Switches are used to connect devices on a LAN, while routers transmit data between different networks, and are most commonly used to connect to the Internet. Most home 'routers' are in fact a router, switch and WAP (see next page) all-in-one.

3) Wired networks can use different cables to connect devices — the choice of cable usually depends on cost, bandwidth and how far you want to transmit data.

Bandwidth is the amount of data that can be sent across a network in a given time.

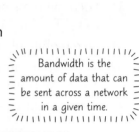

- Fibre optic cables transmit data as light. They are high performance and expensive cables — they don't suffer interference and can transmit over very large distances at a high bandwidth without loss of signal quality.

- CAT 5e and CAT 6 are common types of Ethernet cable. They contain pairs of copper wires which are twisted together to reduce internal interference. They're cheaper than fibre optic cables and have a decent bandwidth, which is why they're commonly used in homes and offices to connect devices on a LAN.

- Coaxial cables are made of a single copper wire surrounded by a plastic layer for insulation and a metallic mesh which provides shielding from outside interference. They tend to be very cheap, although they also have a low bandwidth.

Fibre optic cable

Twisted pair of copper wires

CAT 6 cable

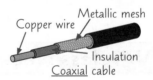

Metallic mesh
Copper wire
Insulation
Coaxial cable

Networking Computers has **Benefits** and **Drawbacks**

Benefits

1) Sharing files is easier — network users can access the same files, work on them at the same time and copy files between machines.

2) You can share the same hardware (like printers) between multiple devices.

3) You can install and update software on all computers at once, rather than one-by-one.

4) You can communicate across a network cheaply and easily, e.g. with email.

5) User accounts can be stored centrally, so users can log in from any device on the network.

Drawbacks

1) They can be expensive to set up, as you often need a lot of extra hardware (see above).

2) Networks can be vulnerable to hacking (see p.111), and malware (p.97) can easily spread between networked computers.

3) Some networks are dependent on one or more servers (see p.91). If those servers go down it can be very disruptive for people trying to use the network.

4) Large networks are difficult to manage and may require employing a specialist to maintain them.

EXAM TIP

Hardware — nothing to do with concrete jackets...

In your exam, you might have to compare fibre optic and copper cables (which include CAT5e/6 and coaxial), or say which you think is more suited to a given situation. You should think in terms of cost (fibre optic = expensive, copper = cheap) and speed (fibre optic = fast, copper = slow).

Wireless Networks

If you don't like the sound of all those cables, don't worry — you can throw them all away and use wireless networking instead. You'll still have to learn about both of them for the exam though, I'm afraid.

Wireless Networks use Radio Waves to transmit data

1) Local wireless networks are called <u>WLANs</u> (wireless LANs). Most people refer to these as <u>Wi-Fi®</u>, but Wi-Fi® is actually a specific <u>family</u> of WLAN <u>protocols</u> (see p.96).

2) Like mobile phones and TVs, wireless networks use <u>radio waves</u> to transmit data.

3) To set up a wireless network, you need a <u>Wireless Access Point (WAP)</u> device. The WAP is basically a <u>switch</u> that allows devices to connect wirelessly.

4) Don't confuse WAPs with <u>hotspots</u> — <u>locations</u> where you can connect to a WAP.

5) To connect, devices need <u>wireless capability</u>. Many modern devices have the necessary hardware built in, but devices that don't can often still connect to a wireless network using a <u>dongle</u>.

- <u>USB dongles</u> can be plugged into computers to allow them to connect wirelessly to the internet.

- <u>HDMI dongles</u> can use wireless networks to stream high-quality video to a TV.

Dongles come in all shapes and sizes (although most of them are roughly the same shape and size).

Wireless Networks have Benefits and Drawbacks

Wireless networks have some <u>great benefits</u>, but they <u>aren't always better</u> than wired networks...

Benefits of wireless networks

1) Wireless networks are <u>convenient</u>, as you can get your device to <u>automatically connect</u> to the network, and can also <u>move around</u> while connected to the network.

2) They can be <u>cheaper</u> and better for the <u>environment</u> as you don't need any <u>wires</u>.

3) It's very easy to <u>add more users</u> to a wireless network — you don't need to install <u>extra wires</u> or do any <u>complex setup</u>.

Drawbacks of wireless networks

1) Wireless networks are generally <u>less secure</u> than wired networks — access points are usually visible to <u>all devices</u>, not just trusted ones, which can allow hackers to gain access.

2) <u>Distance</u> from the WAP, <u>interference</u> from other wireless networks, and physical <u>obstructions</u> (e.g. walls) can all <u>reduce signal strength</u>. This means there's a <u>limit</u> on <u>how far</u> a wireless network can <u>reach</u>.

3) They generally have a <u>lower bandwidth</u> and are <u>less reliable</u> than wired networks.

Remember, WLANs are a separate thing from the Internet...

WLANs allow a device to wirelessly connect to a network with a WAP — that network would then need to be connected to a router in order for the device to be able to access the Internet.

Network Topologies

A topology is essentially the layout of the network. Networks can be arranged in lots of different topologies, but star and bus are the two important ones you'll need to know for the exam.

In a **Star Topology** all devices are connected to the centre

In a star topology, all the devices are connected to a central switch or server that controls the network.

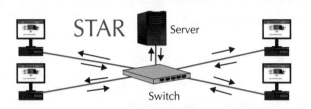

The central switch allows many devices to access the server simultaneously.

Star networks may be wired or wireless.

Pros
- If a device fails or a cable is disconnected, the rest of the network is unaffected.
- It's simple to add more devices to the network, since each device is connected to the switch using a separate cable.
- Star topologies tend to have better performance than other setups — data goes straight to the central device so all devices can transmit data at the same time.
- There are fewer data collisions on a star network compared to other network topologies (e.g. bus).

Cons
- In wired networks, every device needs a cable to connect to the central switch or server. This can be expensive, e.g. for an office building with 50 terminals.
- The switch itself is also an expensive piece of hardware.
- If there is a problem with the switch or server then the whole network is affected.
- The maximum number of possible connections on the network is determined by the switch — if you need more, you might need to buy a new one.

In a **Bus Topology** all devices are connected to a **Single Cable**

1) Bus topologies use a single 'backbone' cable, called a bus, to connect all the devices.

2) Two terminators are placed at the ends of the bus to stop data reflecting back along the bus. Without the terminators, reflected signals would cause interference and potentially make the network unusable.

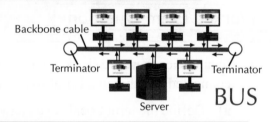

Pros
- Like in a star topology, the network is unaffected if a device fails.
- Bus networks aren't dependent on a central switch working to keep the whole network running.
- They're relatively cheap to set up compared to star networks. The total length of wiring needed is much less, and the hardware you need (the bus cable and terminators) is cheaper than switches, both to buy and to maintain.

Cons
- Data collisions are common on a bus network. When there is a data collision the data must be resent, which slows the network down.
- The more devices you add to the network, the more likely data collisions are. This makes bus topologies unsuitable for large networks.
- To try and avoid data collisions, devices must wait for the bus to be available before they can send any data — this can also slow the network down.
- If the bus cable gets broken (e.g. from nibbling rats), it splits the network into separate parts. Since the separated networks don't have terminators at both ends of the bus, there will be a lot of reflected signals which can shut down the entire network.

"You can't handle a bus network — you've got no backbone"...

Star topologies are pretty common, but relying on the central switch can cause problems if the switch fails. Bus topologies are usually cheaper, but can be really slow when there's heavy traffic — just like real buses.

Warm-Up and Worked Exam Questions

Now that you know what networks are made of and what they look like, test yourself against these questions. If anything catches you out, go back and read over it until you're happy.

Warm-Up Questions

1) Name the type of network that is being described:
   a) An international business has one network connecting all of its offices.
   b) A driver uses a 'dashcam' in her car that records video of the road and wirelessly transmits the data to her smartphone.
   c) A group of friends connect their computers together to play a video game.

2) A laptop, printer and smart TV are connected in a wired LAN using Ethernet cables.
   a) Suggest why Ethernet cables may have been used over other types of cable.
   b) Each device on the network is directly connected to a central switch. What is the name of this network topology?

3) Give one advantage of switching from a wired to a wireless LAN.

4) Are these statements about network devices true or false?
   a) Routers are used to transmit data between networks.
   b) Switches are used to change the network from wired to wireless.
   c) Routers that also include a WAP are always faster than routers that don't.
   d) You can set up a LAN without using a router.

Worked Exam Question

1 In an office there are six computers, a scanner and a router connected together in a Local Area Network (LAN).

   a) Define the term Local Area Network (LAN).

   A group of devices connected to share data over a small geographical area.

   [1 mark]

   b) State **three** advantages of connecting the computers together into a Local Area Network.

   1 The business' six computers can share one Internet connection.

   2 The computers can share the scanner.

   3 It is easier to install and update software.

   They can also share files more easily and store user accounts centrally. *[3 marks]*

   c) Each computer is connected with a wireless keyboard and mouse in a PAN using Bluetooth®. Explain **one** difference between a PAN and a LAN.

   A PAN has a very short range, often connecting devices in the same room,

   whereas a LAN has a slightly bigger range, connecting devices across a site.

   [2 marks]

Exam Questions

2 Suggest a type of network cable that would be appropriate for these businesses.

a) A bank who want the fastest possible connection between their offices at different sites.

....

[1 mark]

b) A hotel who want to put wired Internet access in every hotel room.

....

[1 mark]

3 In a bus topology, all of the devices are connected directly to a bus (main backbone cable) and a terminator is placed at either end of the bus.

a) State the purpose of a terminator.

....

[1 mark]

b) Draw a diagram showing a printer, three computers and a router connected in a bus network.

[2 marks]

c) Explain **one** advantage and **one** disadvantage of bus topologies compared to star topologies.

Advantage ....

....

Disadvantage ....

....

[4 marks]

4 Explain the risks of using computer networks rather than standalone machines.

....

....

....

....

[4 marks]

Network Protocols

Moving data on the network is like going on a car journey — you need a destination, something to tell you how to get there, and rules to stop you crashing into anyone else on the road. That's where protocols come in.

Networks need **Protocols** to set the rules

1) A protocol is a set of rules for how devices communicate and how data is transmitted across a network.

2) Protocols cover how communication between two devices should start and end, how the data should be organised, and what the devices should do if data goes missing.

3) Data sent between networks is split into equal-sized packets. Each packet contains extra information like the destination and source addresses (see p.96) and a checksum (used to find errors).

Network protocols are divided into **Layers**

1) A layer is a group of protocols which have similar functions.

2) Layers are self-contained — protocols in each layer do their job without needing to know what's happening in the other layers.

3) Each layer serves the layer above it — it does the hidden work needed for an action on the layer above. E.g. when you send an email (on layer 4), this triggers actions in layer 3, which triggers actions in layer 2, all the way down to layer 1.

Data can only be passed between adjacent layers. E.g. Layer 2 can pass data to Layers 1 and 3 but Layer 1 can only pass data to Layer 2.

4) The four layers of the TCP/IP model are shown below:

Layer Name	Protocols in this layer cover...	Protocol examples
Layer 4 — Application Layer	Providing networking services to applications — e.g. turning data into websites.	HTTP, FTP, SMTP
Layer 3 — Transport Layer	Setting up communications between two devices, splitting data into packets and checking packets are correctly sent and delivered.	TCP, UDP
Layer 2 — Internet Layer	Adding IP addresses to data packets, directing them between devices and handling traffic. Used by routers.	IP
Layer 1 — Link Layer	Passing data over the physical network. Responsible for how data is sent as electrical signals over cables, wireless and other hardware, e.g. NICs (p.89), and for interpreting signals using device drivers (p.81).	Wi-Fi®, Ethernet

Advantages of Using Layers

1) It breaks network communication into manageable pieces. This helps developers concentrate on only one area of the network without having to worry about the others.

2) As layers are self-contained, they can be changed without the other layers being affected.

3) Having set rules for each layer forces companies to make compatible, universal hardware and software, so different brands will work with each other and always work in basically the same way.

Lots of layers to learn — and plenty of protocols to ponder too...

Make sure you know what the four different layers of the TCP/IP model are, and why layers are so useful.

Network Protocols

The top two layers of the TCP/IP model (application and transport layer), are more closely related to what the user is actually doing. You might have seen HTTP when browsing the web, but there are many others...

Lots of **Important Protocols** work on the **Application Layer**

In the TCP/IP model, the <u>application layer</u> is responsible for things like <u>file</u>, <u>email</u> and <u>data transfer</u>:

Protocol	Stands for...	What is it used for?
HTTP	Hyper Text Transfer Protocol	Used by <u>web browsers</u> to access <u>websites</u> and communicate with <u>web servers</u>.
HTTPS	HTTP Secure	A more <u>secure</u> version of HTTP. <u>Encrypts</u> all information sent and received.
FTP	File Transfer Protocol	Used to access, edit and move <u>files</u> between devices on a network, e.g. to access files on a server from a client computer.
IMAP	Internet Message Access Protocol	Used to <u>retrieve emails</u> from a server.
SMTP	Simple Mail Transfer Protocol	Used to <u>send emails</u>. Also used to transfer emails between servers.

TCP and **UDP** split the data into **Packets**

1) <u>TCP</u> and <u>UDP</u> are <u>transport layer</u> protocols which control the <u>packaging</u> and <u>unpackaging</u> of data.

TCP
- <u>Transmission Control Protocol</u> (TCP) establishes a <u>connection</u> between the sending and receiving devices.
- It then splits the data into <u>numbered packets</u> that can be <u>reassembled</u> into the <u>original data</u> once they reach their destination, even if they arrive <u>out of order</u>.
- It <u>communicates</u> with the receiving device to make sure that <u>all packets</u> have been <u>transferred correctly</u>. If not, the missing/corrupted packets can be <u>resent</u>.
- The sending device gets <u>confirmation</u> when the transfer is complete.

UDP
- <u>User Datagram Protocol</u> (UDP) breaks the data down into packets <u>without numbering</u> them.
- They are <u>read</u> by the receiving device in the <u>order</u> that they <u>arrive</u> — even if that's not the order they were <u>sent</u>.
- UDP only sends each packet <u>once</u> and <u>doesn't check</u> with the receiving device that everything has been <u>received</u>.
- This <u>saves time</u>, but there's <u>no way of knowing</u> if packets have gone <u>missing</u> in transit.

2) UDP is suitable for applications that need <u>fast</u>, <u>efficient</u> transmission, e.g. live video streaming. A hiccup in <u>video quality</u> from a missing packet is better than a <u>delay</u> in the live stream.

3) TCP is better when you need a <u>reliable</u> connection, e.g. downloading files. Missing data packets can cause files to be <u>corrupted</u> and <u>unusable</u>, but you wouldn't want to have to <u>redownload</u> the whole file.

Make sure you know the difference between TCP and UDP...

The next time you're using the Internet, write down any protocols that could be relevant to what you're doing, and what layer they operate on. If you're receiving data from a website, do you think TCP or UDP would be more suitable for transferring the data?

Network Protocols

No surprises here — this page is all about the bottom two layers of the TCP/IP model. The Internet layer and link layer handle the actual transfer of data across the network.

IP is responsible for Packet Switching

1) Internet Protocol (IP) operates on the Internet layer, establishing connections between routers and handling network traffic. IP addresses are unique numbers assigned to every device connected to an IP network — they are added to the header of each packet at the Internet layer.

2) IP is responsible for directing data packets to their destination across the Internet or other IP networks using a process called packet switching.

3) Each packet is sent between a series of routers — each router reads the packet's header and uses the IP address to decide which router to send the packet to next.

4) Which way the data is sent changes depending on network traffic — so the packets can take different routes. If a router receives too many packets at once, it may prioritise some over others.

5) Packet switching is an efficient use of the network because there are so many possible routes that each packet can take — packets can reach their receiving device quickly, even if there's heavy traffic.

Wi-Fi® is the Standard set of Protocols for Wireless LANs

1) Like we mentioned on p.90, Wi-Fi® is a family of protocols commonly used in WLANs. It operates on the link layer — units of data sent on the link layer are called frames instead of packets.

2) Wi-Fi® uses two radio frequency bands — 2.4 GHz and 5 GHz. 2.4 GHz has a greater range and is better at getting through walls and other obstructions, while 5 GHz is faster over short distances.

3) The bands are split into numbered channels that each cover a small frequency range. The channels in the 2.4 GHz band overlap. Networks using adjacent or overlapping channels can cause interference.

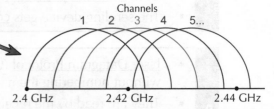

4) It's important that data is encrypted (see p.99) on Wi-Fi® networks. There are security protocols for this, called WPA™ (Wi-Fi® Protected Access) and WPA2™.

Wi-Fi® and Ethernet use switches to direct data frames to a device using its MAC address (p.99).

Ethernet is used on Wired Networks

Ethernet is another family of protocols that operates on the link layer. Like Wi-Fi®, it also handles the transmission of data between devices on LANs, but Ethernet is specifically for wired connections.

They sent me the wrong router — the packets were switched...

IP addresses usually look something like 37.153.62.136. They can be static (you get the same one every time you connect to a network) or dynamic (you can get a different one each time you connect to a network).

Cyber Security Threats

Networks are great for lots of reasons, but they can also be very vulnerable to attacks by criminals.

Cyber Security is important to People and Organisations

1) Cyber security aims to protect networks, data, programs and computers against damage, cyber attacks and unauthorised access. It covers the technologies (e.g. anti-malware software), practices (e.g. network policies) and processes (e.g. penetration testing) used to do this.

2) Cyber attacks can target individuals, organisations or even governments. Hackers (see p.111) often target organisations with the aim of accessing lots of sensitive information at once. There have been cases of millions of people's bank details being compromised by attacks on a single organisation.

Penetration Testing can Test a system's Cyber Security

1) Penetration testing (or pentesting) is when organisations employ specialists to simulate potential attacks to their system. It's used to identify possible weaknesses in their cyber security. The results of the test are then reported back so that vulnerabilities can be fixed.

2) There are two different forms of penetration test — white box and black box.

- White box penetration testing simulates a malicious insider who has knowledge of the current system, e.g. an employee at the organisation. The person carrying out the test will be given user credentials to see what they can do with them.
- Black box penetration testing simulates an external cyber attack. The person carrying out the test will not be given any credentials, but will try to hack the organisation in any way they can.

Malware is software that can harm devices

1) Malware (malicious software) is code that is designed to cause harm or gain unauthorised access to a computer system. It is often installed on someone's device without their knowledge or consent.

2) There are several different ways that malware can get onto a device — for example, being downloaded in an email attachment or hidden on removable media (e.g. USB drive or SD card).

3) Typical actions of malware include:

- Deleting or modifying files.
- Locking files — ransomware encrypts all the files on a computer. The user receives a message demanding a large sum of money be paid in exchange for a decryption key.
- Displaying unwanted adverts — adware can cause pop-up ads that cannot be closed.
- Monitoring the user — spyware secretly tracks actions like key presses and sends info to the hacker, who might be able to work out things like passwords and bank details.
- Altering permissions — rootkits can give hackers administrator-level access to devices.

4) Malware can spread between devices in different ways.

- Viruses attach (by copying themselves) to certain files, e.g. .exe files and autorun scripts. Users spread them by copying infected files and activate them by opening infected files.
- Worms are like viruses but they self-replicate without any user help, meaning they can spread very quickly. They exploit weaknesses in network security.
- Trojans are malware disguised as legitimate software. Unlike viruses and worms, trojans don't replicate themselves — users install them not realising they have a hidden purpose.

Malware can spread like an infectious disease...

You don't need to know every single type of malware out there, but learning all of these examples will give you an idea of how malware gets in to a system, and the damage it can do once it's there.

Cyber Security Threats

Often, security threats arise because organisations fail to secure their network properly — they might forget to encrypt their data or have flaws in their code. Other instances are a result of hackers manipulating employees.

People are often the Weak Point in secure systems

Social engineering is a way of gaining sensitive information or illegal access to networks by influencing people, usually the employees of large companies.

Social engineering comes in many different forms:

Pharming

1) Pharming is where a user is directed to a fake version of a website (often a banking or shopping site), designed to look just like the real thing, with the aim that the user won't notice the difference.

2) When the user inputs their personal information into the website, they're actually handing it all over to the criminals, who can then access their genuine account.

3) Pharming is often carried out using malware that automatically redirects people from legitimate sites to fake ones. Ensuring that anti-malware software is up-to-date can reduce the risk of these attacks.

4) Internet browsers can use web filters to prevent users from accessing these fake sites.

Phishing

1) Phishing is when criminals send emails or texts to people claiming to be from a well-known business, e.g. a bank or online retailer. The emails often lead the victim to a fake website, just like pharming.

2) Phishing emails are often sent to thousands of people, in the hope that someone will read the email and believe its content is legitimate.

3) Many email programs, browsers and firewalls have anti-phishing features that will reduce the number of phishing emails received. There are often giveaways that you can spot, e.g. poor grammar. Emails asking users to follow links or update personal details should always be treated with caution.

Shouldering

1) Shouldering is watching and observing a person's activity (typically over their shoulder).

2) Some examples of this are spying someone's PIN number at a cash machine, or watching someone putting their password into a secured computer.

3) It doesn't require any technical expertise or any planning. It's simple, but it can work. You can reduce risk by being discreet, e.g. covering the keypad when you enter your PIN.

Blagging

1) Blagging is when someone makes up a story or pretends to be someone they're not, to persuade the victim to share information or do things they wouldn't normally do.

2) For example, a potential attacker could email someone, pretending to be one of their friends, saying they are stuck in a foreign country and need them to send money.

3) Another common method is to phone the victim, trying to gain their trust by persuading them that they are someone important — e.g. their boss's boss.

4) Criminals that use these tactics often try to pressure people, or rush them into giving away details without giving it proper thought. One way to reduce risk is to use security measures that can't be given away, e.g. biometrics (see p.100).

No amount of security software can protect against human error...

The best way to prevent social engineering in the workplace is to make employees aware of the dangers. The bottom line is: don't give away any details unless you're sure of who you're giving them to.

Cyber Security Threats

Most organisations have a network policy — a set of rules and procedures that the organisation will follow to ensure their network is protected against any possible security threats, e.g. a cyber attack.

Networks need to be Protected against Threats

Organisations must keep their networks secure from hackers in order to protect sensitive information and comply with data protection laws (see p.111). They can use several methods to help them do this:

Encryption

- Encryption is when data is translated into a code which only someone with the correct key can access, meaning unauthorised users cannot read it.
- Encrypted text is called cipher text, whereas data which has not been encrypted is called plain text.
- Encryption is essential for sending data over a network securely.

Anti-Malware Software

- Anti-malware software is designed to find and stop malware from damaging an organisation's network and the devices on it.
- There are lots of different types of anti-malware software. For example, firewalls examine all data entering and leaving a network and block any potential threats.
- Companies often use firewalls to prevent unauthorised access to their network.

User Access Levels

- User access levels control which parts of the network different groups of users can access.
- For example, business managers are likely to have a higher access level allowing them to access more sensitive data, like pay information.
- User access levels limit the number of people with access to important data, so help to prevent attacks from within the organisation.

Automatic Software Updates

- Automatic software updates are used to patch (fix) any identified security holes in a piece of software.
- Software that is unpatched or outdated could be more easily exploited by hackers, malware and viruses.

MAC Address Filtering

- MAC address filtering is a way of making sure the only people on a network are trusted users.
- It checks the unique identification (MAC address) of each device that tries to connect to the network and only lets allowed devices join the network.

MAC addresses are unique identifiers assigned to network devices by the manufacturer — they can't be changed.

Learn this page and your exam grade should be fairly secure...

Try and find a recent news article about a network attack. Identify the type of attack/malware used. See if you can find out how the attack was carried out and suggest some ways that it may have been prevented. Then try and get over the inevitable fear of ever using the Internet again...

Cyber Security Threats

Good network security involves only allowing trusted users access to sensitive data or information.

Authentication confirms your Identity

User authentication exists to make sure that anyone trying to access a network or use a system is who they say they are. This prevents unauthorised people from accessing data from the network.

Passwords

- Passwords are a simple method of checking someone's identity.
- They should be strong — many characters long, use a combination of letters, numbers and symbols, and be changed regularly.
- Weak or default passwords are a big security risk as they can be more easily cracked. Hackers can use brute force attacks (p.111) to get past short or simple passwords easily, and social engineering (p.98) to figure out commonly used passwords, like birthdays or addresses.

Biometrics

- Biometric measures use scanners to identify people by a unique part of their body, e.g. fingerprint, retina, etc.
- They have many different uses — for example, many smartphones now contain fingerprint scanners to prevent unauthorised access.
- They are usually quite secure and convenient for users (since they don't have to remember a password or carry a keycard etc.) but are often more expensive to implement as they require special hardware.

Email Confirmation

- Email confirmation is used by most web services that require account registration to confirm that the email address belongs to the person registering.
- It is also used to stop people from using fake email addresses to sign up for things. However, since a lot of webmail services are free, people can usually just sign up for a new email address whenever they want, so this isn't always an effective way of confirming somebody's identity.

CAPTCHA

- CAPTCHA stands for 'Completely Automated Public Turing test to tell Computers and Humans Apart'.
- It is designed to prevent programs from automatically doing certain things, like creating user accounts on a website.
- It usually consists of a simple task, like typing out a blurred and distorted word from an image, or recognising things like animals and signposts.
- These tests rely on computers not being able to read images as well as a human can, but as image recognition software and artificial intelligence is developing, machines are becoming more capable of passing these tests.

A typical
CAPTCHA test.

Security measures impact legitimate users as well...

At this point, it might sound like a good idea to use every available security measure all the time. However, having too many layers of authentication can prevent normal users from being able to use the network easily.

Warm-Up and Worked Exam Questions

That's another section down. There are lots of little things to remember, like the different protocols and types of malware, so go over them until they're secure in your mind. Then have a go at some questions.

Warm-Up Questions

1) Complete the table showing the names and functions of various network protocols:

Protocol	Function
HTTP	
	A more secure version of HTTP.
FTP	
	Used to retrieve emails from a server.
	Splits data into numbered packets to be sent over a network.
	Splits data into packets to be sent over a network without numbering them.
IP	

2) Name the type of malware that:
   a) disguises itself as legitimate software.
   b) displays unwanted adverts which often cannot be closed.
   c) secretly tracks user actions, such as key presses.
   d) attaches to files and spreads from users copying the infected files.

Worked Exam Question

1   Hannah often receives fake emails claiming to be from well-known banks and other organisations.

   a) State the name given to the practice of sending fake or spoof emails.

     Phishing
                                   [1 mark]

   b) Explain the purpose of these fake emails.

     They are used to trick people into thinking they are from legitimate organisations

     so that they give away their personal information, e.g. account login details.
                                     [2 marks]

   c) Hannah also receives suspicious emails that contain attachments, sometimes from names in her own contacts list. Explain the dangers of opening untrusted email attachments.

     The email attachment could contain a virus. Opening the attachment

     would activate the virus and cause it to infect the device.
                                     [2 marks]

Exam Questions

2 Kate is a network administrator at a secondary school.
She has assigned access levels to each user account on the network.

a) Explain why the school's network needs to have different user access levels.

....

....

....

[3 marks]

b) Kate notices that a lot of the network's users haven't changed their
default password or have chosen a weak password.

i) Explain why this is a problem.

....

....

[2 marks]

ii) Suggest **two** requirements Kate could impose on passwords to ensure that they are strong.

1 ....

2 ....

[2 marks]

3 Mahindar is live streaming a badminton match over the Internet to his computer.

a) Explain why Mahindar's computer needs an IP address to communicate on the Internet.

....

....

[2 marks]

b) Would it be better to use TCP or UDP when sending the data packets to Mahindar's
computer? Shade **one** oval and explain your answer.

TCP ⬭   UDP ⬭

....

....

....

....

....

....

[5 marks]

Exam Questions

4 Sally is a network manager and deals with layers of network protocols every day.

a) Define the term network protocol.

....

[2 marks]

b) Give **three** benefits of using layers when working with network protocols.

1 ....

....

2 ....

....

3 ....

....

[3 marks]

c) Describe **two** families of protocols that work on the link layer of the TCP/IP model.

Protocol 1: ....

....

....

Protocol 2: ....

....

....

[4 marks]

5 Pharming and shouldering are two social engineering techniques that criminals can use to find out someone's bank account PIN number.

Describe the **two** social engineering techniques mentioned above. You should also explain how people can try to protect themselves against these techniques.

[6 marks]

6 A law firm has 100 members of staff in an office building in London. The firm stores confidential data about its clients on a server.

Discuss the security methods that the law firm could use to protect the data against network threats.

You should consider the threats posed to the firm's network and how they could be prevented.

[9 marks]

Revision Questions for Section Six

From passwords to packets to PANs to protocols — this section has been quite the mouthful...

- Try these questions and <u>tick off each one</u> when you <u>get it right</u>.
- When you've done <u>all the questions</u> for a topic and are <u>completely happy</u> with it, tick off the topic.

Networks, Hardware and Topologies (p.88-91) ☑

1) What's the difference between a LAN and a WAN?
2) What type of network is Bluetooth® used for?
3) What are the following devices used for?   a) NICs   b) switches   c) routers
4) Describe three different types of network cable.
5) Give five benefits and four drawbacks of using a network.
6) What type of network is commonly referred to as 'Wi-Fi®'?
7) Give two benefits and two drawbacks of using wireless networks over wired.
8) Give two advantages and two disadvantages of using a star network topology.
9) Describe the key features of a bus network topology.

Network Protocols (p.94-96) ☑

10) What is the definition of a protocol?
11) List the 4 layers of the TCP/IP protocol model.
12) Give three reasons why we divide protocols into layers.
13) What does each of the following stand for? Describe in a sentence what each one does:
       HTTP   HTTPS   FTP   IMAP   SMTP
14) Explain the differences between how TCP and UDP work.
15) Give one example of when you would use TCP, and one example of when you would use UDP.
16) Briefly describe how packet switching works.
17) Explain the difference between Wi-Fi® bands and Wi-Fi® channels.
18) What does WPA™ stand for and what does it do?
19) Name the family of protocols in charge of transmitting data over wired LANs.

Cyber Security Threats (p.97-100) ☑

20) Give three reasons why someone might carry out a cyber attack.
21) Explain the difference between white box and black box penetration testing.
22) List five actions that malicious software might carry out.
23) Describe three ways that malware can spread between devices.
24) What is meant by social engineering?
25) Give four social engineering methods, and say how you could reduce the risk of each.
26) Briefly describe five ways of protecting networks against threats.
27) What is user authentication?
28) Give three precautions you should take with your passwords.
29) My smartphone has a fingerprint scanner. What is the name for this kind of security measure?
30) Write down the two words in the image below. What kind of test is this and what does it prove?

Ethical Issues

Despite what you might think, computer science doesn't just exist in a well-ventilated bubble — it affects all of our lives. Computers, new technology and the Internet all impact different people in different ways.

Issues created by technology come in Different Flavours

1) <u>Ethical</u> issues are about what would be considered <u>right</u> and <u>wrong</u> by society.

2) <u>Legal</u> issues are about what's actually <u>right</u> and <u>wrong</u> in the eyes of <u>the law</u>.

3) <u>Environmental</u> issues are about how we impact the <u>natural world</u>.

There is often <u>overlap</u> between ethical, legal and environmental issues.

Exam questions on issues could cover topics from earlier sections too, e.g. cloud storage (p.78), wireless networks (p.90) and cyber security (p.97-100).

Digital Technology raises many Ethical Issues

As new digital technology becomes available, it can create a whole bunch of ethical issues.

1) <u>Smartphones</u> have allowed us to keep in touch much more easily, but have also allowed people to <u>neglect face-to-face interaction</u>. Some might say that it is making people <u>more rude</u> and <u>less sociable</u>.

2) <u>Wearable technology</u> has <u>many positive effects</u> — for example, <u>wireless headsets</u> may stop people from using their phone while driving and <u>fitness trackers</u> can help to promote healthy lifestyles. However, it can also cause problems. <u>Smart glasses</u> with built-in cameras have sparked controversy — people say the fact that they could be used to secretly photograph people is an <u>invasion of privacy</u>.

3) <u>Computer based implants</u> (chips that are surgically inserted into the body) may become more common in the future. They could allow better monitoring of our <u>health</u> and might make our daily lives more <u>convenient</u>, but will likely be <u>expensive</u> and may lead to <u>less privacy</u>.

Unequal access to technology has caused a Digital Divide

1) The <u>digital divide</u> is created by some people having <u>greater access</u> to technology than others. E.g. people can use the <u>Internet</u> to apply for jobs or university courses, access a range of services from banking to retail, and keep in touch with friends. People who have a limited access to the Internet are therefore at a heavy <u>disadvantage</u>.

CAUSES OF THE DIGITAL DIVIDE

- Some people don't have enough <u>money</u> to buy new devices like smartphones and laptops, which can be very <u>expensive</u>.

- <u>Urban</u> areas are likely to have greater <u>network coverage</u> than <u>rural</u> areas.

- Some people <u>don't know</u> how to use the Internet and other new technologies, and so are shut out of the opportunities they offer. This is a problem for many <u>older people</u> who haven't grown up with computers and so have little experience with them.

2) The <u>global divide</u> is created by the fact that the level of access to technology is different in different <u>countries</u>. People in richer countries tend to have greater access to technology than people in poorer countries. The Internet and other technologies have created lots of opportunities for the people with access to them, so this has <u>increased</u> the inequality between poorer and richer countries.

Exam questions could ask about any kind of issue...

Extended response questions may ask about ethical, legal <u>and</u> environmental issues. The more points you can make, the better — just make sure all your points are relevant to the question.

Ethical Issues

Technology can do marvellous things, but people abusing it can cause some really serious issues that can damage people's lives. Few technologies are more open to abuse than the Internet.

The **Internet** is the source of a **Lot** of issues

1) People now use the Internet for things they'd traditionally do in person, e.g. online banking and shopping. A lot of money is spent and transferred over the Internet. This means that organisations now store a lot of personal data, including names, addresses and bank details. Because they store this data, they have an ethical (and legal) responsibility to have good cyber security (see p.97) to prevent things like identity theft.

2) This is also true of companies providing the public with wireless access to the Internet (e.g. cafes that offer free Wi-Fi®) — without good cyber security, hackers (see p.111) could monitor what users are doing.

3) Many would argue that these companies also have a responsibility to restrict access to certain websites (such as gambling and pornography sites), as children could be able to gain access. However, since there are so many of these websites, it can be difficult to block them all. Software can block sites based on keywords, but this can end up blocking safe websites as well.

Cyberbullying and **Trolling** are a problem on **Social Media**

Cyberbullying

- Cyberbullying is when somebody uses social media to deliberately harm someone else.
- This includes trying to intimidate, insult, humiliate or defame someone (damage their reputation).
- Cyberbullying can cause serious distress for the victim — people have been driven to suicide because of these attacks.

Trolling

- Trolling is when somebody tries to cause public arguments with others online, only making comments which frustrate other people.
- Trolls normally do this for their own amusement or to gain attention.

1) Problems like cyberbullying and trolling may be a result of the anonymity that the Internet gives people. They say things online that they wouldn't say if talking to someone face-to-face.

2) People can also abuse social media in other ways. For example, by pretending to be someone else as part of a social engineering scheme (see p.98), or by spreading misinformation and fake news.

3) Sexting (sending sexually explicit messages or images to other people) is more common as smartphones and video messaging applications have become more popular. Sexting can be dangerous as the person receiving the images might not be trustworthy — social media allows them to forward someone else's images onto anyone they want. There are now laws which try to prevent this.

Technology has enabled a lot of anti-social behaviour...

These are all sensitive topics, but they're worth mentioning in the exam if they're relevant to the question. The problems on this page can have a damaging impact on the mental wellbeing of the victim — if you ever experience any of them, the best thing to do is to tell someone about it.

Ethical Issues

Computers have had a tremendous impact on society — it's difficult to imagine some of the things we do today without them. Just remember that this technological revolution is not always a good thing...

Technology is changing how we **Access Services**

New technology has provided <u>new ways</u> for people to obtain <u>goods</u> and <u>services</u>, although these modern conveniences can create lots of <u>ethical issues</u>.

1) The ability to <u>wirelessly stream</u> music and television has allowed customers to access media conveniently and cheaply, either for free or through a <u>subscription service</u>. But users of these services often <u>don't own</u> what they're paying for, and they can <u>lose access</u> if their <u>subscription ends</u> or if the service <u>closes down</u>.

2) The rise in popularity of <u>smartphones</u> has lead to certain <u>apps</u> becoming very successful — for example, the Uber app lets you turn your car into a taxi service.

3) These services are often <u>cheap</u> and <u>convenient</u>, but they <u>draw customers away</u> from traditional businesses (e.g. taxi companies). Also, they may be more <u>risky</u> for customers as they are not necessarily <u>regulated</u> as strictly as traditional businesses are.

4) There are also many computing services that are now offered for <u>free</u> — <u>cloud storage</u> (p.78) and <u>webmail</u> are examples of this. Often, these services will have <u>limits</u> on what you can access for free, and a superior '<u>premium</u>' service that costs money. This could help to reduce the <u>digital divide</u> by providing partial services to people who otherwise couldn't afford them.

5) This type of business model can also be seen in <u>mobile games</u> — however, some say that these games <u>exploit</u> people with more <u>impulsive spending habits</u>. There have also been cases of parents <u>accidentally</u> allowing their children to spend <u>hundreds of pounds</u> on these games.

Technology is also changing **How Businesses Operate**

1) A lot of businesses <u>expect</u> people to be able to <u>use technology</u> and <u>access services online</u>. For example, <u>employers</u> may expect people to be able to <u>apply for jobs</u> online, and many require employees to have at least some <u>basic computer skills</u>. However, some people may not have <u>access</u> to technology for various reasons (see p.105), which puts them at an <u>unfair disadvantage</u>.

2) The popularity of <u>mobile devices</u> has lead to some businesses insisting that employees carry a <u>smartphone</u> with them <u>all the time</u>, so that they can <u>always be contacted</u>, either by <u>phone</u> or by <u>email</u>. This can be <u>stressful</u> for employees who feel they can never really <u>switch off</u> from work.

3) In fact, some companies have taken this <u>one step further</u> and have offered their employees <u>computer chip implants</u> (see p.105) that are used to <u>open security doors</u> and <u>access their computer</u>. This is far <u>more secure</u> than traditional password or keycard systems, but many people find the idea of implanting technology in humans to be <u>unethical</u>.

4) <u>Marketing</u> and <u>advertising</u> have also been greatly affected by new technology. <u>Pop-ups</u> appear all over the Internet and <u>targeted adverts</u> are shown to people on social media sites. This has lead to people feeling <u>swamped</u> by advertising online, and has made programs like AdBlock popular. However, lots of <u>free services</u> are funded by <u>advertising money</u>, so if <u>everybody</u> blocked the adverts, then the providers of these services would <u>lose their income</u> and may have to <u>start charging</u> for the service instead.

5) Even though businesses can <u>take advantage</u> of technology in lots of ways, they have to be <u>careful</u> — if they ignored the <u>ethical impact</u> of their actions, even if they were <u>legal</u>, they could lose <u>public trust</u>. Many businesses have a <u>code of conduct</u> (a set of rules that the business and its employees will follow) to show the public that they take these ethical issues seriously.

There are benefits and problems with all technologies...

Pick a new technology that you know quite a lot about. Think about what opportunities and conveniences it can give to its users. Try and come up with some issues that it can cause as well — think about the effects of overusing it, not having access to it, or of people abusing it.

Ethical Issues

It's quite concerning to think how many people have access to your social media profile. However, some people in the world don't get to access social media at all — so maybe you're the lucky one...

It's hard to keep information **Private** on the Internet

1) Most people generally want to be able to keep their personal information <u>private</u>. However, this rarely happens in practice, as many online services require you to provide your details in order to use them:
   - Many websites (shopping, banking, etc.) require users to provide <u>personal information</u> in order to set up an account, e.g. date of birth and address.
   - <u>Social media</u> websites actively <u>encourage</u> you to post even more personal information, including photographs and details of your job and social life.

2) Users will accept a <u>privacy agreement</u> before using many websites and software. The trouble is that very few people actually read these, so most are <u>unaware</u> of what they're agreeing to. Even if they <u>do</u> read the terms, users often have <u>no choice</u> but to agree if they want to use the website or software at all.

3) Companies can do lots of things with your details as long as they stay <u>within the bounds</u> of the privacy agreement. They can make your information available to <u>other people</u>, or <u>sell</u> your <u>personal details</u>, <u>buying habits</u> etc. to other organisations (who could use it to send you <u>targeted adverts</u> or <u>spam</u> emails).

4) Users can take steps to make the information they share more <u>private</u>, e.g. change their <u>privacy settings</u> on social media sites (which are often fairly relaxed by <u>default</u>).

5) Users have to trust companies to keep their data <u>secure</u>. But this doesn't always happen — there have been various <u>high profile cases</u> where customer data held by large companies has been <u>leaked</u> or <u>stolen</u>.

Surveillance and Censorship are controversial issues

Surveillance

1) <u>Computer surveillance</u> is when someone <u>monitors</u> what other people are accessing on the Internet.

2) Many countries use some form of surveillance. Government <u>security services</u> may use packet sniffers and other software to <u>monitor Internet traffic</u>, looking out for certain <u>key words</u> or <u>phrases</u> that might alert them to illegal activities, terrorism, etc. Often, governments will push for <u>greater powers</u> (e.g. access to private emails) to assist in catching criminals, but might face <u>opposition</u> from the public.

3) In some countries, <u>Internet Service Providers</u> (ISPs) <u>keep records</u> of all websites visited by all its customers for a certain amount of time, and may be <u>legally required</u> to share data with <u>security services</u>.

Censorship

1) <u>Internet censorship</u> is when someone tries to <u>control</u> what other people can access on the Internet. Some countries' governments use censorship to restrict access to certain information.

2) One of the strictest countries for censorship is <u>China</u>, where they restrict access to websites which are <u>critical</u> of the government. China also censors many major <u>foreign websites</u>, including Facebook®, YouTube™ and Twitter. In <u>Cuba</u>, citizens can only access the Internet from government-controlled <u>access points</u>.

3) Many governments use <u>some form</u> of censorship. Many countries (including the UK) restrict access to pornography, gambling and other inappropriate websites in order to <u>protect children</u>.

Censorship and surveillance are <u>controversial</u> topics. Some people support them in some form, e.g. to protect children or to stop terrorism. Others are completely against them, including several non-profit organisations which campaign against what they call <u>cyber censorship</u> and <u>mass surveillance</u>.

You should have seen this page before it was censored...

The weird thing about this stuff is that everyone knows it's happening but most do nothing about it — the Internet is such a big part of modern life that for many people their loss of privacy is a price worth paying. Other people aren't so keen about losing their privacy though, which is why these issues are so controversial.

Warm-Up and Worked Exam Questions

You're probably already aware of some of the issues on these pages, but it's worth going back over any that are new to you. The more you can remember, the more marks you'll be able to bank in the exam.

Warm-Up Questions

1) What is meant by the 'digital divide'?
2) Give one disadvantage of a subscription-based digital service.
3) Tick one box in each row to show whether it concerns censorship or surveillance.

	Censorship	Surveillance
A business monitors what their employees view online.		
A country's government blocks access to Facebook®.		
A government agency intercepts emails containing certain words.		
A school restricts access to harmful websites.		
An Internet Service Provider collects data on browsing habits.		

Worked Exam Question

1 Jasmine uses several social media apps on her smartphone.
She has recently been the victim of severe cyberbullying and trolling.

a) What is meant by cyberbullying?

The use of social media to deliberately harm someone else.

[1 mark]

b) Suggest **one** reason why cyberbullying and trolling have become more commonplace.

Social media gives people greater anonymity than they would have in real life.

[1 mark]

c) Jasmine's parents suggest that the social media apps should automatically screen all messages for abusive and inappropriate language. Explain **one** problem with this suggestion.

Other users of the apps may consider it an invasion of their privacy

if they knew the app was 'reading' their personal messages.

[2 marks]

d) Jasmine's teacher tells her that she should avoid using social media apps altogether.
Do you agree with this attitude? Explain your answer.

No — it is the cyberbullies who should be banned from social media apps.

It isn't fair to force Jasmine to stop using them because of their actions.

[2 marks]

As long as you explain your answer, you can argue for either side.
You don't even have to give your real opinion if you don't want to.

Exam Questions

2   Some governments censor and monitor what their citizens view online.
    Explain **one** benefit and **one** drawback of governments censoring certain online content.

Benefit   ....

....

....

Drawback ....

....

....

[4 marks]

3   Tom works for a smartphone company. Tom is stressed
    because he feels he can never switch off from work.

   a)   Explain how new technology could have allowed work to intrude into other areas of Tom's life.

....

....

....

[2 marks]

   b)   The company that Tom works for are looking for new staff, but they only accept
            online applications. Suggest **one** ethical issue that this could raise.

....

....

[1 mark]

   c)   The company have been criticised for making unethical decisions in order to reduce costs.
            Explain why it may be in the company's interest to act ethically, even if it is more costly.

....

....

....

[2 marks]

4   In recent years, a number of technology companies have developed 'smart glasses'. These are
    devices that can be worn like glasses, and have built-in screens, microphones, cameras, etc.

    Discuss the benefits and risks of smart glasses. In your answer you should
    consider any ethical issues related to the use of smart glasses.

[6 marks]

Legal Issues

Since computers went mainstream, the law has had to keep up with the way people use and abuse them. The Internet causes lots of issues, since it's so difficult to police what people do online.

Laws Control the use of your **Personal Data**

1) When an organisation stores someone's personal data on their system, that person is entitled to certain rights, stated in data protection laws. These rights can be summarised by the principles shown here.

2) Before collecting personal data, an organisation must register with the government, saying what data they'll collect, and how they'll use it.

3) Organisations have a legal obligation to have good cyber security (p.97) on their networks to keep personal data secure. This can be hard for small businesses, who may not be able to afford top-of-the-range security software.

4) Companies using cloud storage (see p.78) to store personal data must ensure that the service is trustworthy and reliable. They should also understand how and where the data is stored, especially when servers in other countries are used.

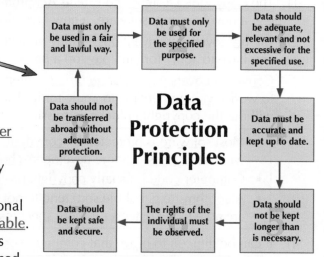

Data must only be used in a fair and lawful way.

Data must only be used for the specified purpose.

Data should be adequate, relevant and not excessive for the specified use.

Data should not be transferred abroad without adequate protection.

Data Protection Principles

Data must be accurate and kept up to date.

Data should be kept safe and secure.

The rights of the individual must be observed.

Data should not be kept longer than is necessary.

The **Computer Misuse Act** prevents illegal access to files

The Computer Misuse Act was introduced to stop cyber crime (see below). It introduced three new offences:

1) Gaining unauthorised access to a private network or device, e.g. through hacking (just accessing a network could get you a fine or prison sentence).
2) Gaining unauthorised access to a network or device in order to commit a crime, like stealing data or destroying the network.
3) Unauthorised modification of computer material — e.g. deleting or changing files. The Act also makes it illegal to make, supply or obtain malware.

Cyber Crime is a major problem

1) Cyber crime refers to any illegal activity that involves computers. Hackers are a type of cyber criminal.

> Hacking refers to gaining access to a system by exploiting weaknesses in its security. This is usually done to steal or destroy data, or to infect the system with malware (p.97). However, some companies employ 'good' hackers to identify vulnerabilities through penetration testing (p.97).

2) There are lots of different methods that hackers use to attack systems, including:
   • passive attacks — monitoring data on a network, e.g. using packet sniffer software.
   • active attacks — using malware or other means to attack a system directly.
   • brute force attacks — using automated software and trial-and-error to crack passwords.
   • denial-of-service attacks — preventing people from using a network by flooding it with useless traffic.

3) Since cyber criminals tend to have a good understanding of networks and security measures, they often know how to avoid being tracked down, making it very difficult to catch and prosecute them.

The law has to keep up with developing technology...

You don't need to memorise all of the data protection principles given above, but the more you know about them, the more points you'll be able to make in the exam.

Legal Issues

Another important legal area is intellectual property — stuff people create. When it comes to computers, intellectual property often involves things like hardware, software, computer code and algorithms.

Copyright and Patents protect innovation

1) The Copyright, Designs and Patents Act protects intellectual property (anything someone has created, e.g. a novel, a song, software, a new invention) from being copied or stolen by other people.

2) Patents cover new inventions — they protect ideas and concepts rather than actual content. Normally, you have to apply for (and pay for) a patent. In computing, patents mostly apply to pieces of hardware.

3) Copyright covers written or recorded content, e.g. books, music, and films. Copyright usually applies to works without needing to apply for it. The Act makes it illegal to share copyrighted material without the copyright holder's permission, or to plagiarise (copy) somebody else's work.

   - Most software is protected by copyright. It's illegal to use or share a piece of copyrighted software without a license. Some developers choose to make their software open source (see below).
   - Computer code is usually copyright protected, although it's hard to protect smaller pieces of code.
   - Algorithms (e.g. bubble sort) tend to not be copyright protected. In certain countries, developers are able to get patents for more specific algorithms (e.g. filtering algorithms used in search engines).

4) It can be difficult to prove that computer code has been copied, because:

   - Similarities in code may just be down to coincidence, particularly if both programs were written to perform the same task. It is very difficult to measure how 'original' a piece of code is.
   - Creators of paid software will often want to keep their source code secret to prevent competitors from seeing and copying it. However, not being able to directly compare the source code makes it hard to identify where code has been copied.

5) The Internet has made it harder to protect copyrighted content due to the ease of file sharing. Developers often include DRM (digital rights management) with software — this attempts to prevent unauthorised use of software with things like activation keys and online authentication.

6) Software with DRM is a common target of cracking. Cracking is where users illegally modify the software to remove or bypass unwanted features. The cracked software is often distributed online, which leads people to argue that DRM doesn't work and that it only inconveniences legitimate users. Some DRM can even make older software unusable if the authentication service is no longer available.

7) As well as being illegal, using cracked software can lead to a loss of income for the software creator. This could discourage them from fixing bugs in the software or developing new software. Hackers also often use cracked software to distribute malware, e.g. by including a virus (see p.97).

Some content can be Copied and Shared Legally

1) There is a lot of open source software available online, where users are allowed to freely download and modify the source code (see p.42). Well-known examples include Apache HTTP Server™ (runs web servers), GIMP (image editing), Mozilla® Firefox® (web browser), and VLC media player.

2) Open source software is often distributed using Creative Commons (CC) licences. These allow users to legally share the software, while specifically allowing and disallowing certain actions (e.g. modifying the code, using it for profit, etc.).

3) Popular open source software is often supported by a strong online community, where people work together to improve the software and fix bugs.

Intellectual property covers loads of different media...

Search the Internet for something (e.g. software, music, an image, etc.) that is open source, or has a Creative Commons licence. What benefits does this give to the people who want to use it, and to the creator? What problems might it cause that a stricter copyright licence would avoid?

Environmental Issues

Devices have a huge environmental impact. Take a smartphone — it's made of materials that have to be mined from the Earth, when it's used it consumes energy, and when it's thrown away it could end up on a landfill site.

When we **Make** devices we use up **Natural Resources**

1) Electronic devices contain lots of <u>raw materials</u>.
2) <u>Plastics</u> (which are used for casing and other parts) come from <u>crude oil</u>.
3) Devices also contain many <u>precious metals</u> like gold, silver, copper, mercury, palladium, platinum, and indium. Many of these metals only occur naturally in <u>tiny quantities</u>.
4) Extracting these materials uses lots of <u>energy</u>, creates <u>pollution</u> and depletes scarce <u>natural resources</u>.

When we **Use** devices we use **Energy**... lots of it

All the billions of devices in the world today are consuming energy in the form of <u>electricity</u> — a lot of it.

1) Most electricity is made using <u>non-renewable</u> resources like coal, oil and gas. <u>Extracting</u> these resources and <u>producing electricity</u> in power stations causes lots of <u>pollution</u> including greenhouse gases.
2) All computers generate <u>heat</u> and require cooling. The powerful <u>servers</u> used by businesses and the Internet are a particular problem. They're very <u>power hungry</u> and require special <u>air-conditioned</u> rooms to keep them cool. That means using even more energy and more pollution.
3) Devices also <u>waste</u> a lot of energy. Servers normally only use a <u>small proportion</u> of their <u>processing power</u>. People often leave their desktops, laptops and smartphones <u>idle</u>. This means these devices are using a lot of energy without actually doing <u>anything</u>.
4) There are several ways to <u>reduce</u> the amount of energy wasted by devices:

- <u>Virtual servers</u> are <u>software-based</u> servers rather than real machines. Multiple virtual servers can run on one physical server, so the physical server can run at <u>full capacity</u>.
- <u>Switching off</u> mobile devices <u>overnight</u>, or putting them into <u>sleep</u> mode, can save power.
- Devices often use more energy when searching for a <u>wireless</u> connection. Disabling this, or using a <u>wired</u> connection, could preserve battery life.

When we **Throw Away** devices we create loads of **E-waste**

1) <u>E-waste</u> is a huge problem — the world creates <u>20-50 million tonnes</u> of e-waste every year. Modern devices have a very <u>short life</u> before they're discarded — either because they <u>break</u> or because people want to <u>upgrade</u> (particularly with smartphones).
2) <u>Device manufacturers</u> and <u>retailers</u> are part of this problem. They provide short <u>warranties</u> (e.g. 1 year), use <u>marketing</u> to convince people to upgrade and have pricing policies that make it <u>cheaper to replace</u> than to repair.
3) The Waste Electric and Electronic Equipment (<u>WEEE</u>) directive was created to tackle the e-waste problem. The WEEE has rules for disposing of e-waste <u>safely</u>, to promote <u>reuse</u> (e.g. refurbishing broken devices to use again) and <u>recycling</u> (e.g. extracting the devices' <u>precious metals</u>).
4) To <u>cut costs</u> a lot of e-waste is sent to certain African and Asian countries where regulations are less strict. Here, most of it ends up in <u>landfill</u> and can be a hazard — toxic chemicals can leak into the <u>ground water</u> and harm wildlife.

Don't (e-)waste your time — use your energy to learn this page...

From manufacture right through to when they're thrown away, our devices put a strain on the environment. But it's not all bad — they let us communicate without having to travel long distances in pollution-spouting vehicles, and reduce our need for paper. However, whether these make enough of a difference is debatable.

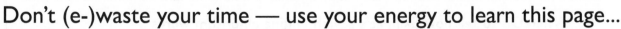

Warm-Up and Worked Exam Questions

Make sure you know what each law is about — it's easy to mix them up and drop some marks. Once you're confident with the last few pages, try out these questions — then go back over anything that slips you up.

Warm-Up Questions

1) Describe the overall aim of the following laws:
   a) data protection laws   b) Computer Misuse Act   c) Copyright, Designs and Patents Act

2) For each situation below, state which of the laws from question 1 it is against (if any):
   a) Obtaining malware from the Internet and distributing it.
   b) An employer backing up their employees' personal details on a secure server.
   c) Removing copy protection from a piece of paid software and distributing it online.
   d) Using pop-up adverts on your website.
   e) Breaking into a company's network and stealing their data.
   f) Throwing a smartphone into the general waste rather than recycling it properly.
   g) A business storing customers' personal information without their permission.

Worked Exam Questions

1 The average household can spend almost £100 a year on wasted electricity.

   a) Give **two** ways that electronic devices waste electricity.

   1 _Users sometimes leave devices idle / on standby._

   2 _Devices generate excess heat due to inefficiency._

   [2 marks]

   b) Explain how hardware manufacturers can limit the amount of electricity wasted by electronic devices.

   Manufacturers can include sleep or hibernation modes in new devices

   to reduce their energy consumption when they are idle.

   [2 marks]

2 A new algorithm has been developed for the search engine WhereDis. The algorithm uses a new method for prioritising search results. The developers have obtained a patent for the algorithm.

   a) Explain **one** drawback of allowing people to patent algorithms.

   Patenting algorithms prevents other people from using them,

   which can prevent innovation and development of the algorithm.

   [2 marks]

   b) WhereDis suspect another search engine, Skippee, of using their algorithm. Explain why it might be difficult for WhereDis to prove that Skippee have copied their algorithm.

   Skippee may not be willing to share their source code, so it might be impossible

   for WhereDis to tell how Skippee's search engine algorithm works.

   [2 marks]

Exam Questions

3 People who crack software could be infringing upon the copyright of the software's developers.

    a) Define the following terms:

        i) software cracking

        ....
[1 mark]

        ii) copyright

        ....
[1 mark]

    b) Many developers have implemented digital rights management (DRM), such as compulsory online authentication, into their software. Give **one** benefit and **one** drawback of this.

    Benefit ....

    Drawback ....
[2 marks]

    c) Some pieces of software are open-source. Explain what is meant by open-source software.

    ....

    ....
[2 marks]

4 The average smartphone is only used for two years before it is discarded as e-waste.

    a) Suggest **two** reasons why smartphones are only used for a short amount of time before they are discarded.

    1 ....

    2 ....
[2 marks]

    b) Explain **one** way in which e-waste can be managed to limit its impact on the environment.

    ....

    ....
[2 marks]

5 A fitness company have developed a wearable wristband that collects data while you exercise, including your heart rate and location. The wristband uploads this data wirelessly over the Internet to the company's servers. The user can then access their data by signing in to their online account.

Discuss the potential security risks of this technology. In your answer you should consider any legal issues related to these security risks.

Think about how hackers could abuse the technology, and the data protection laws the company must follow. *[6 marks]*

Revision Questions for Section Seven

Well, that section had a lot of issues — thankfully you're not here to solve its problems, just learn its content.
- Try these questions and <u>tick off each one</u> when you <u>get it right</u>.
- When you've done <u>all the questions</u> for a topic and are <u>completely happy</u> with it, tick off the topic.

Ethical Issues (p.105-108) ☑

1) Define each type of issue in a sentence: a) ethical   b) legal   c) environmental ☑
2) Give one positive and one negative ethical issue caused by:
a) mobile devices   b) wearable technology   c) the Internet ☑
3) Give three reasons why a digital divide exists. ☑
4) What is: a) cyberbullying?   b) trolling? ☑
5) Give a reason why cyberbullying and trolling have become so common. ☑
6) Give three examples of services that have been changed by new technology. ☑
7) Explain, in 30 words or less, how businesses can be affected by each of the following:
a) mobile devices   b) the Internet   c) computer-based implants ☑
8) Give two reasons why someone might give their personal details to a website. ☑
9) Give two problems with many online companies' privacy agreements. ☑
10) What can you do to make the information you share online more private? ☑
11) Explain the difference between censorship and surveillance. ☑
12) Give one argument for and one against Internet censorship. ☑
13) Give one argument for and one against governments carrying out Internet surveillance. ☑

Legal Issues (p.111-112) ☑

14) a) When do data protection laws apply?
b) Give three data protection principles. ☑
15) What three offences does the Computer Misuse Act cover? ☑
16) a) What is a hacker?
b) Describe four methods that a hacker might use to attack a system. ☑
17) Define: a) intellectual property   b) patents   c) copyright ☑
18) Explain how copyright and patents apply to:
a) software   b) computer code   c) algorithms ☑
19) Describe two reasons why someone may find it difficult to prove if their code has been copied. ☑
20) a) What does DRM stand for? What is it used for?
b) What is meant by cracking? ☑
21) What is meant by 'open source' software? Give two examples. ☑
22) Why might a software developer want to use a Creative Commons licence? ☑

Environmental Issues (p.113) ☑

23) Give three examples of natural resources which are used to make computers. ☑
24) Explain how a device's need for energy impacts the environment. ☑
25) Give three ways to reduce the amount of energy devices waste. ☑
26) What is e-waste and why do we generate a lot of it? ☑
27) Describe an environmental danger caused by e-waste left in landfill sites. ☑

Once you've been through all the questions in this book, you should be starting to feel prepared for the final exams. This practice paper will test you on Sections 1-5 of this book and assess your computational thinking and problem solving skills — this will be the case in the real exams as well.

GCSE AQA Computer Science

Practice Paper 1

Centre name				
Centre number				
Candidate number				

Time allowed:

- 1 hour 30 minutes

Surname	
Other names	
Candidate signature	

You **may not** use a calculator

Instructions to candidates

- Write your name and other details in the spaces provided above.
- Answer **all** questions in the spaces provided.
- Some questions will require you to shade an oval.
  If you make a mistake, cross through the incorrect answer.
- Do all rough work in this book. Cross through any work you do not want to be marked.

Information for candidates

- There are 80 marks available on this paper.
- The marks available are given in brackets at the end of each question.

For examiner's use						
Q	Attempt Nº		Q	Attempt Nº		
1			6			
2			7			
3			8			
4			9			
5			10			
Total						

Answer **all** questions in the spaces provided

1 Mike is developing a program for a publisher of an online magazine.
The program will manage user subscriptions.

(a) Shade **one** oval to show the term that best describes
the thought process behind each statement.

(i) "The colour of the magazine isn't important, but the price of a subscription is."

A Decomposition ◯   **B** Abstraction ◯   **C** Computation ◯

[1 mark]

(ii) "I should write separate subprograms for setting up new accounts
and making changes to existing accounts."

A Decomposition ◯   **B** Abstraction ◯   **C** Computation ◯

[1 mark]

(b) Mike writes the algorithm below to calculate the monthly cost (in £)
of a basic and a premium subscription to the online magazine.

```
cost ← 5.0
OUTPUT 'Premium or basic?'
subType ← USERINPUT
IF subType = 'basic' THEN
    cost ← cost * 0.5
ELSE
    cost ← cost + 1.0
ENDIF
OUTPUT cost
```

What is the difference in monthly cost between a basic and a premium subscription?

....

....

[2 marks]

2 St Colin's Hospital has many computers and medical devices.

(a) Most of the medical devices, such as heart rate monitors, contain embedded systems.
Explain **two** benefits of using embedded systems in medical devices.

1 ....

....

2 ....

....

[4 marks]

(b) The computers are all connected to the hospital network and have access to patient data. Explain, with examples, how application and utility software could help to manage this data.

....

....

....

....

....

[4 marks]

The network was recently taken offline during a cyber attack. The IT team at St Colin's need to manually install a 3 GB security patch on every computer in the hospital.

(c) Explain whether each of the following types of storage media would be appropriate for distributing the patch.

(i) CDs

....

....

....

....

[2 marks]

(ii) USB flash drives

....

....

....

....

[2 marks]

(iii) External hard disk drives

....

....

....

....

[2 marks]

Turn over ▶

3 Harry wants to store information about the animals at his local zoo in a data structure.

(a) What is a data structure?

....

....

[1 mark]

Harry decides to store this information in records.
An example of the data he wants to store is shown in the table below.

animal	numberInZoo	averageWeight	continent	carnivore
Giraffe	5	1200.2	Africa	false

(b) Shade **one** oval to show the most suitable data type for these fields.

(i) animal

    A Boolean ⬭   **B** Integer ⬭   **C** Real ⬭   **D** String ⬭

[1 mark]

(ii) numberInZoo

    A Boolean ⬭   **B** Integer ⬭   **C** Real ⬭   **D** String ⬭

[1 mark]

(iii) averageWeight

    A Boolean ⬭   **B** Integer ⬭   **C** Real ⬭   **D** String ⬭

[1 mark]

(iv) carnivore

    A Boolean ⬭   **B** Integer ⬭   **C** Real ⬭   **D** String ⬭

[1 mark]

(c) Harry creates records for all of the zoo animals, and stores all of these records in an array. Explain why storing the records in an array might be useful.

....

....

....

[2 marks]

4   Every 5 minutes, an app on a mobile phone records the electrical
current (in mA) passing through a pair of connected headphones.

A sample of the readings is shown below.

| 10 mA | 15 mA | 12 mA | 18 mA | 20 mA |

(a)   Show the stages of a linear search to find the value '12 mA' in the list above.

....

....

....

....

....

....

[2 marks]

(b)   If a reading is greater than 30 mA the mobile phone will buzz and then the program
will stop. If not, the program will wait 5 minutes before taking another reading.
Draw a flowchart to show this program.

[6 marks]

Turn over ▶

5 Adam wants to write an algorithm to randomise which type of tea he should drink each morning. His different options are stored in an array, called `teaTypes`.

The start of Adam's program is shown below. Extend the algorithm so that it randomly selects a tea from the array, and outputs a suitable message.

```
teaTypes ← ['ginger', 'chamomile', 'chai', 'mango', 'lemon']
```

....

....

....

....

....

....

....

[3 marks]

6 A radio broadcast transmits an analogue signal. A digital recording of the broadcast is made by sampling different points of the analogue wave.

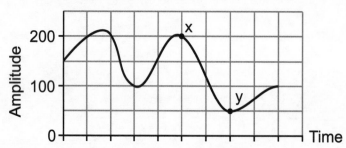

(a) Complete the table below for point x.

	x	y
Decimal Value		50
Binary Value		00110010
Hex Value		32

[3 marks]

(b) The broadcast was recorded with a sample rate of 40 000 Hz and a sample resolution of 2 bytes. The broadcast lasted approximately 10 000 seconds.

(i) Estimate how many bytes will be needed to store the whole sound file.

....

....

[2 marks]

(ii) Explain how increasing the sample rate can affect the quality of the sound file.

....

....

[2 marks]

(c) Explain why the broadcasters might want to compress the sound file.

....

....

[2 marks]

7 The subroutine `test` takes an array as a parameter.

```
SUBROUTINE test(arr)
    x ← 0
    y ← 0
    FOR k ← 0 TO (LEN(arr)-1)
        IF arr[k] > x THEN
            y ← x
            x ← arr[k]
        ELSE IF arr[k] > y THEN
            y ← arr[k]
        ENDIF
    ENDFOR
    OUTPUT x
    OUTPUT y
ENDSUBROUTINE
```

(a) Complete the trace table for the subroutine call `test([4, 2, 7, 1, 9])`.

k	arr[k]	x	y

[4 marks]

(b) Explain what the purpose of this subroutine is.

....

....

[2 marks]

Turn over ▶

8   Yifei is using structured programming to develop a program to manage an online mailing list. She has designed multiple subroutine interfaces as part of a module that will manage adding someone to the mailing list.

(a)   Which of the following is not a property of a subroutine interface? Shade **one** oval only.

   A Subroutine name   ◯

   B Parameters   ◯

   C Comments   ◯

   D Return value   ◯

[1 mark]

One of Yifei's subroutines is shown below. It checks whether an email address input by the user contains an '@' symbol.

```
SUBROUTINE checkEmail(i)
    b ← false
    FOR x ← 0 TO 10
        IF SUBSTRING(x,x,i) = '@' THEN
            b ← true
        ENDIF
    ENDFOR
    RETURN b
ENDSUBROUTINE
```

(b) (i)   Explain, with an example, how Yifei could improve the variable naming in her code.

....

....

....

....

[2 marks]

(ii)   State **one** logic error in Yifei's code and explain why it is a logic error.

Logic error ....

Explanation ....

....

....

[2 marks]

(c) Yifei's program can only manage email addresses containing a maximum of 64 characters. Write a validation subroutine that will check that the input is of a valid length. It should:

- Output a suitable message to the user if the input is too long, or if the input is left blank.

- Return true if the input is valid, and return false if not.

....

....

....

....

....

....

....

....

....

....

....

....

....

[5 marks]

(d) Yifei needs to translate her program from a high-level language into machine code. Describe **two** differences in the way a compiler and an interpreter would translate her program.

1 ....

....

....

2 ....

....

....

[4 marks]

Turn over ▶

126

9 The table below shows information on two standard character sets.

Character Set	ASCII	Unicode®
Bit Length	8	32

(a) (i) Describe in general how the bit length affects the size of the character set.

....

....

[1 mark]

(ii) Ed claims that Unicode® can represent 4 times as many characters as ASCII. Is he correct? Explain your answer.

....

....

[2 marks]

(b) Suggest **two** benefits of using Unicode® to encode each character.

Benefit 1: ....

....

Benefit 2: ....

....

[2 marks]

(c) In ASCII, the character q is represented by the binary code 0111 0001. What binary code represents the letter t?

....

....

[1 mark]

10 RW Games have built an arcade game, and sold 100 units to arcades across the country. Each unit automatically sends its top 10 high scores to RW Games at the end of every day.

The 2D array called topScores stores the high scores. For example, topScores[0][0] is the highest score for unit 1, topScores[0][1] is the second-highest score for unit 1, etc.

The start of an algorithm used by RW Games is shown below.

```
01   inUse ← 0
02   FOR unit ← 0 TO 99
03       IF topScores[unit][0] = 0 THEN
```

(a) Shade **one** oval to show which type of statement is given in:

(i) line 02

A Selection	◯	**C** Indefinite Iteration	◯
B Definite Iteration	◯	**D** Validation	◯

[1 mark]

(ii) line 03

A Selection	◯	**C** Indefinite Iteration	◯
B Definite Iteration	◯	**D** Validation	◯

[1 mark]

(b) Extend the algorithm so that it:

- Outputs a suitable message for units that are not in use
  (units that are not in use have a high score of 0).

- Calculates the average score for units that are in use
  (i.e. the sum of all 10 scores divided by 10) and outputs the result.

- Outputs the total number of units in use.

```
01    inUse ← 0
02    FOR unit ← 0 TO 99
03        IF topScores[unit][0] = 0 THEN
```

....

....

....

....

....

....

....

....

....

....

....

....

[7 marks]

END OF QUESTIONS

Practice Paper 2

This practice paper will test you on Sections 4-7 of this book and contains a mix of short answer and longer answer questions. It also has two extended response questions.

GCSE AQA Computer Science

Practice Paper 2

Centre name				
Centre number				
Candidate number				

Time allowed:

• 1 hour 30 minutes

You **may not** use a calculator

Surname	
Other names	
Candidate signature	

Instructions to candidates

• Write your name and other details in the spaces provided above.

• Answer **all** questions in the spaces provided.

• Some questions will require you to shade an oval.
If you make a mistake, cross through the incorrect answer. ⊗

• Do all rough work in this book. Cross through any work you do not want to be marked.

Information for candidates

• There are 80 marks available on this paper.

• The marks available are given in brackets at the end of each question.

	For examiner's use				
Q	Attempt N°		Q	Attempt N°	
1			6		
2			7		
3			8		
4			9		
5			10		
		Total			

Answer **all** questions in the spaces provided

1 A series of transistors make the two-level logic circuit (NOT A) AND (B AND C).

(a) Complete the truth table below.

A	B	C	NOT A	B AND C	(NOT A) AND (B AND C)
0	0	0			
0	0	1			
0	1	0			
0	1	1			
1	0	0			
1	0	1			
1	1	0			
1	1	1			

[3 marks]

(b) Draw the logic diagram that represents (NOT A) AND (B AND C).

[3 marks]

Turn over ▶

2   The control unit, arithmetic logic unit, registers and cache memory are all parts of the CPU.

(a)   State **two** functions of the control unit.

1 ....

2 ....

[2 marks]

(b)   Describe the function of the arithmetic logic unit (ALU).

....

....

....

[2 marks]

(c)   Explain the purpose of CPU registers.

....

....

[2 marks]

(d)   Explain how cache memory is used by the CPU.

....

....

....

[3 marks]

(e)   Which of the following statements about Von Neumann architecture is true?
Shade **one** oval only.

A   Only instructions are stored in main memory.   ⬭

B   Only data is stored in main memory.   ⬭

C   Instructions and data are stored together in the same main memory.   ⬭

D   Instructions and data are stored in separate main memories.   ⬭

[1 mark]

3 A Yorkshire-based television company has two studios, one based in Leeds and the other based in York. The company's computer network is shown in the diagram below.

Leeds — Local Area Network (LAN)   York — Local Area Network (LAN)

The Leeds studio uses wired connections, while the York studio uses wireless connections.

(a) Which of these is a family of network protocols used on wired networks?
Shade **one** oval only.

A Ethernet ⬭   **B** Wi-Fi® ⬭   **C** WLANs ⬭   **D** WAPs ⬭

[1 mark]

(b) What type of topology is being used at the Leeds studio? Shade **one** oval only.

A Bus ⬭   **B** Ring ⬭   **C** Star ⬭   **D** Mesh ⬭

[1 mark]

(c) State the name of the hardware device inside each computer that connects it to a LAN.

....

[1 mark]

(d) Describe the advantages and disadvantages of each LAN setup.

The Leeds studio's wired setup: ....

....

....

....

The York studio's wireless setup: ....

....

....

....

[4 marks]

Turn over ▶

(e) The studios are connected in a Wide Area Network (WAN) using fibre optic cables.

    (i) State **one** advantage of using fibre optic cables rather than copper cables in a WAN.

    ....

    ....

    [1 mark]

    (ii) Suggest **one** reason why the company uses leased lines for its WAN.

    ....

    ....

    [1 mark]

4 Binary shifts can be used to quickly multiply and divide binary numbers.

    (a) Complete a 3 place left shift on the binary number 00011010.

    ....

    ....

    [1 mark]

    (b) State an appropriate binary shift to divide a binary number by 4
    and use it on 11010100.

    ....

    ....

    ....

    [2 marks]

    (c) Yasha says "Adding a binary number to itself is the same as a 2 place left shift."
    Is he correct? Explain your answer.

    ....

    ....

    ....

    ....

    [2 marks]

5 Sinead is a college lecturer. She usually does research for her lectures on a laptop connected to her home network.

(a) Sinead connects her smartphone and headphones wirelessly to her laptop in a PAN. Which of these statements about PANs are true? Shade **two** ovals only.

A PANs can only be used to transfer images and music. ◯

B PANs connect devices over a very short range. ◯

C Devices on a PAN are always connected wirelessly. ◯

D PANs can connect devices without needing any additional hardware. ◯

[2 marks]

(b) While researching on the Internet, Sinead notices that some website addresses have HTTP before them and some have HTTPS before them. Explain what is meant by each one, including why some websites use one instead of the other.

....

....

....

....

[3 marks]

(c) Sinead often takes her laptop into the college and connects it to the college's WLAN. Describe a potential network security risk of connecting a laptop to a network.

....

....

[2 marks]

(d) Explain **two** network security measures that could reduce the risks posed by users like Sinead connecting devices to a network.

1 ....

....

....

2 ....

....

....

[4 marks]

Turn over ▶

6 Kadijah is a graphic designer for a publishing company. The image editing software that she uses represents each unique colour as a six digit hex code.

(a) Explain **one** benefit to programmers of using hex codes to represent the different colours.

....

....

[2 marks]

(b) One of the colours Kadijah is using, named Vibrant Pink, is given by the code E0078F, which is 1110 0000 0000 0111 1000 1111 in binary.

(i) Compress this binary data using run-length encoding (RLE).

....

....

....

....

[3 marks]

(ii) Explain whether RLE will reduce the data's size if a total of 1 byte is used for each data pair.

....

....

[2 marks]

7 Cochlear implants are electronic devices that are surgically implanted into the inner ear. They allow people who are deaf, or hard of hearing, to be able to hear. It has been suggested that this technology could be adapted to enhance a person's hearing so they can pick up sounds that would usually be impossible to hear.

Discuss why people may be opposed to this adapted technology. In your answer you should suggest ways in which the technology could be used, and consider any related legal, ethical and environmental issues.

....

....

....

....

....

....

....

....

....

....

....

....

[6 marks]

8   Packets can be sent across the Internet using network protocols.

(a)   Describe what is meant by a packet.

....

....

....

[2 marks]

(b)   Shade **one** oval to indicate which of these network protocols is responsible for:

(i)   routing the packets across the network.

A IP ◯   **B** UDP ◯   **C** FTP ◯   **D** TCP ◯

[1 mark]

(ii) numbering the packets.

A IP ◯   **B** UDP ◯   **C** FTP ◯   **D** TCP ◯

[1 mark]

(c)   IMAP is another network protocol. State which layer of the TCP/IP model
it operates on and describe the layer's main function.

Layer name: ....

Layer function: ....

....

[2 marks]

Turn over ▶

9 Hardeep wants to try a new operating system on his computer. His current PC specs and the minimum system requirements for the new OS are given below.

	Hardeep's PC	**OS Minimum Requirements**
Processor:	1.4 GHz, 4 cores	2.0 GHz, 4 cores
RAM:	2 GB	2 GB
Storage:	256 GB, 25 GB free	19 GB free space

(a) Which component does Hardeep need to upgrade in his computer before the new operating system can be installed? Shade **one** oval only.

    A Processor ◯   **B** RAM ◯   **C** Storage ◯

[1 mark]

(b) Explain why Hardeep may also want to upgrade the other two components mentioned above.

....

....

....

....

....

[4 marks]

(c) Describe how having more processor cores can improve a system's performance.

....

....

[2 marks]

(d) Explain why the OS requires the computer to have a certain amount of RAM.

....

....

[2 marks]

(e) The new operating system has a user interface that is optimised for touchscreen use. Describe **one** feature that an interface may include to take advantage of touchscreen technology.

....

....

[2 marks]

10 Most smartphones can wirelessly connect to global positioning systems (GPS).
This has lead to many apps being developed that track and use the user's location.

Discuss the advantages and disadvantages of using GPS technology in smartphones.
In your answer you should consider any related legal, ethical and environmental issues.

....

....

....

....

....

....

....

....

....

....

....

....

....

....

....

....

....

....

....

....

....

....

[9 marks]

END OF QUESTIONS

Answers

Section One — Algorithms

Page 4 (Warm-Up Questions)

1 Decomposition, Abstraction and Algorithmic Thinking

2 An algorithm is a process or set of instructions used to solve a problem or carry out a task.

3 B and D

4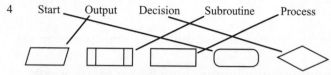

Page 5 (Exam Questions)

2 a) It asks the user to input a height and width. *[1 mark]*
   It then multiplies these values together *[1 mark]*
   to get the area and outputs the value of the area. *[1 mark]*

   b) D *[1 mark]*

3 a) E.g. Abstraction is picking out important details and ignoring irrelevant ones. The file uploading service will focus on the important details like the file name and ignore the unimportant details like the contents of each file.
   [3 marks available — 1 mark for a definition of abstraction, 1 mark for an example of a detail to ignore, 1 mark for an example of a detail to focus on]

   b) E.g. Decomposition breaks the programming task down into smaller problems. A programmer might focus on 'How will the service keep track of files already uploaded?' or 'How will the service compare file names?' and try to solve each programming problem individually.
   [3 marks available — 1 mark for a definition of decomposition, 1 mark for each example of decomposition up to a maximum of 2 marks]

4 Using Start / Begin. *[1 mark]*
   Asking user to input x, y. *[1 mark]*
   Using SqMove (with correct subroutine box). *[1 mark]*
   Decision box with appropriate question. *[1 mark]*
   Creating a loop to repeat SqMove. *[1 mark]*
   Using Stop / End. *[1 mark]*
   E.g.

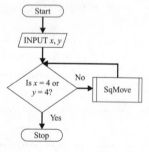

Page 9 (Warm-Up Questions)

1 a) Middle item = (7 + 1) / 2 = 4th item = 11
   11 is bigger than 8 so take left hand side.
   3, 6, 8
   Middle item = (3 + 1) / 2 = 2nd item = 6
   6 is smaller than 8 so take right hand side.
   8
   Middle item = (1 + 1) / 2 = 1st item = 8
   Stop searching as 8 has been found.

   b) Check 1st item: $3 \neq 11$.
   Check 2nd item: $6 \neq 11$.
   Check 3rd item: $8 \neq 11$.
   Check 4th item: $11 = 11$.
   Stop searching as 11 has been found.

2 See page 7.

---

3 a) *1st pass (2 swaps):*

Chris	Beth	Dalia	Ahmed
Beth	Chris	Dalia	Ahmed
Beth	Chris	Ahmed	Dalia

   2nd pass (1 swap):

   | Beth | Chris | Ahmed | Dalia |
   | Beth | Ahmed | Chris | Dalia |

   3rd pass (1 swap):

   | Beth | Ahmed | Chris | Dalia |
   | Ahmed | Beth | Chris | Dalia |

   4th pass (no swaps — list is in order):

   | Ahmed | Beth | Chris | Dalia |

   You don't necessarily need to do the last pass — since there are four items in the list, the algorithm will only take at most three passes to get the list in order.

   b)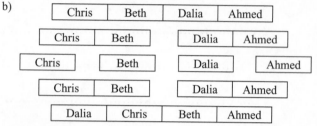

4 Merge Sort

Page 10 (Exam Questions)

3 a) Compare butterscotch to mint. *[1 mark]*
   Mint is greater so split and take the left side. *[1 mark]*
   A further comparison. *[1 mark]*
   Correct identification of butterscotch. *[1 mark]*
   E.g.
   Middle item = (5 + 1) / 2 = 3rd item = mint.
   Compare mint with butterscotch.
   Butterscotch comes before mint, so take left hand side.
   The list is: Butterscotch, Chocolate.
   Middle item = (2 + 1) / 2 = 1.5 = 2nd item = chocolate.
   Compare chocolate to butterscotch.
   Butterscotch comes before chocolate, so take left hand side.
   Middle item = (1 + 1) / 2 = 1st item = butterscotch.
   Stop searching as butterscotch has been found.

   b) It takes fewer steps for large lists of items, so will run in less time. *[1 mark]*

   c) There will be 11 items in total — so the middle item will be the (11 + 1) / 2 = 6th item. *[1 mark]*
   The 9th item is after the 6th so take the right side. *[1 mark]*
   This reduced list includes the 7th to 11th items of the original list — so 5 items in total.
   Check the middle item which will be the (5 + 1) / 2 = 3rd item of the reduced list (which is the 9th item of the original list).
   It has taken 2 iterations to find the 9th item. *[1 mark]*

4 a)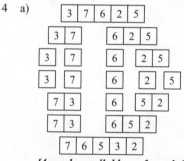

   [4 marks available — 1 mark for correctly splitting the list into single items, 1 mark for each correct merging row]

   b) A *[1 mark]* and C *[1 mark]*

Page 11 (Revision Questions)

8 E.g.

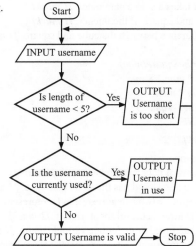

11 a) Binary Search:
The middle item is the 4th item, *Dagenham,* which comes before *Morpeth.* So lose first half of list to leave:
Morpeth, Usk, Watford
The middle item of the new list is the 2nd item, *Usk,* which comes after *Morpeth* so lose second half of list to leave:
Morpeth
The middle item of the new list is the 1st item, which is *Morpeth*, so you've found the correct item.
Even when there is one entry left you still have to carry on with the algorithm to check that it is the correct entry.

b) Linear Search:
Ashington ≠ Morpeth
Brecon ≠ Morpeth
Chester ≠ Morpeth
Dagenham ≠ Morpeth
Morpeth = Morpeth
You've found the correct item.

13 b) *1st pass (4 swaps):*
O, B, A, P, G, L
B, O, A, P, G, L
B, A, O, P, G, L
B, A, O, G, P, L
B, A, O, G, L, P

2nd pass (3 swaps):
B, A, O, G, L, P
A, B, O, G, L, P
A, B, G, O, L, P
A, B, G, L, O, P

3rd pass (no swaps — list is in order):
A, B, G, L, O, P

15 a)
8	7	5	1	3	6	4	2
8	7	5	1		3	6	4	2
8	7	5	1	3	6	4	2
8	7	5	1	3	6	4	2
7	8	1	5	3	6	2	4
1	5	7	8	2	3	4	6
1	2	3	4	5	6	7	8

b) *1st pass (4 swaps):*
8 7 5 1 3 6 4 2
8 7 5 3 1 6 4 2
8 7 5 3 6 1 4 2
8 7 5 3 6 4 1 2
8 7 5 3 6 4 2 1
2nd pass (2 swaps):
8 7 5 3 6 4 2 1
8 7 5 6 3 4 2 1
8 7 5 6 4 3 2 1
3rd pass (1 swap):
8 7 5 6 4 3 2 1
8 7 6 5 4 3 2 1
4th pass (no swaps):
8 7 6 5 4 3 2 1

Section Two — Programming

Page 17 (Warm-Up Questions)

1 a) String   b) Integer   c) Real/Float   d) Boolean
2 a) 40   b) 1   c) 4   d) 19
3 a) True   b) True   c) False   d) True
4 E.g. The value of a constant is set at design time and does not change as the program is running. The value of a variable might change as the program is running.
5 a) 7   b) lob   c) 5   d) bst

Page 18 (Exam Questions)

3 C *[1 mark]*
4 a) Boolean *[1 mark]* — the variable can only take two values, either pressed or not pressed, i.e. true or false. *[1 mark]*
b) Integer *[1 mark]* — it's measuring the number of whole seconds and whole numbers are best stored as integers. *[1 mark]*
5 a) Joining together two or more strings. *[1 mark]*
b) ora2000 *[1 mark]*
c) 05 fruit ← SUBSTRING(0, 2, fruit)
06 prodID ← fruit + volume
[2 marks available — 1 mark for correct use of SUBSTRING function and 1 mark for correct use of string concatenation]
If you assume volume is an integer, you would need to use the INT_TO_STRING function to cast it as a string on line 06.

Page 25 (Warm-Up Questions)

1 a) Iteration   b) Selection   c) Selection
d) Iteration   e) Selection   f) Iteration
2 E.g. A CASE statement makes selections based solely on the value of one variable, an ELSE-IF statement makes selections based on any conditions that are true or false.
3 a) Count-controlled loop: FOR loop
Condition-controlled loop: E.g. REPEAT-UNTIL loop
b) A FOR loop will iterate a specified number of times. A REPEAT-UNTIL loop will keep iterating until a specific condition is satisfied.
4 a) False   b) True   c) True   d) True
5 3, 4, 5, 6, 7, 8

Page 26 (Exam Questions)

3 a) B *[1 mark]*

b) 2 hrs 30 mins *[1 mark]*

4 E.g. The RANDOM_INT function could produce the same number more than once, which would produce the same card twice. *[1 mark]* This is not intended, as when a card is drawn it should be removed from the deck. *[1 mark]*

5 Using an appropriate selection statement. *[1 mark]*
A Boolean condition that checks each of the conditions. *[1 mark]*
Allowing the dryer to start if conditions are met. *[1 mark]*
E.g.
IF (weight > 1.5 AND weight < 15.0) AND doorClosed = true
THEN
    allowStart ← true
ELSE
    allowStart ← false
ENDIF

6 Count controlled loop to allow 10 games. *[1 mark]*
Asking for an input of the winner's name for each game. *[1 mark]*
A selection statement for the winner of each game. *[1 mark]*
Adding 1 to the winner's score. *[1 mark]*
A selection statement to find the overall winner. *[1 mark]*
Outputting the correct message depending on the scores. *[1 mark]*
E.g.
karlWin ← 0
johnWin ← 0
FOR i ← 1 TO 10
    OUTPUT 'Who won the game?'
    winner ← USERINPUT
    CASE winner OF
        'Karl': karlWin ← karlWin + 1
        'John': johnWin ← johnWin + 1
    ENDCASE
ENDFOR
IF karlWin > johnWin THEN
    OUTPUT 'The winner is Karl.'
ELSE IF johnWin > karlWin THEN
    OUTPUT 'The winner is John.'
ELSE
    OUTPUT 'The game is a draw.'
ENDIF
To make your algorithm more robust you could have used input validation to make sure the winner was either 'Karl' or 'John'. You could also have named the variables differently so that the code would make sense regardless of who was playing.

Page 33 (Warm-Up Questions)

1 a) 440 500   b) 81 000

2 a) Assigns the 4th element in the array to the variable "player".

b) Replaces the 6th element of the array with the string 'Pele'.

3 a) OPEN()   b) WRITE() or WRITELINE()

c) CLOSE()   d) READ() or READLINE()

4 E.g.
- A record can store different data types.
- Names can be given to the different fields.
- Record structures cannot accidently be changed later on.

5 E.g.
- You only have to write them once so you don't have to repeat blocks of code.
- You can call them from anywhere in the program.
- You only have to debug them once.
- They will improve the readability / maintainability of the code.
- They break the program down into smaller more manageable chunks.

Pages 34-35 (Exam Questions)

2 A subroutine that takes a single parameter. *[1 mark]*
Finding the cube and square of the integer. *[1 mark]*
Returning the difference between the cube and square. *[1 mark]*
E.g.
SUBROUTINE cubeSquare(num)
    *cube ← num * num * num*
    *square ← num * num*
    RETURN (cube – square)
ENDSUBROUTINE

3 a) String *[1 mark]*

b) Any **three** reasons, e.g.
- Multiple items of data need to be stored. *[1 mark]*
- All the data being stored has the same data type. *[1 mark]*
- The data is split by two categories / can be represented in a table so a 2D array is useful for storing it. *[1 mark]*
- Stores the data together under one variable name. *[1 mark]*
- Accessing the information is more efficient. A single command, e.g. *sportsDay[position][event]* can be used to access any name from the array. *[1 mark]*

[3 marks available in total — at least one reason must specifically mention 2D arrays.]

4 a) String *[1 mark]*

b) E.g. Storing the data in records allows the different fields to have different data types *[1 mark]* while if they used an array, they would all have to be the same data type. *[1 mark]*

5 Opening and closing the story properly. *[1 mark]*
Using a condition-controlled loop. *[1 mark]*
Exiting the loop when 'THE END' is outputted. *[1 mark]*
Using a selection statement to check the user's input. *[1 mark]*
Outputting the next line of the story. *[1 mark]*
E.g.
story ← OPEN('adventure.txt')
REPEAT
    keypress ← USERINPUT
    IF keypress = 'y' THEN
        currentLine ← READLINE(story)
        OUTPUT currentLine
    ENDIF
UNTIL currentLine = 'THE END'
CLOSE(story)

6 a) OUTPUT distanceRun[4][3] *[1 mark]*

b) Accepting user input of the runner number. *[1 mark]*
Using a FOR loop. *[1 mark]*
Adding all elements correctly. *[1 mark]*
Outputting the total distance. *[1 mark]*
E.g.
totalDistance ← 0
OUTPUT 'Choose a runner number from 0-3'
runner ← USERINPUT
FOR i ← 0 TO 6
    totalDistance ← totalDistance + distanceRun[i][runner]
ENDFOR
OUTPUT totalDistance

c) Using a FOR loop nested in another FOR loop. *[1 mark]*
Having one loop from 0 to 3 and the other from 0 to 6. *[1 mark]*
Using milesConvert() on each element of the array. *[1 mark]*
E.g.
FOR i ← 0 TO 3
    FOR j ← 0 TO 6
        distanceRun[i][j] ← milesConvert(distanceRun[i][j])
    ENDFOR
ENDFOR

7 a) Any **two** reasons, e.g.
- Local variables can only be changed and accessed from within the subroutine they're declared in. *[1 mark]* This prevents programmers from accidentally affecting things in different parts of a program. *[1 mark]*
- A local variable 'disappears' outside of the subroutine, *[1 mark]* which means that you could declare the same variable name twice without it creating a conflict. *[1 mark]*
- A subroutine with only local variables is self-contained *[1 mark]* so you could reuse it in a different program without having to declare any variables beforehand. *[1 mark]*

[4 marks available in total]

b) A subroutine that takes the number of sides the dice have as a parameter. *[1 mark]*
Using a condition controlled loop. *[1 mark]*
Using the rollTwo function. *[1 mark]*
Increasing the score by 1 after each roll. *[1 mark]*
Returning the score. *[1 mark]*
E.g.

```
SUBROUTINE rollGame(sides)
    score ← 0
    REPEAT
        results ← rollTwo(sides)
        score ← score + 1
    UNTIL results[0] = results[1]
    RETURN score
ENDSUBROUTINE
```

Page 36 (Revision Questions)

2 a) STRING_TO_INT('1234')

b) REAL_TO_STRING(0.578)

c) INT_TO_STRING(8)

d) STRING_TO_REAL('0.75')

5 b) (i) 7   (ii) 2   (iii) 'mage'

9 first_day ← USERINPUT
```
IF first_day = 'Sunday' OR first_day = 'Monday' THEN
    OUTPUT 5
ELSE
    OUTPUT 4
ENDIF
```

10 FOR i ← 1 TO 100
```
    roll ← RANDOM_INT(1, 8)
    OUTPUT roll
ENDFOR
```

12 a) *OUTPUT chars[4]*

b) *chars[2] ← 'D'*

c) FOR i ← 0 to 9
```
    chars[i] ← 'N'
ENDFOR
```

13 FOR i ← 0 TO 9
```
    FOR j ← 0 TO 9
        multiply[i][j] ← i * j
    ENDFOR
ENDFOR
```

Section Three — Design, Testing and Translators

Page 43 (Warm-Up Questions)

1 E.g. It makes coding easier because each module only carries out a simple task. Programmers can fix and update modules without affecting the rest of the program.

2 a) Presence check   b) Look-up table

3 E.g.
- Clear comments
- Indentation
- Properly named variables/subprograms
- Use of local (rather than global) variables where possible

4 a) False   b) True   c) True   d) False

5 High-level languages are programming languages that are easy for humans to read and write, but that computers need to translate before they can execute the code.

6 A compiler translates all of a program's source code into one executable file of machine code.

Pages 44-45 (Exam Questions)

2 a) E.g. Time efficiency is a measure of how 'quickly' an algorithm completes a task. *[1 mark]* The 'quicker' an algorithm completes a task, the better its time efficiency. *[1 mark]*

b)
a	b
11	4
10	3
9	2
8	1
7	0

[2 marks available — 1 mark for each column with the correct values in the correct order]

c) E.g. He is wrong because time efficiency is affected by more than the length of an algorithm. *[1 mark]* The subroutine *numDiff* would be more time efficient *[1 mark]* — e.g. when a and b are far apart, *diffNums* would have to repeat the loop many times. *[1 mark]* *numDiff* would have a more consistent run-time regardless of the values of a and b. *[1 mark]*

3 a) Any **two** reasons, e.g.
- They may need to have a greater control over the program in order to make a program with lower memory use. *[1 mark]*
- They may need to have a greater control over what the CPU does in order to make a program run quicker. *[1 mark]*
- They may be trying to maintain old code or hardware. *[1 mark]*

[2 marks available in total]

b) Assembly languages are more readable for humans than machine code *[1 mark]* so can be programmed / edited more easily. *[1 mark]*

c) C *[1 mark]*

4 a) E.g. a test plan should take the user down all possible paths of the program. *[1 mark]* It should use normal, extreme and erroneous test data. *[1 mark]* If any of the tests get a result not equal to the expected outcome then the user knows there is a logic error. *[1 mark]*

b)
Test Data	Expected Outcome	Reasons for test
Group_Size = 4	210	Check program with data user is likely to input.
Group_Size = 10	510	Check program works with values on the limit.
Group_Size = 12	Display an error message	Check what happens if input is too large.

[5 marks available — 1 mark per box]

5 a) Any **two** advantages, e.g.
  - Coding is easier as objectives are smaller and simpler. *[1 mark]*
  - Multiple programmers can work on one program at once by working on different modules separately. *[1 mark]*
  - Modules can be tested individually to find errors more easily. *[1 mark]*
  - Modules can be updated separately without it affecting the rest of the program. *[1 mark]*
  - Modules can be reused in different programs. *[1 mark]*
  [2 marks available in total]

  b) i) Any **two** suitable modules, e.g.
    - Updating a user's details. *[1 mark]*
    - Deleting a user account. *[1 mark]*
    - Changing user access levels. *[1 mark]*
    - Searching for users. *[1 mark]*
    [2 marks available in total]

  ii) E.g.

Name	Inputs	Processes	Return Values
Enter user details	None	Prompt user to enter details	Array of user details
Generate email address	Array of user details	Create email address from user details	User's email address

[3 marks available — 1 mark for each suitable entry]

Page 46 (Revision Questions)

8 Range check — the program checks if the user has entered a year between 1900 and 2019 before breaking out of the REPEAT-UNTIL loop.

13 E.g.
  - Normal input data (e.g. 'art')
  - No input (e.g. ' ')
  - A string with no anagram (e.g. 'x')
  - Mixed case string (e.g. 'aRT')
  - Other characters (e.g. '2?#')

15

x	arr[x]	total
		1
0	2	2
1	5	10
2	1	10
3	2	20
4	3	60

Section Four — Data Representation

Page 50 (Warm-Up Questions)

1 a)

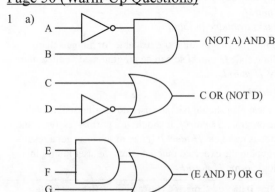

  b)

A	B	NOT A	(NOT A) AND B
0	0	1	0
0	1	1	1
1	0	0	0
1	1	0	0

C	D	NOT D	C OR (NOT D)
0	0	1	1
0	1	0	0
1	0	1	1
1	1	0	1

E	F	G	E AND F	(E AND F) OR G
0	0	0	0	0
0	0	1	0	1
0	1	0	0	0
0	1	1	0	1
1	0	0	0	0
1	0	1	0	1
1	1	0	1	1
1	1	1	1	1

2 TB

3 a) 80 000 bits

  b) 3 000 000 MB

Page 51 (Exam Questions)

3 a) 100 kB = 100 × 1000 = 100 000 bytes *[1 mark]*
    100 000 bytes = 100 000 × 8 = 800 000 bits *[1 mark]*

  b) 5000 × 100 kB = 500 000 kB *[1 mark]*
    500 000 kB = 500 000 ÷ 1000 = 500 MB
    500 MB = 500 ÷ 1000 = 0.5 GB *[1 mark]*

  c) Computers are made up of logic circuits *[1 mark]* which use high and low voltages to represent 1s and 0s. *[1 mark]*

4 a)

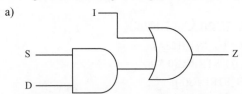

  [3 marks available — 1 mark for inputs S and D going into an AND gate, 1 mark for the output of the AND gate and input I going into an OR gate, 1 mark for Z being the OR gate output]

  b) (S AND D) OR I = Z *[1 mark]*

  c) i) S = 0, D = 1, I = 0, Z = 0 *[1 mark]*

    ii) S = 1, D = 1, I = 1, Z = 1 *[1 mark]*
      S = 1, D = 0, I = 1, Z = 1 *[1 mark]*

Page 57 (Warm-Up Questions)

1 a) 89   b) 1000101

2 11110010

3 00010111

4 Multiplying the number by 2.

5 a) 30   b) 198   c) A2   d) 111101

Page 58 (Exam Questions)

3 a) 2^8 or 256 *[1 mark]*

  b) 6 bits *[1 mark]*
    $2^6 = 64$ is enough, but $2^5 = 32$ isn't, so 6 bits are needed.

4 a) Split bytes into nibbles and convert to hexadecimal.
    0100 = 4, 0011 = 3, so 01000011 = C = 43. *[1 mark]*
    0100 = 4, 0001 = 1, so 01000001 = A = 41. *[1 mark]*
    0101 = 5, 0100 = 4, so 01010100 = T = 54. *[1 mark]*

  b) i) D = 44 = 01000100 *[1 mark]*

    ii) From CAT, 43 = C and from DOG, 44 = D and 4F = O.
      E is 1 more than D (= 44) so 45 = E. *[1 mark]*
      The password is CODE. *[1 mark]*

5 a) decimal(A) = 10 and decimal(C) = 12 *[1 mark]*
    So, decimal(A) + decimal(C) = 10 + 12 = 22 *[1 mark]*

b) Taking a hexadecimal as an input. *[1 mark]*
Splitting hexadecimal into characters. *[1 mark]*
Multiplying first character in decimal by 16. *[1 mark]*
Adding the second character in decimal to the first. *[1 mark]*
E.g.
OUTPUT 'Enter a two digit hexadecimal'
hexadecimal ← USERINPUT
char1 ← SUBSTRING(0, 0, hexadecimal)
char2 ← SUBSTRING(1, 1, hexadecimal)
ans ← 16 * decimal(char1) + decimal(char2)
OUTPUT ans

Page 66 (Warm-Up Questions)

1 ASCII uses fewer bits to represent each character but is a much smaller character set.

2 16

3 a) The file size would increase.

   b) The file size would decrease.

4 a) The file size and quality would both increase.

   b) The file size and quality would both increase.

5 E.g. Lossy compression will make file sizes a lot smaller. Lossless compression will maintain the quality of the original file.

6 E.g. Run-length encoding is a form of lossless compression. It looks for runs of data and stores the number of times data is repeated and one copy of the data as a data pair.

7 E.g. The code for 'e' is shorter than the code for 'z', so 'e' is likely to appear more frequently than 'z' in the text file.

Pages 67-68 (Exam Questions)

3 a) A character set is a collection of characters a computer recognises from their binary representation. *[1 mark]*

   b) E.g. Binary code sent to computer. *[1 mark]*
   Character set used to translate binary code. *[1 mark]*

4 a) Recording 2 would have a better sound quality *[1 mark]* because it has a higher sampling rate and sample resolution, both of which are indications of better overall sound quality. *[1 mark]*

   b) The file size would be larger. *[1 mark]*

5 a) (7, 0), (6, 1), (11, 0)
   [3 marks available — 1 mark for each correct data pair]
   *You could give your answer in a different format
   — e.g. 0716011 would also be acceptable.*

   b) Original = 24 bits, encoded = 3 × 6 = 18 bits. *[1 mark]*
   So the encoding saves 24 – 18 = 6 bits. *[1 mark]*

6 a) In image A, 1 bit is needed to represent each pixel (black or white) and there are 15 pixels. 15 × 1 = 15 bits. *[1 mark]*
   In image B, 2 bits are needed to represent each pixel (4 different colours) and there are 9 pixels. 9 × 2 = 18 bits. *[1 mark]*
   In image C, 1 bit is needed to represent each pixel and there are 16 pixels. 16 × 1 = 16 bits. *[1 mark]*
   So image B requires the most bits to represent it. *[1 mark]*

   b) 10101 01011 01101 *[1 mark]*

7 a)
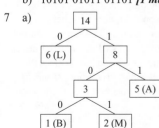

   [4 marks available — 1 mark for each pair of branches connecting to the correct nodes (for a total of 3 marks), 1 mark for each branch correctly labelled with 0/1]

b)

Letter	L	A	M	B
Huffman Code	0	11	101	100

[2 marks available — 2 marks for all three codes correct, otherwise 1 mark for at least two codes correct]

c) 0 | 0 | 11 | 101 | 11
    L | L | A | M | A

[2 marks available — 1 mark for correct method, 1 mark for correctly decoded text]

Page 69 (Revision Questions)

2

A	B	C	A OR B	(A OR B) AND C
0	0	0	0	0
0	0	1	0	0
0	1	0	1	0
0	1	1	1	1
1	0	0	1	0
1	0	1	1	1
1	1	0	1	0
1	1	1	1	1

5 a) 0.2 gigabytes

   b) 1 600 000 bits

6 1000 1111

8 a) i) 10001   ii) 10010100   iii) 11110000

   b) i) 11   ii) 94   iii) F0

9 a) i) 56   ii) 159   iii) 43

   b) i) 38   ii) 9F   iii) 2B

10 a) i) 74   ii) 117   iii) 3033

    b) i) 1001010

       ii) 1110101

       iii) 101111011001

22 a) (4, P), (2, Q), (3, R), (6, S), (5, P), (3, Q)

    b)
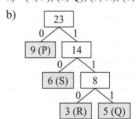

    c) i) 23 × 8 = 184 bits

       ii) The number of bits needed for each character using the Huffman coding is shown in the table below:

Char.	Code	Freq.	Bits
P	0	9	9
Q	111	5	15
R	110	3	9
S	10	6	12

       This gives a total of 9 + 15 + 9 + 12 = 45 bits.

       iii) 8 × 2 × 6 = 96 bits

Section Five — Components of a Computer System

Page 73 (Warm-Up Questions)

1 E.g.
- Power supply
- Case cooling fan
- CPU
- Heat sink
- Optical drive
- RAM
- Hard Disk Drive/HDD
- Graphics card/GPU
- Motherboard

2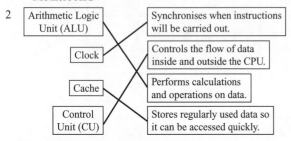

3 **A** should be labelled as 'Registers' and
   B should be labelled as 'Memory'.

Page 74 (Exam Questions)

2 a) A computer system built into another device. *[1 mark]*

   b) Any **two** devices, e.g.
   - Dishwasher *[1 mark]*
   - Mp3 player *[1 mark]*
   - Digital thermometer *[1 mark]*
   - Washing machine *[1 mark]*
   - Manufacturing machinery *[1 mark]*
   [2 marks available in total]

   c) Any **two** benefits with explanation, e.g.
   - Embedded systems are usually smaller than non-embedded systems *[1 mark]* which means devices with embedded systems can be made more compact. *[1 mark]*
   - Embedded systems are cheaper to produce than non-embedded systems *[1 mark]* which can help to keep down the cost of the devices they're used in. *[1 mark]*
   - Embedded systems are usually designed for a specific purpose, *[1 mark]* while non-embedded systems can be adapted to perform many different tasks. *[1 mark]*
   - Embedded systems tend to be more reliable than non-embedded systems, *[1 mark]* so they might last longer and require less maintenance. *[1 mark]*
   - Embedded systems are likely to use ROM for their main memory (which is cheap), *[1 mark]* while non-embedded systems are likely to use RAM (which can be expensive). *[1 mark]*
   [4 marks available in total]

3 a) E.g.
   Fetch:
   - The CU reads the memory address of the next instruction. *[1 mark]*
   - The instruction is fetched from memory. *[1 mark]*
   - The fetched instruction is copied to one of the registers. *[1 mark]*
   - The address in the CU is changed to point to the address of the next instruction. *[1 mark]*
   Decode:
   - The fetched instruction is decoded by the control unit. *[1 mark]*
   - A new value may be loaded into registers to prepare for the execute step. *[1 mark]*
   Execute:
   - The decoded instruction is carried out / executed, *[1 mark]* e.g. data is loaded from memory / data is written to memory / a calculation is done / a program is halted. *[1 mark]*
   - The cycle is repeated. *[1 mark]*
   [6 marks available in total — fetch, decode and execute stages must all be covered for full marks.]

   b) D *[1 mark]*

Page 79 (Warm-Up Questions)

1 RAM is volatile memory that can be read from and written to, used to store files and applications while they are in use. ROM is non-volatile memory that can generally only be read, which contains the startup instructions for the computer.

2 A clock speed of 3 GHz means that the single-core processor can process 3 billion instructions per second.

3 a) E.g. Solid state drive (SSD) / USB pen drive / SD memory card

   b) E.g. Optical disc / CD / DVD / Blu-Ray™

   c) Hard disk drive (HDD)

4 E.g.
- Data can be easily accessed and shared.
- It can be cheaper than other options.
- Automatic backups might be provided by the cloud host.

Page 80 (Exam Questions)

3 a) E.g.
   - Secondary storage is needed to store data and software in the long term. *[1 mark]*
   - Secondary storage is non-volatile memory, so retains data when there is no power. *[1 mark]*
   - Computers could not function without permanent data storage, as all software and data would be lost when switched off. *[1 mark]*
   - Secondary storage has a high capacity, so you can store a lot more data. *[1 mark]*
   [3 marks available in total]

   b) Any **two** advantages and **two** disadvantages, e.g.
   Advantages:
   - Optical discs have a low cost per GB. *[1 mark]*
   - They are highly portable. *[1 mark]*
   - They are durable against shock and water damage. *[1 mark]*
   Disadvantages:
   - They are very slow to write to. *[1 mark]*
   - They require an optical drive to be read / written. *[1 mark]*
   - They can be scratched easily. *[1 mark]*
   - They have a low capacity compared to other forms of storage, e.g. flash memory cards. *[1 mark]*
   [4 marks available in total]

4 a) Cache is much faster than RAM. *[1 mark]* The larger the cache, the more data can be stored for quick access by the CPU, meaning the CPU should perform better. *[1 mark]*

   b) E.g. Jackson's CPU has more cores than Will's CPU, which should mean better performance. *[1 mark]* It also has a larger cache than Will's, which should again lead to better CPU performance. *[1 mark]* On the other hand Will's CPU has a higher clock speed than Jackson's, so there is a chance that Will's may give better performance than Jackson's. *[1 mark]* Overall, it is hard to tell whether Will's CPU will offer better performance, therefore it seems unwise to buy Will's CPU, as it may be no better than Jackson's current one. *[1 mark]*
   If you'd decided that Will's CPU was the best option, you'd still get the marks as long as you'd put together a sensible argument based on comparisons of the CPU specs.

c) E.g. Increasing the amount of RAM increases the amount of data / number of applications that the computer can hold in memory. *[1 mark]* Jackson may not use all of the current RAM in his computer, as he may use undemanding software or he may not open many programs at once *[1 mark]* so adding more RAM will not improve performance. *[1 mark]*
[2 marks available in total]

Page 85 (Warm-Up Questions)

1

	System Software	Not System Software
Operating System	✓	
Word Processor		✓
Email Client		✓
Disk Defragmenter	✓	

2 a) System cleanup

b) Compression

c) Virus scanner

d) Encryption

e) Backup

Page 86 (Exam Questions)

2 a) Any **three** functions, e.g.
  • The OS communicates with I/O devices. *[1 mark]*
  • The OS provides a user interface. *[1 mark]*
  • The OS provides a platform for software / applications to run on. *[1 mark]*
  • The OS manages memory and system resources. *[1 mark]*
  • The OS manages the CPU and processes. *[1 mark]*
  • The OS deals with file and disk management. *[1 mark]*
  • The OS provides some system security measures. *[1 mark]*
  [3 marks available in total]

b) Any **two** features, e.g.
  • It may allow different user accounts, giving each user access to their own personal data and desktop, which cannot be accessed by other users. *[1 mark]*
  • It may have anti-theft measures, like password or pin protection. *[1 mark]*
  • It may include encryption software, to allow users to protect their files. *[1 mark]*
  • It may include anti-virus software or a firewall to help protect against unauthorised users / software. *[1 mark]*
  [2 marks available in total]

3 a) Utility software is software that helps to configure, optimise or maintain a computer. *[1 mark]*

b) E.g. Over time, as files are moved and deleted on a hard drive, gaps appear that result in files getting split up (fragmented). *[1 mark]* Defragmentation software puts the files back together and collects all the gaps together *[1 mark]* to allow the drive to read these files faster. *[1 mark]*

4 E.g.
  • When applications are opened, the OS moves the necessary parts to memory. *[1 mark]*
  • The OS will remove unneeded data from memory, e.g. when applications are closed. *[1 mark]*
  • When multiple applications are run at once, their data is placed into different locations in memory *[1 mark]* so that their processes cannot overwrite or interfere with each other. *[1 mark]*
  • The OS divides CPU time between running applications, as it can only process one at a time. *[1 mark]*
  • The OS uses scheduling to determine the most efficient order to deal with each process. *[1 mark]*

• Processes are allocated a 'priority' by the OS. *[1 mark]*
• The OS can interrupt processes if higher-priority processes become available. *[1 mark]*
• The CPU switches between processes for different applications at a rapid rate, which allows both applications to run at once. *[1 mark]*
[6 marks available in total — both memory management and processor management must be covered for full marks]

Section Six — Networks

Page 92 (Warm-Up Questions)

1 a) WAN   b) PAN   c) LAN or WAN

2 a) E.g. Ethernet cables are cheaper than fibre optic cables / have higher bandwidth than coaxial cables.

b) Star topology

3 E.g.
  • New devices on the LAN could connect automatically.
  • Devices like laptops could be moved and stay connected.

4 a) True   b) False   c) False   d) True

Page 93 (Exam Questions)

2 a) Fibre optic cable *[1 mark]*

b) Ethernet / Copper cable *[1 mark]*

3 a) To absorb signals and stop data reflecting back along the bus. *[1 mark]*

b)

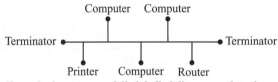

[2 marks for a correct fully labelled diagram, otherwise 1 mark for a correct but unlabelled diagram]
The devices on the network can be in any order apart from the terminators — they have to be on the ends.

c) Any **one** advantage with matching explanation, e.g.
  • A bus network isn't reliant on a central server or switch *[1 mark]* whereas a star network will completely fail if the central device stops working. *[1 mark]*
  • Bus networks require less cabling / don't require a switch *[1 mark]* so are often cheaper and easier to set up. *[1 mark]*
  [2 marks available in total]

  Any **one** disadvantage with matching explanation, e.g.
  • Data collisions are common in a bus network *[1 mark]* as all devices want to use the same cable at the same time. *[1 mark]*
  • Bus networks are reliant on a single cable, *[1 mark]* so if that cable was to fail then the whole network would stop working. *[1 mark]*
  [2 marks available in total]

4 E.g.
  • Networks can be vulnerable to malware *[1 mark]* because once one computer is infected it can quickly spread to other computers on the network. *[1 mark]*
  • Networks are more vulnerable to hacking *[1 mark]* as hackers only need to gain access to one computer in order to access the whole network. *[1 mark]*
  • Networks often store data on a server rather than on each machine *[1 mark]* so if the servers go down it can disrupt everyone on the network. *[1 mark]*
  • Networks can be difficult to set up and maintain *[1 mark]* as large networks need lots of hardware and often require a network specialist to maintain them. *[1 mark]*
  [4 marks available in total]

146

Page 101 (Warm-Up Questions)

1

Protocol	Function
HTTP	Used by web browsers to access websites / communicate with web servers.
HTTPS	A more secure version of HTTP.
FTP	Used to access, edit and move files on other devices.
IMAP	Used to retrieve emails from a server.
TCP	Splits data into numbered packets to be sent over a network.
UDP	Splits data into packets to be sent over a network without numbering them.
IP	Manages packet switching over a network.

2 a) Trojan   b) Adware   c) Spyware   d) Virus

Pages 102-103 (Exam Questions)

2 a) E.g.
- Different user access levels prevent students from accessing the same data as teachers, including sensitive data like their peers' personal information. *[1 mark]*
- Different user access levels prevent a student from maliciously deleting or editing data. *[1 mark]*
- Different user access levels prevent students accidentally deleting or editing important files. *[1 mark]*
- Different user access levels allow network administrators to flexibly change the amount of access students and staff have to certain files. *[1 mark]*

[3 marks available in total]

   b) i) Default and weak passwords are easy for hackers to crack *[1 mark]* by using automated software to try all likely combinations. *[1 mark]*

      ii) Any **two** requirements, e.g.
- Make passwords require a mix of characters (uppercase, lowercase, numbers and symbols). *[1 mark]*
- Make passwords have to be a minimum length. *[1 mark]*
- Make users change passwords regularly. *[1 mark]*

[2 marks available in total]

3 a) E.g. IP addresses are used to identify devices on the Internet. *[1 mark]* Routers use IP addresses to direct data packets to the correct destination. *[1 mark]*

[2 marks available in total]

   b) UDP *[1 mark]*
E.g.
- UDP doesn't require retransmission of lost or corrupted packets *[1 mark]* which means that there will be no delay when sending packets. *[1 mark]*
- UDP doesn't order packets *[1 mark]* so the receiving device can just read packets whenever they arrive, which can speed up transmission. *[1 mark]*
- The packets are probably being transmitted to multiple devices. *[1 mark]* UDP doesn't have to keep track of which devices have and haven't received each packet. *[1 mark]*
- UDP doesn't need to establish a connection between the sending and receiving devices, *[1 mark]* which prevents delays in transmission. *[1 mark]*

[5 marks available in total — 1 mark for choosing UDP and 4 marks for explanation]

4 a) A set of rules *[1 mark]* for how devices communicate across a network. *[1 mark]*

   b) Any **three** benefits, e.g.
- Layers break network communication into manageable pieces. *[1 mark]*
- Layers allow developers to focus on one area of the network without worrying about the others. *[1 mark]*
- Layers are self-contained. *[1 mark]*
- There are set rules for each layer. *[1 mark]*
- Layers allow interoperability / layers make companies produce compatible, universal hardware and software. *[1 mark]*

[3 marks available in total]

   c) Protocol 1: Wi-Fi® *[1 mark]* is a family of protocols that manage wireless data transfer on WLANs. *[1 mark]* Protocol 2: Ethernet *[1 mark]* is a family of protocols that manage data transfer on wired LANs. *[1 mark]*

5 E.g. Pharming is a cyber attack that redirects a user from a legitimate website to a fake site by infecting their computer (or the actual site's servers) with malware. *[1 mark]* They then willingly enter their personal data, thinking they are using the genuine website. *[1 mark]* This type of attack can be protected against by using anti-malware software and web filters on browsers to prevent users from being redirected to these fake sites. *[1 mark]*

E.g. Shouldering is when somebody monitors a person's activity *[1 mark]* in order to see them entering personal information like passwords. *[1 mark]* This type of attack can be protected against by covering the keyboard or keypad when you are entering personal data, or checking that you are not being watched. *[1 mark]*

6 Points you might include:

The threats posed to the firm's network
- Hackers could use rootkits, spyware and other malware to steal confidential information.
- Employees unaware of the potential dangers could be tricked into giving criminals sensitive information through social engineering.
- Disgruntled employees could use their position to attack the network, e.g. by releasing malware onto the network from a USB drive.
- Hackers with packet sniffers or other similar tools could intercept and read information entering or leaving the company's network.
- Hackers could use automated software to crack weak passwords.

Methods to improve network security
- Automatic encryption of all data leaving and entering the network could prevent intercepted data from being read by hackers and criminals.
- Installing anti-malware and firewall software and keeping it up-to-date could prevent harmful malware from entering the network.
- Regular penetration testing (both white box and black box) to find problems in the network security.
- Educating employees on the dangers of social engineering could protect against it.
- Mandatory use of strong passwords / passwords that are changed regularly.
- An acceptable use policy that all employees must sign.
- Controlling physical access to hardware / the network, e.g. by using biometric measures like retina scanning to access high security areas.
- Different user access levels given to different groups of users to limit the dangers of an attack from within the firm.

How to mark your answer:
- Two or three points with very little explanation. *[1-3 marks]*
- Three to five points with detailed explanation. *[4-6 marks]*
- Six or more detailed points that form a well-written, balanced discussion. *[7-9 marks]*

Section Seven — Issues

Page 109 (Warm-Up Questions)

1   The digital divide is the separation between people who have ready access to technology and those who don't, who tend to be at a disadvantage because of this.

2   E.g. Users of the subscription service can lose access if the service closes down.

3

	Censorship	Surveillance
A business monitors what their employees view online.		✓
A country's government blocks access to Facebook®.	✓	
A government agency intercepts emails containing certain words.		✓
A school restricts access to harmful websites.	✓	
An Internet Service Provider collects data on browsing habits.		✓

Page 110 (Exam Questions)

2   Any **one** benefit, e.g.
- Censoring certain websites can prevent citizens from accessing illegal sites. *[1 mark]* This can help to reduce crime rates, drug abuse, etc. *[1 mark]*
- Certain websites contain content that is inappropriate for children, e.g. pornography. *[1 mark]* Censoring these sites would prevent children from accessing them. *[1 mark]*

Any **one** drawback, e.g.
- Censoring websites would damage the freedom of citizens, *[1 mark]* as the government is controlling what people can and cannot access. *[1 mark]*
- Trying to censor websites might not work *[1 mark]* as other alternative websites might keep popping up. *[1 mark]*
- Censorship could be used to oppress certain ethical or political views *[1 mark]* and could damage the citizens' right to free speech. *[1 mark]*
[4 marks available in total]

3   a)   E.g.
- The Internet / social media / email mean Tom can be contacted at any time of day. *[1 mark]*
- Tom may be expected to carry a smartphone so he can be contacted by his boss at all times. *[1 mark]*
- Tom's smartphone may alert him when he receives work emails from clients. These can be hard to ignore. *[1 mark]*
[2 marks available in total]

   b)   Any **one** issue, e.g.
- They might be excluding people who cannot afford to buy electronic devices. *[1 mark]*
- They might be excluding people who live in a rural area with poor network coverage. *[1 mark]*
- Their might be excluding people who are not able to use technology, e.g. because of a disability. *[1 mark]*
[1 mark available in total]

   c)   E.g. If they act ethically, they might gain public trust. *[1 mark]* Having a good reputation might earn them more customers and more money in the long term. *[1 mark]*

4   Points you might include:
Benefits of smart glasses
- Smart glasses could be a very convenient technology, e.g. by displaying reminders, helping to navigate, etc.
- Smart glasses could be used while exercising to display information like speed and heart rate.
- Smart glasses could use the Internet to allow instant communication with other people, which could help people to stay connected in their daily lives.
- Smart glasses could provide benefits to those with impaired vision, e.g. by zooming in on far away objects. *(ethical)*
- Developing the technology could lead to further innovations and new beneficial technology. *(ethical)*

Risks of smart glasses
- Smart glasses could be used to covertly record people without their knowledge, which could be seen as an invasion of privacy. *(ethical)*
- People might not be happy having wireless technology so close to their brain, as there could be a risk of negative health effects. *(ethical)*
- Hackers may be able to exploit the technology to find out what a person can see and hear. *(ethical)*
- Depending on how it was implemented, the technology might not be available to people who already wear glasses or have other visual impairments. *(ethical)*
- They may be expensive, which would make them unavailable to certain members of society and contribute to the digital divide. *(ethical)*

How to mark your answer:
- One or two brief benefits or risks with very little explanation. *[1-2 marks]*
- Three or four detailed points covering benefits and risks, including some ethical issues. *[3-4 marks]*
- Four or more detailed points covering benefits and risks, that form a well-written, balanced discussion and cover a range of ethical issues. *[5-6 marks]*

Page 114 (Warm-Up Questions)

1   a)   Data protection laws aim to prevent the misuse of peoples' personal data that is used by organisations or the government.

   b)   The Computer Misuse Act aims to prevent cyber crime (such as hacking and the spread of malware).

   c)   The Copyright, Designs and Patents Act aims to protect intellectual property from being copied or stolen.

2   a)   Computer Misuse Act
   b)   Not against any of these laws
   c)   Computer Misuse Act / Copyright, Designs and Patents Act
   d)   Not against any of these laws
   e)   Computer Misuse Act
   f)   Not against any of these laws
   g)   Data protection laws

Page 115 (Exam Questions)

3   a)   i)   Illegally modifying a piece of software to remove unwanted features, e.g. copy protection. *[1 mark]*

        ii) A way of protecting intellectual property / a way of protecting something that has been created / a way of protecting written and recorded content, e.g. books, music, films, software and video games. *[1 mark]*

   b)   Any **one** benefit, e.g.
- DRM can prevent people from pirating the software. *[1 mark]*
- Online authentication can ensure all users have the most up-to-date version. *[1 mark]*
- Online authentication could be used to track how many copies of a piece of software have been sold. *[1 mark]*

Any **one** drawback, e.g.
- DRM can make the software less convenient to use. *[1 mark]*
- Online authentication might make the software unusable to someone who does not have internet access. *[1 mark]*
- If the authentication service becomes unavailable, e.g. for older programs, then the software may become unusable. *[1 mark]*
[2 marks available in total]

c) E.g. Open source software can legally be modified and distributed *[1 mark]* allowing users to customise and improve the software as they like. *[1 mark]*

4 a) Any **two** reasons, e.g.
- Smartphones are portable, so can be broken easily, for example by dropping them. *[1 mark]*
- Smartphones are not built to last more than a few years. *[1 mark]*
- It is often cheaper to replace a smartphone than it is to repair it. *[1 mark]*
- Smartphone manufacturers release new devices on a regular basis and use advertisements to influence people into buying them. *[1 mark]*
- People often want to buy the newest technology and are happy to discard their old smartphones regularly. *[1 mark]*
- Retailers only provide short warranties on many smartphones. *[1 mark]*
- Many people feel pressured by their peers to upgrade to the latest smartphone. *[1 mark]*

[2 marks available in total]

b) Any **one** way, e.g.
- People can take devices to local collection facilities to be correctly disposed *[1 mark]* rather than throwing them out with general waste. *[1 mark]*
- The government can put pressure on companies or local authorities to ensure e-waste regulations are being followed, *[1 mark]* e.g. by setting targets on the amount of e-waste that they are recycling. *[1 mark]*
- Old devices can be refurbished and reused *[1 mark]* and their raw materials can be recycled. *[1 mark]*

[2 marks available in total]

5 Points you might include:

Security risks
- Hackers could break into the company's servers and steal the data.
- Hackers could directly attack the servers, e.g. with a denial-of-service attack.
- Hackers could intercept the wireless signal to steal a person's data.
- Hackers could use the wristband's connection to upload malware to the company's servers.
- If someone obtained a user's location data, they could use it to track them and possibly commit crimes against them.
- If someone obtained a user's account data, they may be able to access things like their bank details.
- If someone obtained a user's phone number or email address, they may be able to attack them using social engineering.

Legal issues
- Hackers who exploit any of these risks could be breaking the law.
- If personal data was stolen by hackers, the company might be accountable for not keeping the data safe and secure.
- If stolen data led to other crimes being committed against the user, the company might be considered responsible.

How to mark your answer:
- One or two brief points with very little explanation. *[1-2 marks]*
- Three or four detailed points that show a good understanding of security risks and the relevant legal issues. *[3-4 marks]*
- Four or more detailed points that show a good understanding of security risks and the relevant legal issues, and clearly apply them to the situation. *[5-6 marks]*

Practice Paper 1

1 a) i) B *[1 mark]*
   ii) A *[1 mark]*

b) A basic subscription would cost 5 × 0.5 = £2.50 and a premium subscription would cost £5 + £1 = £6. *[1 mark]* The difference is £6 – £2.50 = £3.50. *[1 mark]*

2 a) Any **two** benefits with suitable explanation, e.g.
- Embedded systems are often very small, *[1 mark]* so they can easily fit into medical equipment. *[1 mark]*
- Embedded systems are cheap, *[1 mark]* which can keep the cost of medical devices down. *[1 mark]*
- Embedded systems are good at carrying out a single specific task *[1 mark]* and most medical devices only need to perform one function. *[1 mark]*
- Most medical devices are only needed for simple functions and do not need much, if any, memory, *[1 mark]* so embedded systems would be suitable. *[1 mark]*

[4 marks available in total]

b) E.g. Application software, such as database managers, *[1 mark]* can be used to organise and process the patients' data. *[1 mark]* Utility software, such as encryption utilities, *[1 mark]* can keep the data safe and secure from cyber attacks. *[1 mark]*

c) i) E.g. Not suitable, as CDs have only around 700 MB capacity, *[1 mark]* so they would need multiple discs for the update. *[1 mark]*
   ii) E.g. Suitable, as most USB flash drives would have enough space for the entire update. *[1 mark]* They are also cheap, easy to obtain and shock-proof. *[1 mark]*
   iii) E.g. Suitable, as HDDs have relatively quick read/write speeds and plenty of capacity. *[1 mark]* They're usually not too expensive and are long-lasting. *[1 mark]*
   For each of these, it's ok if you answered differently, as long as you justify your decision. Each type of storage has lots of advantages and disadvantages that you could mention.

3 a) A data structure is a format for storing multiple data values under one variable name. *[1 mark]*

b) i) D *[1 mark]*
   ii) B *[1 mark]*
   iii) C *[1 mark]*
   iv) A *[1 mark]*

c) E.g. It allows all of the records to be held together under one variable name *[1 mark]* which makes it easier to loop/search through all of the records at once. *[1 mark]*

4 a) Check each item in order.
Check the first item: 10 mA ≠ 12 mA
Check the second item: 15 mA ≠ 12 mA
Check the third item: 12 mA = 12 mA.
Stop searching as the item has been found.
[2 marks available — 1 mark for starting with 10 mA, 1 mark for checking items in order until you find 12 mA]

b) Using Start / Begin. *[1 mark]*
Input to check reading. *[1 mark]*
Decision box with appropriate question. *[1 mark]*
'Buzz' as an output. *[1 mark]*
Wait 5 minutes as a process. *[1 mark]*
Using Stop / End. *[1 mark]*
E.g.

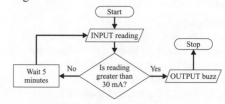

5   Generating a random integer from 0 to 4 *[1 mark]*
Using this to choose a tea from the array   *[1 mark]*
Outputting a suitable message using the chosen tea *[1 mark]*
E.g.
teaTypes ← ['ginger', 'chamomile', 'chai', 'mango', 'lemon']
number ← RANDOM_INT(0, 4)
chosenTea ← teaTypes[number]
OUTPUT ('This morning, have a ' + chosenTea + ' tea.')

6   a)   Decimal Value = 200 *[1 mark]*
       Binary Value = 11001000 *[1 mark]*
       Hex Value = C8 *[1 mark]*

   b)   i)   40 000 × 2 × 10 000 *[1 mark]*
           = 800 000 000 bytes *[1 mark]*

       ii)   Increasing the sampling rate means that more samples are taken every second. *[1 mark]* The sound quality will be better as the file will more closely match the original. *[1 mark]*

   c)   E.g. The sound file is large, so compression would greatly reduce its file size. *[1 mark]* This would make it easier to store the file and allow them to store more broadcasts. *[1 mark]*

7   a)

k	arr[k]	x	y
		0	0
0	4	4	0
1	2		2
2	7	7	4
3	1		
4	9	9	7

[4 marks available — 1 mark for each column with the correct values in the correct order]
It doesn't matter if you've put spaces in different places to the table above, or if you've not got any spaces at all, as long as the values that each variable takes are correct.

   b)   The algorithm finds the largest two numbers in an array of positive numbers *[1 mark]* and outputs them, largest first. *[1 mark]*

8   a)   C *[1 mark]*

   b)   i)   E.g. She could rename 'i' as 'email' or 'input'. *[1 mark]* This would make it easier for other developers to understand and edit her code. *[1 mark]*

       ii)   Logic error: FOR x ← 0 TO 10 *[1 mark]*
Explanation: The @ symbol might appear after the first 11 characters. *[1 mark]*

   c)   A subroutine accepting one input. *[1 mark]*
Checking the length of the input. *[1 mark]*
Suitable output message if length is 0. *[1 mark]*
Suitable output message if length is greater than 64. *[1 mark]*
Returning true/false based on whether input is valid. *[1 mark]*
E.g.
SUBROUTINE checkLength(email)
    valid ← false
    IF LEN(email) = 0 THEN
       OUTPUT 'Please enter an email address'
    ELSE IF LEN(email) > 64 THEN
       OUTPUT 'Email address too long'
    ELSE
       valid ← true
    ENDIF
    RETURN valid
ENDSUBROUTINE

   d)   Any **two** ways, e.g.
- A compiler would produce an executable file *[1 mark]* while an interpreter would not. *[1 mark]*
- A compiler would list any errors at the end of the translation *[1 mark]* while an interpreter would return the first error it found then stop. *[1 mark]*
- A compiler would translate the code all at once *[1 mark]* while an interpreter would translate and run the code line by line. *[1 mark]*

[4 marks available in total]

9   a)   i)   In general using more bits to represent characters increases the size of the character set. *[1 mark]*

       ii)   He is incorrect. *[1 mark]* Unicode® could represent 2^{32} characters which is much more than 4×2^8. *[1 mark]*

   b)   Any **two** benefits, e.g.
- It can support a large number of characters. *[1 mark]*
- Can use the same character set to type in lots of different languages. *[1 mark]*
- Easier for systems to operate globally. *[1 mark]*

[2 marks available in total]

   c)   0111 0100 *[1 mark]*
t is 3 letters away from q, so to find the binary representation of t, add 3 (in binary) to q, i.e. 01110001 + 00000011.

10   a)   i)   B *[1 mark]*

       ii)   A *[1 mark]*

   b)   Outputting a suitable message if unit is not in use. *[1 mark]*
Using the inUse variable to count how many units are in use. *[1 mark]*
Using a loop to access all of the scores for each unit in use. *[1 mark]*
Adding up all of the scores for each unit in use. *[1 mark]*
Calculating the average by dividing the total by 10. *[1 mark]*
Outputting the average. *[1 mark]*
Outputting the total number of units in use. *[1 mark]*
E.g.
inUse ← 0
FOR unit ← 0 TO 99
    IF topScores[unit][0] = 0 THEN
       OUTPUT ('Unit ' + INT_TO_STRING(unit)
               + ' not in use')
    ELSE
       inUse ← inUse + 1
       total ← 0
       FOR score ← 0 TO 9
          total ← total + topScores[unit][score]
       ENDFOR
       average ← total/10
       OUTPUT ('Unit ' + INT_TO_STRING(unit)
               + ' has an average score of '
               + INT_TO_STRING(average))
    ENDIF
ENDFOR
OUTPUT (INT_TO_STRING(inUse) + ' units are in use')

Practice Paper 2

1 a)

A	B	C	NOT A	B AND C	(NOT A) AND (B AND C)
0	0	0	1	0	0
0	0	1	1	0	0
0	1	0	1	0	0
0	1	1	1	1	1
1	0	0	0	0	0
1	0	1	0	0	0
1	1	0	0	0	0
1	1	1	0	1	0

[3 marks available — 1 mark for each correct column]

b)

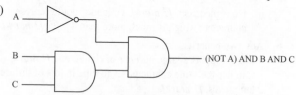

(NOT A) AND B AND C

[3 marks available — 1 mark for input A going into a NOT gate, 1 mark for inputs B and C going into an AND gate, 1 mark for outputs going into an AND gate with one output]

2 a) Any **two** functions, e.g.
   • The control unit executes instructions. *[1 mark]*
   • It follows the fetch-decode-execute cycle. *[1 mark]*
   • It controls the flow of data within the CPU. *[1 mark]*
   • It controls the flow of data between the CPU and other parts of the computer system (such as memory, and input and output devices). *[1 mark]*
   [2 marks available in total]

b) E.g. The ALU carries out arithmetic operations, e.g. addition, subtraction and multiplication (using repeated addition). *[1 mark]* It performs logic operations on binary data, such as AND, NOT, and OR. *[1 mark]*

c) The registers are super fast memory that store tiny amounts of data or instructions *[1 mark]* that the CPU can access extremely quickly. *[1 mark]*

d) E.g. Cache memory is extremely fast memory in the CPU. *[1 mark]* It stores regularly used data or instructions. *[1 mark]* The CPU can access data stored in the cache much faster than retrieving it from RAM. *[1 mark]*

e) C *[1 mark]*

3 a) A *[1 mark]*

b) C *[1 mark]*

c) Network Interface Controller/Card (NIC) *[1 mark]*

d) E.g.
   The Leeds studio's wired setup:
   • Wired connections have a more reliable performance as there is no loss of signal no matter where the devices are in the building. *[1 mark]*
   • Wired connections are more restrictive as it is harder to add new devices / access the network while moving through the building. *[1 mark]*

   The York studio's wireless setup:
   • Wireless connections are easier for the employees to connect to (e.g. no need for cables to add a laptop or mobile device to the network). *[1 mark]*
   • Wireless connections can suffer from signal problems caused by building interference or interference from other wireless signals nearby. *[1 mark]*
   To get all four marks, you'll need one advantage and one disadvantage for wired connections, as well as one advantage and one disadvantage for wireless connections.

e) i) Any **one** advantage, e.g.
      • Fibre optic cables tend to have greater bandwidth / can carry more data than copper cables. *[1 mark]*
      • Fibre optic cables can carry data over longer distances / don't suffer signal degradation or interference. *[1 mark]*
      • Fibre optic cables are easier to maintain than copper cables so cost less in the long term. *[1 mark]*
      [1 mark available in total]
   ii) E.g.
      • Laying its own cables between Leeds and York could be too expensive for the company. *[1 mark]*
      • Leased lines are likely to be more reliable and faster than other WAN connections. *[1 mark]*
      [1 mark available in total]

4 a) 11010000 *[1 mark]*

b) A 2 place right shift *[1 mark]* gives 00110101. *[1 mark]*

c) He is not correct.
   E.g. 0001 + 0001 = 0010 is a 1 place left shift.
   [2 marks available — 1 mark for not correct, 1 mark for a valid explanation]

5 a) B *[1 mark]* and D *[1 mark]*

b) HTTP is an application layer protocol used to access websites and communicate with web servers. *[1 mark]* HTTPS is the secured version of HTTP where all information sent is encrypted. *[1 mark]* Websites where the user needs to enter personal information will tend to use HTTPS to keep the information secure. *[1 mark]*

c) E.g. The laptop could contain malware *[1 mark]* which could spread to the network, infecting other devices using the network. *[1 mark]*

d) Any **two** security measures with explanation, e.g.
   • MAC address filtering could be used *[1 mark]* so that only trusted devices are allowed to access the network. *[1 mark]*
   • A firewall *[1 mark]* will help to stop any malware on user devices from spreading onto the network. *[1 mark]*
   • Regular software patches and updates *[1 mark]* will help prevent security holes from being exploited. *[1 mark]*
   • Authentication (e.g. passwords) could be used *[1 mark]* to make sure anyone accessing the network is an authorised user. *[1 mark]*
   [4 marks available in total]

6 a) E.g. It would be easier to remember the hex code for a particular colour *[1 mark]* because the hex code would be shorter than the binary or decimal equivalents. *[1 mark]*

b) i) (3, 1), (10, 0), (4, 1), (3, 0), (4, 1)
      [3 marks available — 3 marks for all data pairs correct, otherwise 2 marks for four data pairs correct or 1 mark for at least 2 data pairs correct]
      There are other formats you could give your answer in.
   ii) The original data took up 3 bytes, but the encoded data would take up 5 bytes *[1 mark]* so no, it will not reduce the size of the data. *[1 mark]*

7 Points you might include:

Ways that the technology may be used
- Certain jobs, e.g. doctors, may be able to make use of the technology in their work.
- Governments may be able to use the technology to aid security services in catching criminals and terrorists, which would help to keep people safe.
- The technology could be used by people to listen in on private conversations.
- It could be able to record things people have said without them knowing.

Reasons why people may be opposed to the technology
- People might be worried that their privacy may be at risk from people using the technology to listen in on them. *(ethical)*
- People might not be comfortable with the government using the technology to catch criminals and might be worried that they may be using it to carry out surveillance. *(ethical)*
- If the procedure to implant the device in a person is dangerous, then it could potentially cause people to suffer injuries that they wouldn't have otherwise. *(ethical)*
- If the device can record sound, then it could easily be used to record private conversations without people knowing they are being recorded. *(legal)*
- Hackers may be able to attack the implant with malware or otherwise affect its function. *(legal)*
- People could see modifying the body with technology in this way as 'playing God' and fundamentally unethical. *(ethical)*
- Creating the devices would probably require the use of precious natural resources. *(environmental)*
- The devices would need power to run, so they would consume energy and have a negative environmental impact. *(environmental)*

How to mark your answer:
- One or two brief points with very little explanation. *[1-2 marks]*
- Three to four detailed points covering uses and some ethical, legal or environmental issues. *[3-4 marks]*
- Four or more detailed points that form a well-written explanation, covering uses and a range of ethical, legal and environmental issues. *[5-6 marks]*

8 a) A packet is a unit of data sent over a packet-switching network *[1 mark]* that contains the main data and extra information, e.g. source and destination addresses. *[1 mark]*

   b) i) A *[1 mark]*
      ii) D *[1 mark]*

   c) Layer name: Application layer *[1 mark]*
      Layer function: Provides networking services to applications. *[1 mark]*

9 a) A *[1 mark]*

   b) E.g. Hardeep might want to upgrade his RAM as he only just has enough to meet the minimum requirements, *[1 mark]* so the OS may not run very smoothly once it's installed. *[1 mark]* He might want to upgrade his storage as he will not have much remaining free space left after installing the OS. *[1 mark]* Free space will be needed if the OS needs to install an update or Hardeep wants to download more files/programs. *[1 mark]*

   c) Having more cores allows a computer to process more instructions at once, *[1 mark]* which can decrease the amount of time it takes to process certain tasks. *[1 mark]*

d) RAM stores data and applications that are currently in use. *[1 mark]* As operating systems are running all the time, a large amount of the OS is kept in RAM. *[1 mark]*

e) Any **one** feature, e.g.
   - Large buttons and icons *[1 mark]* that can be pressed to open applications and windows. *[1 mark]*
   - Screens and menus *[1 mark]* that can be navigated / controlled by swiping or dragging with a finger. *[1 mark]*
   - Support for finger gestures *[1 mark]* such as pinching to zoom out / tap and hold to open additional options / four finger swipes to swap between apps etc. *[1 mark]*
   - Virtual on-screen keyboard *[1 mark]* to allow the user to type without attaching an external keyboard. *[1 mark]*
   [2 marks available in total]

10 Points you might include:

Advantages of GPS technology
- It can be used for navigation and route-planning, which could mean people spend less time driving around lost and consume less petrol in their car. *(environmental)*
- It can reduce the need for standalone sat nav devices, and the environmental impact of producing them. *(environmental)*
- It can be used to locate a lost or stolen phone, which can help to combat theft. It can also reduce the demand for new mobile phones, and the environmental impact of producing them. *(legal/environmental)*
- It can provide very convenient services, such as showing you what the nearest restaurants are, or alerting you when one of your friends is nearby. *(ethical)*
- Security services can use the technology to track the positions of criminals and terrorists, or of people who have gone missing. *(ethical/legal)*

Disadvantages of GPS technology
- It may be difficult to keep location data private while using these apps. The data may be shared with third-party services, or collected on servers that could be hacked into. *(ethical/legal)*
- Apps may not explain exactly how the location data is being used, or might make the user agree to a long user agreement that they are unlikely to read. *(ethical/legal)*
- If governments or law enforcement have access to this data, people may consider it an invasion of privacy, and may see it as surveillance. *(ethical)*
- If a smartphone gets hacked, the hacker could use the technology to track the owner's location, and target them for other crimes, e.g. robbery. *(legal)*
- Use of GPS services can quickly drain battery power, which would lead to increased energy consumption from extra charging. *(environmental)*
- The GPS chip in the device may require additional precious resources to create. *(environmental)*

How to mark your answer:
- Two or three brief points with very little explanation. *[1-3 marks]*
- Three to five detailed points covering some ethical, legal or environmental issues. *[4-6 marks]*
- Six or more detailed points that form a well-written, balanced discussion, covering a range of ethical, legal and environmental issues. *[7-9 marks]*
[Award a maximum of 5 marks for an answer that covers only advantages or only disadvantages]

Glossary and Index

Glossary and Index

Glossary and Index

H

hacker A person who tries to access or attack a computer network or device by exploiting weaknesses in its security. **111**

hard disk drive (HDD) Traditional internal storage for PCs and laptops that stores data magnetically. **70, 77**

hardware The physical parts of a computer system. **70, 81, 89**

heat sink Pulls heat away from the CPU to help maintain its temperature. **70**

hexadecimal A counting system using base-16 consisting of the digits 0-9 and the letters A-F. **55, 56**
  converting to/from binary 56
  converting to/from decimal 55

high-level language A programming language like C++ and Java™ that is easy for humans to understand. **42**

hotspot A location where people can access a wireless access point. **90**

HTTP (Hyper Text Transfer Protocol) Used by web browsers to access websites and communicate with web servers. **95**

HTTPS (HTTP Secure) A version of HTTP that encrypts data. **95**

Huffman coding A type of lossless compression that assigns codes of varying length to data based on its frequency. **64, 65**

I

IF statement A type of selection statement. **19**

image resolution The number of pixels in an image. **60**

IMAP (Internet Message Access Protocol) A protocol used to retrieve emails from a server. **95**

indefinite iteration A type of iteration statement where the number of times it repeats depends on a condition. **21**

indentation Spaces put at the beginning of lines of code to help show a program's structure. **39**

input validation Checking that an input meets certain criteria. **38**

integer (data type) A numerical data type for whole numbers. **12**

intellectual property An original piece of work (or an idea) that someone has created and belongs to them. **112**

Internet The biggest WAN in the world, based around the TCP/IP protocol. **88**

Internet layer One of the layers in the TCP/IP network protocol model. **94, 96**

Internet Protocol (IP) The protocol responsible for packet switching. **96**

interpreter A translator that turns source code into machine code and runs it one instruction at a time. **42**

I/O (input/output) device 81

IP address A unique identifier given to a device when it accesses an IP network. **96**

iteration statement A statement which makes the program repeat a set of instructions. **21, 22**

K

kilobyte 1000 bytes. **49**

L

LAN (Local Area Network) A network which only covers a single site. **88**

layers (network) Groups of protocols that have similar functions. **94**

legal issue An issue relating to what's right and wrong in the eyes of the law. **105, 111, 112**

linear search algorithm 6

link layer One of the layers in the TCP/IP network protocol model. **94, 96**

local variable A variable that is only defined and usable within certain parts of a program. **32**

logic circuit An electronic circuit for performing logic operations on binary data. It may have more than one logic gate and more than two inputs. **48**

logic error When a program does something that was not intended. **40**

logic gate An electronic circuit component that performs a Boolean operation (e.g. AND, OR or NOT). **47**

loop (programming) A set of instructions that the program repeats until a condition is met or count is reached. **21, 22**

lossless compression Temporarily removing data from a file to decrease the file size. **62**

lossy compression Permanently removing data from the file to decrease the file size. **62**

low-level language A programming language that is close to what a CPU would actually do and is written for specific hardware (i.e. CPU type). E.g. machine code and assembly languages. **42**

M

MAC address A unique identifier assigned to a device that cannot be changed. **99**

MAC address filtering A way of keeping networks secure by blocking devices from accessing the network unless their unique identification (MAC address) is known and trusted. **99**

machine code The lowest-level programming language consisting of 0s and 1s. CPUs can directly process it as a string of CPU instructions. **42**

magnetic storage Hard disk drives and magnetic tapes that hold data as magnetised patterns. **77**

mainframe (or supercomputer) An extremely powerful (and expensive and reliable) computer for specialist applications. **70**

malware Malicious software created to damage or gain illegal access to computer systems. **97, 99**

megabyte 1000 kilobytes. **49**

memory Hardware used to store data that a CPU needs access to. **72, 75, 82**

merge sort algorithm 8

module (structured programming) Each independent part of a program after decomposition. **37**

motherboard The main circuit board in a computer that other hardware connects to. **70, 75**

multitasking (OS) When an operating system runs multiple programs and applications at the same time. **82, 83**

N

nested statement A selection or iteration statement made up of multiple statements inside each other. **19, 22**

network interface card (NIC) An internal piece of hardware that allows a device to connect to a network. **89**

network policy A set of rules and procedures an organisation will follow to ensure their network is protected against attacks. **99**

network security Protection against network attacks. **99, 100**

nibble 4 bits. **49**

non-volatile memory Memory that retains its contents when it has no power. **75**

normal data Test data that simulates the inputs that users are likely to enter. **40**

NOT One of the Boolean operators.
  logic gate 47
  operator 23

Glossary and Index

O

open source (software) Software that can be modified and shared by anyone. **112**

operating system (OS) A piece of software responsible for running the computer, managing hardware, applications, users and resources. **81-83**

operator A special symbol like +, *, =, AND, ←, that carries out a particular function. **13, 14**

optical disc CD, DVD or Blu-Ray™ disc that is read / written to with lasers. **78**

optical drive Device used to read and write to optical discs. **70, 78**

OR One of the Boolean operators.
logic gate 47
operator 23

overclocking Running a CPU at a higher clock speed than was intended. **76**

P

packets (networks) Small, equal-sized units of data used to transfer files over networks. **94-96**

packet switching The process of directing data packets on a network using routers and the IP protocol. **96**

PAN (Personal Area Network) A small network used to transmit data over a short range. **88**

parameter A variable that a subroutine requires in order to run — it's only defined within the subroutine. **31**

passive attack A network attack where a hacker monitors data travelling on a network. **111**

password A string of characters that allows access to certain parts of a computer or program. **38, 83, 100**

patent A licence that protects new inventions, ideas and concepts. **112**

penetration testing (pentesting) The process of simulating attacks on a network to identify weaknesses. **97**

peripherals External hardware connected to a computer. **70, 81, 82**

pharming Directing users to fake versions of websites in order to get them to input their personal data. **98**

phishing When criminals send emails or texts to someone claiming to be a well-known business. **98**

pixels Small dots that make up a bitmap image. **60**

R

platform (OS) A computer system that other applications can run on. **82**

power supply A piece of hardware that gives the other pieces of hardware the energy they need to run. **70**

primary storage Memory that can be accessed directly by the CPU. **75, 77**

privacy 108

procedure A subroutine that carries out instructions but doesn't return a value. **31, 32**

processing The execution of program instructions by the CPU. **71, 83**

program A set of instructions that can be executed on a computer.
programming 12-32

program flow The order in which statements are executed in a program (controlled with selection and iteration statements). **19-22**

protocols (networks) A set of rules for how devices communicate over a network. **94-96**

pseudo-code A set of instructions in the style of a programming language but using plain English. **2**

R

RAM (Random Access Memory) The main memory of a computer. **70, 75, 76**

random number generation 24

ransomware A type of malware that uses encryption to lock a user out of their files. **97**

real (data type) A numerical data type for decimal numbers. **12**

record A data structure used to store multiple items of data about one 'thing' together. **29**

register A temporary data store inside a CPU. **71, 72**

REPEAT-UNTIL loop A type of indefinite iteration statement. **21**

ROM (Read Only Memory) Memory that can be read but not written to. **75**

rootkit A type of software used by hackers which can alter permissions on a system to give the hacker administrator-level access. **97**

router A piece of hardware responsible for transmitting data between networks. **89, 96**

run-length encoding A form of lossless compression that looks for repeating data. **63, 64**

S

sample rate The number of audio samples that are taken per second. **61**

sample resolution The number of bits available for each audio sample. **61**

sampling The process of converting analogue signals to digital data. **61**

scope Determines which parts of a program a variable can be used in. **32**

search algorithm A set of instructions that you can follow to find an item in a list. **6**

secondary storage External data storage accessed indirectly by the CPU. It's used to store data so that the computer can be switched off. **77, 78**

selection statement A statement which causes the program to make a choice and flow in a given direction — e.g. IF and CASE statements. **19, 20**

server A device which provides services for other devices (clients), e.g. file storage / web pages / printer access. **91**

shouldering Watching over a person's shoulder to gain access to a secure system. **98**

SMTP (Simple Mail Transfer Protocol) Used to send emails and transfer emails between servers. **95**

social engineering A way of gaining illegal access to data or networks by influencing people. **98**

social media Web applications which allow people to communicate and share content with others online. **108**

software Programs or applications that can be run on a computer system. **70, 81-84**

software licence A legal agreement that states how software can be used and distributed. **112**

solid state drive (SSD) Alternative to a traditional magnetic hard disk drive that uses flash memory. **77**

sorting algorithm A set of instructions that you can follow to order a list of items.
bubble sort 7
merge sort 8

sound 61

source code The actual written code of a program. **42**

spyware A type of malware which secretly monitors and records user actions. **97**

star topology A type of network topology where all devices are connected to a central switch or server which controls the network. **91**

storage device A device used to read and write data to a storage medium. **77, 78**

Glossary and Index